# Between Athens and Jerusalem

SUNY series in the Thought and Legacy of Leo Strauss
Kenneth Hart Green, editor

# Between Athens and Jerusalem

## Philosophy, Prophecy, and Politics in Leo Strauss's Early Thought

David Janssens

STATE UNIVERSITY OF NEW YORK PRESS

Published by
State University of New York Press, Albany

For information, contact State University of New York Press, Albany, NY
www.sunypress.edu

Production by Judith Block and Eileen Meehan
Marketing by Anne M. Valentine


**Library of Congress Cataloging-in-Publication Data**

Janssens, David, 1971–
  [Tussen Athene en Jerusalem. English]
  Between Athens and Jerusalem : philosophy, prophecy, and politics in
Leo Strauss's early thought / David Janssens.
     p. cm. — (SUNY series in the thought of Leo Strauss and his legacy)
  Includes bibliographical references (p.    ) and index.
  ISBN-13: 978-0-7914-7391-7 (hardcover : alk. paper)
  1. Strauss, Leo.  I. Title.
B945.S84J3613 2008
181'.06—dc22

2007017443

10 9 8 7 6 5 4 3 2 1

For Margot and Camille

*Idesthe tôde tô kasignètô, philoi*

# Contents

# Abbreviations

| | |
|---|---|
| AAPL | *The Argument and the Action of Plato's Laws* |
| CM | *The City and Man* |
| EW | *The Early Writings* |
| FPP | *Faith and Political Philosophy* |
| GS 1 | *Gesammelte Schriften, Vol. 1* |
| GS 2 | *Gesammelte Schriften, Vol. 2* |
| GS 3 | *Gesammelte Schriften, Vol. 3* |
| JPCM | *Jewish Philosophy and the Crisis of Modernity* |
| LAM | *Liberalism Ancient and Modern* |
| NRH | *Natural Right and History* |
| OT | *On Tyranny* |
| PAW | *Persecution and the Art of Writing* |
| PL | *Philosophy and Law* |
| PPH | *The Political Philosophy of Hobbes* |
| RCPR | *The Rebirth of Classical Political Rationalism* |
| SA | *Socrates and Aristophanes* |
| SCR | *Spinoza's Critique of Religion* |
| SPPP | *Studies in Platonic Political Philosophy* |
| TM | *Thoughts on Machiavelli* |
| WPP | *What Is Political Philosophy?* |

# Leo Strauss's Early Years
# Chronology of Major Events and Writings
# (1899–1937)

1899      Born in Kirchhain, Hessen, on September 20, 1899.

1912–1917      Attends the Gymnasium Philippinum in Marburg. Is "converted" to political Zionism in 1916. Joins Zionist student organization Jüdischer Wanderbund Blau-Weiss.

1917–1921      Studies philosophy, mathematics, and natural sciences at the universities of Marburg, Frankfurt am Main, Berlin, and Hamburg. Performs military service in Belgium from July to December 1918. Acquaintance with Jacob Klein, Hans-Georg Gadamer, Karl Löwith, Gerhard Krüger, and Hans Jonas.

1921      Obtains PhD at the University of Hamburg with a dissertation titled "The Problem of Knowledge in the Philosophical Doctrine of Fr. H. Jacobi," supervised by Ernst Cassirer.

1922      Spends postdoctoral year at the University of Freiburg, where he attends the lectures of Julius Ebbinghaus, Edmund Husserl, and Martin Heidegger.

1922–1925      Participates in the Free Jewish House of Learning (Freies jüdisches Lehrhaus) in Frankfurt am Main, founded by Franz Rosenzweig. Acquaintance with Nehama Leibowitz, Julius Guttmann, and Nahum Glatzer.

1923      "Response to Frankfurt's 'Word of Principle'"; "The Holy"; "A Note on the Discussion of 'Zionism and Anti-Semitism'"; "The Zionism of Nordau."

1924            "Paul de Lagarde"; "Sociological Historiography?"; "Review
               of Albert Levkowitz, *Contemporary Religious Thinkers*"; "On
               the Argument with European Science"; "Cohen's Analysis of
               Spinoza's Bible Science."

1925–1932      Appointed by Julius Guttmann as researcher at the Acad-
               emy for the Science of Judaism (Akademie für die Wis-
               senschaft des Judentums) in Berlin.

1925           "Ecclesia Militans"; "Biblical Science and History"; "Com-
               ment on Weinberg's Critique."

1926           "On the Bible Science of Spinoza and His Precursors."

1927           Acquaintance with Gershom Scholem.

1928           "Review of Sigmund Freud, *The Future of an Illusion*."

1929           "Franz Rosenzweig and the Academy for the Science
               of Judaism"; "Conspectivism"; "On the Ideology of Politi-
               cal Zionism."

1930           *Spinoza's Critique of Religion*; "Religious Situation of
               the Present."

1931           "Cohen and Maimonides"; "Review of Julius Ebbinghaus,
               *On the Progress of Metaphysics*"; "Introductions to Moses
               Mendelssohn, *Collected Works*"; "Preface to a Projected Book
               on Hobbes."

1932           Obtains a Rockefeller Foundation Fellowship and relocates
               to Paris. Acquaintance with Alexandre Kojève, Alexandre
               Koyré, Raymond Aron, and Louis Massignon. "The Testa-
               ment of Spinoza"; "Comments on Carl Schmitt, *The Concept
               of the Political*"; "The Religious Situation of the Present";
               "Introductions to Moses Mendelssohn, *Collected Works*."

1933           Marries Mirjam Bernson. "Some Remarks on Hobbes's
               Political Science"; "Hobbes's Critique of Religion: A Con-
               tribution to the Understanding of the Enlightenment."
               Attempts to secure a position at the Hebrew University of
               Jerusalem, without success.

1934           Relocates to London. Acquaintance with Ernest Barker.
               "Hobbes's Critique of Religion: A Contribution to the
               Understanding of the Enlightenment."

1935            Moves to Cambridge. Acquaintance with Richard H.
               Tawney. *The Political Philosophy of Hobbes: Its Basis and
               Its Genesis*; *Philosophy and Law: Contributions to the Under-
               standing of Maimonides and His Predecessors.*

1936            "Some Remarks on the Political Science of Maimonides
               and Alfarabi"; "A Lost Writing of Alfarabi"; "Introductions
               to Moses Mendelssohn, *Collected Works.*"

1937            Relocates to the United States. Appointed Research Fellow
               in the Department of History at Columbia University, New
               York. "The Place of the Doctrine of Providence in the Opin-
               ion of Maimonides"; "On Abravanel's Philosophical Ten-
               dency and Political Teaching"; "On Abravanel's Critique of
               Kingship"; "Introductions to Moses Mendelssohn, *Collected
               Works*"; "A Recollection/Reminder of Lessing."

# Introduction

*Was verlangt ein Philosoph am ersten und letzten von sich?*
*Seine Zeit in sich zu überwinden, "zeitlos" zu werden.*
*Womit also hat er seinen härtesten Strauss zu bestehen?*
*Mit dem, worin gerade er das Kind seiner Zeit ist. Wohlan!*

—Nietzsche, *Der Fall Wagner*

"The story of a life in which the only real events were thoughts is easily told."[1] With these words, Allan Bloom, author of *The Closing of the American Mind*, began an "in memoriam" for the man he regarded as his most important teacher: Leo Strauss. Of course, in a historical light, Bloom's phrase appears to stretch the truth somewhat. Born in 1899 in Germany, Strauss was forced to flee to the United States in the 1930s, along with many other intellectuals. There he died, in 1973, after a richly filled career at a number of American universities, most notably the University of Chicago. The course of his life, then, runs parallel to the anything-but-uneventful twentieth century.

On further consideration, nevertheless, Bloom's words do contain a grain of truth. Whoever opens a book by Strauss for the first time will soon be under the impression of dealing with a *Kammergelehrte*, a scholar secluded from all public life. The majority of his academic work is devoted to the interpretation of great texts, primarily of philosophy, but also of theology and even of classical poetry. Because of this, he has often been labeled a historian of ideas. However, his interpretive method is bound to strike the reader as particularly unhistorical and untimely, if not antiquarian. At times, his interpretations are reminiscent of medieval commentaries, with their patient, long-winded, and sometimes slightly awkward paraphrases. For Strauss, only the text and nothing but the text seems to matter, or more precisely: nothing but the thoughts contained therein. References to the historical context, both of the past and of the present, are very rare indeed.

The fact that Strauss's life largely took place within the four walls of a study does not prevent his thought from having led to a whole range of

1

"events" in the conventional sense of the word. Already during his lifetime, his work was the object of heated and sometimes bitter controversies within the American academic world. Since his death, the discussion has continued *crescendo* and has even spread far beyond the context of the academy. When in 1996 *Time* magazine declared him to be "one of the most influential people in American politics," these words offered only an inkling of what was yet to come.[2] In the wake of the September 11, 2001, attacks and the American response, Strauss's putative connection to the neoconservative movement within the U.S. government sparked a widespread and passionate debate that continues to this very day. This is no small achievement for a German immigrant of Jewish origin, a quarter of a century after his death.

How can a reclusive scholar raise so much dust, and for so long, outside the confines of his study, and even beyond the confines of the academy? Of course, the responsibility of an author for the reception of his work is always difficult to ascertain. Nevertheless, the most important points of debate can be clearly delineated. The controversy concerns, first, the motivation and intention at the heart of Strauss's work. His research into the sources of political thought, after all, goes hand in hand with a critical attitude toward modernity and its characteristic political form: liberal democracy. In this respect, he is often mentioned in conjunction with Hannah Arendt and Eric Voegelin, two other immigrants of his generation. With these authors he shares the view that the modern project reveals certain structural shortcomings, which have led, ultimately, to a deep crisis. The most conspicuous symptoms of this crisis are not only the predominance of positivism, relativism, and historicism, but also the painful incapacity of liberal democracy to defend itself against the undermining effect of these ideas. In order to ward off the dangers that they kindle, a thorough rethinking of the philosophical, moral, and political foundations of modernity is necessary. This project cannot succeed, however, without a keen willingness to study and learn from thinkers of the past.

It is hardly surprising that these views met with opprobrium and opposition, as they did in the case of his two better-known contemporaries, especially in a country considered to be a model liberal democracy and a bulwark of modernity, freedom, and progress. In the strongly polarized American political landscape, Strauss came to be generally regarded as a conservative thinker. While this label has generated the inevitable criticism from the other side of the political spectrum, the tone is often considerably sharper and more dismissive than in the cases of Arendt and Voegelin. One of the principal reasons is the remarkable position he develops and defends in his interpretation of texts.

According to Strauss, a considerable number of great philosophers of the past were faced with the phenomenon of political and religious persecution. To circumvent this danger, they were forced to employ exceptional care in the way they expressed themselves in their writings. Each in his way made use of a technique Strauss called "the art of writing carefully" or "the art of writing between the lines": through diverse literary means, they hid their unconventional and even subversive ideas behind a conventional facade adjusted to reigning opinion. In this way, they made sure that their ideas were only accessible to kindred spirits. With the birth of the Enlightenment and the diffusion of philosophy to a much larger public, this art was largely forgotten. An adequate understanding of premodern authors therefore demands that this art be learned anew—among other things, by paying as much attention to the form of their writings as to the content—but also that one reflect on the changes that have occurred in the course of time in the relationship between philosophy and political society.

Even though Strauss developed this thesis with the greatest caution, documenting it carefully and extensively, it has been seen by many as highly provocative, not to say offensive. It is not difficult to see that Strauss's approach radically calls into question the conventional historical interpretation of philosophical works, which is mainly the fruit of the Enlightenment. Among other things, it leads to the notion that the real opinions of an author can differ strongly from those ascribed to him by conventional readings. The idea that an author is the stepchild rather than the child of his time is bound to evoke suspicion and even resistance in an era that celebrates historicity. Hence, it is hardly surprising that Strauss's hermeneutics have been strongly criticized by contemporary philosophers.

Even more than for its hermeneutical and philosophical aspects, Strauss's approach has been attacked for its political implications. The suggestion that the relationship between philosophy and society is a fundamental problem that also deserves attention in a liberal and democratic society has led to reactions ranging from suspicion and insinuation to outright denunciation, aimed not merely at the work, but at the person as well. According to some of the more extravagant critics, Strauss considers the truth to be too dangerous for society, and his work is a covert plea for the rule of a philosophical elite controlling the masses for their own good by means of salutary myths. "Elitist," "sectarian," "antiliberal," "antidemocratic," and "antimodern" are but a few of the epithets ascribed to him over the years.[3]

That the criticism has taken on such extreme forms, however, is not only the accomplishment of his antagonists, but also that of some of his allies. In the course of his long career in the United States, Strauss undoubtedly made his mark. He is reputed to have been an inspiring teacher with a great intellectual power of attraction.[4] Several generations of students followed his example in studying a wide range of authors.[5] Some of them, who identify themselves explicitly as "Straussians," have developed his critical dialogue with modernity and his recovery of premodern thought into an avowedly conservative political position. A few actually embarked on a political career, which led many critics, often with little or no knowledge of his work, to denounce Strauss as the *maître à penser* of American neoconservatism. In that unlikely position, his name appeared in 1996 in the pages of *Time*, and, after 9/11, in almost all other media.

The result of this overly politicized polemic is that both sides combat each other in the name of what is often a caricature. Indeed, Strauss made no secret of the fact that his political preferences tended toward conservatism, even if he was acutely aware of the limitations of every political stance.[6] Still, it is doubtful whether he would have recognized himself in the fierce cultural criticism and the passionate political commitment of some of his intellectual descendants. Only too often the fundamental questions he tried to raise anew have been welded all too rashly into ready-made answers by some. In addition, one would be hard put to attribute to him virulently antiliberal or antidemocratic tendencies. As a refugee from the violence of totalitarianism, he explicitly expressed his debt as well as his loyalty to the country that received him. This did not prevent him, however, from emphasizing that the friend of liberal democracy cannot be its flatterer, but must be the one who approaches its claims critically in order to be able to defend it when necessary.[7]

Compared to the American reception, European scholarship, which has been developing for some time, appears to be less charged with political and ideological differences. As a result, its appraisal of Strauss's work is often more balanced and nuanced, not least because more attention is paid to the historical and the intellectual context in which Strauss's thought developed. In France, where large parts of his work have been translated, his reputation is by now firmly established. A host of eminent political philosophers—Raymond Aron, Pierre Manent, and Claude Lefort among them—have devoted studies to him, in which they point to the philosophical value of his hermeneutics and the critical potential of his thought.[8] In Germany, his country of origin, interest is growing steadily after a long period of near silence, not least thanks to a careful edition of his complete works, several volumes of which have already appeared.[9] This edition has made clear that a considerable and important part of Strauss's thought and work in fact predates his relocation to the United States. As a result, Strauss is slowly being recognized as a major *European* thinker in his own right.

The aim of this book is to introduce the early European Strauss to an English-speaking readership, as well as to show that an appreciation of this Strauss is a vital prerequisite for understanding the later American Strauss. On a number of occasions, Strauss expressly stated that, from the very beginning, his investigations were guided by a single theme. Different commentators, some of whom knew him personally, confirm that he had developed his key questions and issues at a very early stage, only to further develop and deepen them over time. Thus, the German philosopher Hans Jonas, who attended Martin Heidegger's seminars together with Strauss in the early 1920s, testifies as follows: "Strauss came to Heidegger with his questions fully formed."[10] Similarly, the French philosopher Rémi Brague, an astute longtime reader of Strauss, has claimed: "In any case, it seems to be legitimate to presume that . . . Strauss never strayed from his initial positions concerning the fundamental questions, and that he held on to them for a very long time, not to say during his entire life."[11] Finally, his student Allan Bloom confirms: "A survey of Strauss' entire body of work will reveal that it constitutes a unified and continuous, ever deepening investigation."[12] Hence, an in-depth study of his early writings proves to be a valuable complement to that of his later works.

Oddly enough, however, the early writings that came about before his migration to the United States, and in which his questioning takes form, have hardly been studied in the vast body of secondary literature. Whenever they are referred to, in general this is merely to make a biographical point. This lacuna is rather peculiar, since the authors who refer to the early work never fail to stress its great importance. Thus, we find the following remark in the introduction to an American collection of essays on Strauss: "what can be considered as the 'European Strauss' still needs to receive necessary attention."[13] In the same vein, two German authors state bluntly: "All of Strauss's writings, in German and in English, find their origins in the seminal studies done during the Weimar Republic."[14] Even the great historian and classicist Arnaldo Momigliano called the early work "essential to whoever seeks to reconstruct the genesis of Strauss' thought."[15]

The characteristics I have discussed here—the great unity, consistency, and continuity of Strauss's work—are central to the design and organization of this book. Among other things, they offer a unique opportunity to combine an introductory work with a contribution to contemporary scholarship. The adjective "introductory" must be taken literally: in the following chapters the genesis of Strauss's thought is reconstructed from the start by means of an analysis of the early work. Moreover, at every step the connection to his later American work is brought to light wherever possible, either within the analysis itself or in the notes. In the epilogue, these various threads are gathered in an attempt to bring out the relationship between the early and the later Strauss. In this way, the reconstruction of the European Strauss aims to contribute to identifying and clarifying the core or "unifying center" of his thought.[16] As will hopefully become clear, this approach ab ovo produces several valuable insights that are harder to perceive starting from the later work.

For the same reasons, this cannot be a complete, detailed, and exhaustive discussion of Strauss's complete oeuvre. The main intention of this book is to acquaint the reader with the principal elements of his thought, and to offer a number of tools with which to start reading his works. Strauss himself wrote his interpretations in order to guide the curious and attentive reader to the works of the great philosophers, theologians, and poets themselves. If the present work contributes something to that end, it will have succeeded.

This volume is based on a book originally written and published in Dutch in 2001.[17] The State University of New York Press's (SUNY) offer to publish an English translation gave me the opportunity to thoroughly revise and enlarge it in the light of new material, both primary and secondary, that was published in the meantime. This endeavor would not have succeeded without the help and encouragement of a number of people to whom I wish to express my gratitude. Joseph Cropsey graciously granted me access to the Leo Strauss Papers in the University of Chicago Library. Kenneth Hart Green, editor of SUNY's series in the Thought and Legacy of Leo Strauss, enthusiastically welcomed the project. Nathan Tarcov, Heinrich Meier, and Mark Lilla, who continued to show interest in my work through the years, provided me with valuable and welcome comments and advice. Daniel Tanguay generously gave me the benefit of his work as well as of his friendship. Finally, I am indebted to my colleagues at Tilburg University—Bert van Roermund, Hans Lindahl, and Luigi Corrias—for their unstinting support.

# CHAPTER 1

# "In the Grip of the Theological-Political Predicament"

## The Theological-Political Problem and the Jewish Question

In many respects, 1965 marks a special occasion in the academic career of Leo Strauss. In that year, two of his earliest books are republished in translation. An American publisher brings out *Spinoza's Critique of Religion*, the English translation of his first book, which had originally appeared in German in 1930. Concurrently, a German publisher issues *Hobbes' politische Wissenschaft*, the German original of a text of 1936, which until then had only been available in English as *The Political Philosophy of Hobbes*.[1] In both cases, something of an old debt is settled. With the first book, Strauss's English-speaking audience finally gains access to a scholarly debut that was received as an important achievement in its day. Conversely, the publication of the original book on Hobbes offers the German readership a further opportunity to get acquainted with his work. Moreover, it provides a belated compensation for the disappointments Strauss had to endure in the 1930s, when he found no German publisher prepared to print the work of a Jewish scholar.[2]

As is customary on such occasions, Strauss adds a foreword to both texts, in which he looks back at the road traveled and supplies elements of an intellectual biography. Reading these forewords in conjunction, the reader cannot fail to be struck by two passages. The preface to *Spinoza's Critique of Religion* begins as follows: "This study . . . was written between the years 1925–1928 in Germany. The author was a young Jew, born and raised in Germany, who found himself in the grip of the theological-political predicament."[3] In the foreword to the Hobbes book, Strauss refers to his research on Baruch Spinoza while adding an important declaration: "My

study of Hobbes began in conjunction with an investigation of the origins of
the critique of the Bible in the seventeenth century, in particular of Spinoza's *Theologico-Political Treatise* . . . Since then the theological-political
problem has remained *the* theme of my investigations."[4]

In the case of an exceptionally careful reader and writer like Strauss,
any coincidence can safely be ruled out. By dividing a single message over
two distinct audiences, he not only bridges the two worlds of his native and
his adoptive country, but he also joins two halves of a life devoted to scientific research and intersected by a world war. With unusual emphasis, moreover, he points to what he regards as the core and Leitmotiv of his life and
work. In almost four decades, we may infer, the "grip of the theological-
political predicament" has not slackened, even though his understanding of
it may have changed, as the shift from "predicament" to "problem" seems to
indicate. At any rate, it seems that, by Strauss's own directions, any attempt
to understand his work must focus on "the theological-political problem."

However, the picture proves to be more intricate. In 1962, presumably while composing the preface to the book on Spinoza, Strauss gave a
lecture at the Hillel House of the University of Chicago. On this occasion,
he told his audience, many of whose members were Jewish: "I believe that
I can say without exaggeration that since a very, very early time the main
theme of my reflections has been what is called 'the Jewish Question'"[5] No
less deliberate and no less emphatic than the other two, this statement is
apparently directed to yet another audience, and it complicates our initial
question, what does Strauss mean by "the Jewish Question," and how is it
related to the "theological-political problem"? Are they identical, or is the
former rather an instance of the latter? In order to answer these questions,
we do well to turn to the beginnings. In the 1920s, the young Strauss was
an adherent of political Zionism who energetically participated in a number of debates concerning what was then called "the Jewish Question": the
conditions, the identity, and the future of the Jews in Europe. At this "very,
very early time," his commitment was marked by a keen interest in the
relationship between political and religious-theological issues.

## Back to Reality: Emancipation, Assimilation, and Zionism

The historical issues underlying the Jewish Question can be defined with
some accuracy. The term became current during the second half of the nineteenth century when, following a period of relative quiet and stability,
the presence and the place of Jews in Europe was called into question with
unprecedented vehemence. In Eastern Europe, thousands of mostly orthodox

Jews were killed or put to flight in violent pogroms. However, the secularized and assimilated Jews living in the liberal democracies of Western Europe did not remain unaffected either. Notwithstanding their formal equality before the law as citizens, they were put apart once again, in many cases more intensely than before. What had been known for centuries as *rishus*, vicious-ness against Jews, had returned in pseudoscientific garb under the name of "anti-Semitism." Before long, the Jewish Question was put on a par with other great issues of the time, such as the "Social Question" and the "Labor Question."

Profound disillusionment with the failure of liberal democracy pushed many assimilated Jews into a crisis. While assimilation proved unable to live up to its promises—to end discrimination and promote legal and social equality—doubts regarding its effectiveness produced a feeling of powerless-ness. The Jewish individual who had assimilated in order to escape what the poet Heinrich Heine had called "*das dunkle Weh*," the "dark pain" or "dark misfortune" of being a Jew, found himself in a situation hardly more enviable and hardly less precarious.[6] Confronted with the persistence of discrimina-tion, he had to do without the resilience of his ancestors, who had been able to invoke and emulate a glorious and heroic Jewish past. The wealth of this past, the meaning it had acquired in the course of long and profound suffer-ing, had been discounted by assimilation in a potentially endless historical progress.[7] The option of a liberal, secularized modernity thus appeared as a painfully superficial and unsatisfying solution. For this reason, many assimi-lated Jews engaged in active political self-organization. By constructing their own state, they aimed to build a safe haven where physical and spiritual per-secution and repression would come to an end, if necessary by enforcing recognition. The Zionist movement originated when, at the end of the nine-teenth century, the passage of large groups of Jewish refugees from Eastern Europe, fleeing the violence of the pogroms, rekindled the dream of a return to Palestine among many West European Jews.[8]

Initially, however, the efforts of the small and insular Zionist societies—orthodox as well as assimilated—to aid the so-called *Ostjuden* in building a new life were hardly organized or coordinated, and of a humanitarian and philanthropic rather than a political nature. For most German Zionists, the idea of a Jewish nation was at best a beautiful dream that in no way affected their loyalty to the German state. Only by the turn of the century did Zion-ism evolve into a full-blown Jewish nationalism. With his classic pamphlet *The Jewish State* (*Der Judenstaat*, 1896), the Austrian journalist and writer Theodor Herzl attempted to unify and focus the dormant and dispersed Zionist ambitions, giving them a markedly political turn. Deeply impressed by the Russian pogroms as well as by the Dreyfus Affair in France, Herzl announced the failure of emancipation and assimilation: in spite of their exalted promises, they had proved unable to end the discrimination of Jews. Banishing anti-Jewish sentiments to the margins of society had, in fact, allowed them to proliferate and intensify.[9] In the face of renewed anti-Semitism, assimilation proved to be powerless and blind, insofar as it denied or trivialized the gravity of the situation. In Herzl's view, assimilation proved to be merely a continuation of *galut*, the Jewish exile, and thus also of the discomfort and the dangers that accompanied it.

Instead of emancipation from without, promoted and organized by the European nation states, Herzl advocated the self-emancipation of the Jewish people. This goal could be realized only by political means, he argued: any legal or social solution was precluded a priori by the problems inherent in liberalism, so that the Jews had no other recourse than to develop into a united and organized power.[10] Moreover, Herzl's strictly political approach to the Jewish Question implied that he attached no primary importance to Jewish language, culture, tradition, or even religion in the establishment of a Jewish state. In reaction, other currents within Zionism emerged that sought to correct and remedy this putative one-sidedness. Thus, motivated by what it saw as political Zionism's neglect of the Jewish tradition, so-called *cultural* Zionism emerged. Its founder, the writer Ahad Ha'am, argued that a purely political approach to the Jewish Question was untenable, insofar as the pursuit of a *Jewish* state as such implied a decisive concession to the Jewish tradition. According to Ahad Ha'am, a Jewish nation could not exist if it did not make room for a proper Jewish national culture, the so-called Jewish content (*Jüdische Inhalte*) in which Jewish religious experience expressed itself.

Going beyond cultural Zionism, religious Zionism, founded in 1902, argued that the nationalist struggle could only be a means to the religious end of reuniting the Jewish people under the Torah, the revealed law. For this reason, it opposed the approach of both political and cultural Zionism. Finally, opposed to Zionism in all its varieties was Jewish neoorthodoxy. Founded by Samson Raphael Hirsch at the end of the nineteenth century and led in the 1920s by his grandson Isaac Breuer, it anathemized Zionism as *apikorsuth*, or Epicureanism, a synonym for apostasy, atheism, and the self-centered pursuit of this-worldly comfort.

In spite of disagreement and opposition, Herzl managed to play off against each other the Jewish interests and those of the international powers with an exceptional feeling for diplomacy and an acute political instinct, in such a way that Jewish unity became a possibility, if not a reality. In this way, he ushered in a second phase in which Zionism, albeit not without great effort, gradually gathered political momentum. The First World War did not so much interrupt this process as subject it to a profound revision. As Jehuda Reinharz argues in his study of the German Zionist movement, the war threw Zionism back on itself and forced it to reflect on its own foundations and presuppositions, at a point in time when discord between different Zionist groups seemed to have been more or less overcome. In the light of these new conditions, Herzl's diplomatic approach turned out to be as insufficient as the initial philanthropy. Heated debates erupted again, and, as Reinharz points out, "they required new, far-reaching commitments of every Zionist, as well as a revision of his identity as a Jewish nationalist living in Germany."[11] As a result of their experiences in Germany as well as abroad, young Zionists found themselves in a tangled web of conflicting claims: the political pursuit of a Jewish state, the requirements of German citizenship, the role of the Jewish tradition, and the influence of German culture.

## "God and Politics"

This third phase of Zionism, its postwar introspection, is the stage on which Leo Strauss, a young graduate in philosophy, makes his first appearance. Raised in an orthodox family, he was, in his own words, "converted to simple, straightforward political Zionism" at the age of seventeen.[12] As an active but by no means uncritical member of a Zionist student organization, Strauss espoused the strictly secular political approach advocated by Herzl.[13] Thus, one of his earliest writings begins with the following programmatic assertion: "It is the view of political Zionism that the plight of the Jews can only be alleviated by the establishment of a Jewish state, by the consolidation of the power of Jewish individuals into the Jewish power of the people."[14] In other writings of the same period, Strauss makes clear that this endeavor is essentially and irrevocably *modern*. It is a struggle to end Jewish exile predicated on the destruction of its religious foundations:

> Political Zionism has repeatedly characterized itself as the will to normalize the existence of the Jewish people, to normalize the Jewish people . . . In truth, the presupposition of the Zionist will to normalization, that is, the Zionist negation of *galut*, is the conviction that "the power of religion has been broken."[15]

Political Zionism's claim to legitimacy vis-à-vis contemporary Jews is thus ultimately founded on the success of the critique of religion in the seventeenth and eighteenth centuries, Strauss explains that:

when Europe criticized itself, that is, its Christianity, it *eo ipso* criticized Judaism. That this critique *made an impact on* the Jewish context, is illustrated historically by the fact that the Jewish tradition, insofar as it was not able to reconstruct itself with regard to this critique, succumbed to the European attack. Here lies the decisive cause of what is known as assimilation, which therefore is Jewishly legitimate also from this perspective.[16]

As a necessary consequence, Strauss points out, "Political Zionism, wishing to ground itself radically, must ground itself in unbelief (*sich als ungläubig begründen*)."[17] Elsewhere, he formulates this implication in a way that leaves nothing to be desired in the way of clarity: "Political Zionism is the organization of unbelief within Judaism; it is the attempt to organize the Jewish people on the basis of unbelief."[18] This sober, uncompromising understanding of political Zionism is characteristic of the position Strauss takes in the postwar debates. First, it leads him to challenge Herzl's view that assimilation is merely a continuation of Jewish exile, and that only political Zionism can make a radical break with this past.[19] Rather, he argues, this break can be shown to precede *both* assimilation *and* Zionism, insofar as *both* are essentially opposed to the "lack of reality" (*Entwirklichtheit*) of the exile. Under *galut*, Jewish existence was literally "abnormal": it stood outside the historical process in which the other nations faced each other as political entities. By the same token, the unity and cohesion of the Jewish people in the *galut* were based on the complete absence of a political center. Deprived of the natural conditions of existence, the vitality of the Jewish people was sustained and nourished only by faith in divine providence, but precisely this faith precluded normal political action. Thus, the essence of *galut* consists in the fact that "*it provides the Jewish people with a maximal possibility of existence by means of a minimum of normality*."[20]

In the long run, however, this unreal, apolitical existence proved to be untenable, Strauss continues. The modern critique of religion and its political correlate, the liberal political thought of the French Revolution, offered a way out. Among other things, the secular separation of church and state offered Jews the opportunity to join the "normal" historical, economic, social, and political reality of the non-Jewish world.[21] Initially, this "return to reality" (*Einwirklichung*) occurred on the individual level, when individual Jews detached themselves from Jewish faith and tradition, and participated actively in non-Jewish life. When the achievements of this process were subsequently called into question both by Jews and non-Jews alike, it became apparent that the return to reality could be successful only to the extent that it was undertaken on a collective, political level.

Hence, assimilation and political Zionism are not opposed, Strauss holds. They are two distinct but complementary phases within the same process of the return to reality. What is more, political Zionism would never have been possible without assimilation and its attendant contact with European culture. Assimilation primarily meant that religious matters were relegated from the public sphere to the private sphere. This created a space in which assimilated Jews could submit to a profound "Germanization" (*Eindeutschung*), an immersion in German culture and its characteristic blend of historical consciousness and nationalism.[22] Therefore, Strauss asserts, political Zionism is essentially a *modern* movement, a child of the nineteenth century, just as assimilation was a child of the eighteenth.[23]

More importantly, however, Strauss's understanding of political Zionism as essentially based on unbelief leads to a sharp critique of other contemporary currents within Zionism that nevertheless attempt to integrate religion in their pursuit of a Jewish state. Thus, he repeatedly attacks cultural Zionism, and its attempts to reintegrate the Jewish content. Strauss firmly rejects this approach on two grounds:

> This "content" cannot simply be adopted, not only because the content is conditioned by, and supportive of *galut* and therefore endangers our Zionism but also because inherent in this content as religious content is a definite claim to truth that is not satisfied by the fulfillment of national demands.[24]

At the core of this claim to truth, he goes on to explain, is the independent existence of God, which cannot be reduced to mere human culture or human experience: "That religion deals *first* with 'God' and *not* with the human being, that this conception is the great legacy of precisely the Jewish past—this our ancestors have handed down to us, and this we wish to hold on to honestly and clearly."[25] By reducing this legacy to mere culture, cultural Zionism proves to be based on modern atheism, in spite of its own claims to the contrary.

In his autobiographical prefaces, Strauss spells out his critique of cultural Zionism in more detail. As he argues there, cultural Zionism's alleged return to Jewish tradition was insincere and bound to fail, since it was based on a profound modification of the Jewish tradition. Inspired by the thought of German Idealist thinkers like G. W. F. Hegel and Johann Gottlieb Fichte, cultural Zionism understood the Jewish tradition as "high culture" (*Hochkultur*), the product of the Jewish "folk spirit" (*Volksgeist*). In doing so, however, it departed from the tradition's self-understanding, which traced the origin of Jewish culture not to a human, but to a divine act. According to the tradition, the people of Israel were distinguished from all other peoples by divine election through receiving the revealed law. As a result, the Jewish people is what it is by dint of something that cannot be reduced to the "folk spirit," national culture, or national consciousness. Strauss observes:

> And if you take these things with a minimum of respect or seriousness, you must say that they were not meant to be products of the Jewish mind. They were meant to be ultimately "from Heaven" and this is the crux of the matter: Judaism cannot be understood as a culture. . . .The substance is not culture, but divine revelation.[26]

If cultural Zionism wanted to remain consistent in its objections to political Zionism, it had no choice but to transform itself into religious Zionism, Strauss asserts. This, however, implied a profound change in priorities: "when religious Zionism understands itself, it is in the first place Jewish faith and only secondarily Zionism."[27] If religion prevails over political concerns, the reconstitution of the Jewish state is no longer exclusively nor essentially a matter of human intervention, but it becomes dependent on the coming of the Messiah, who will inaugurate *tikkun*, the great restoration. Religious Zionism is based on the conviction that the Jewish Question is an absolute problem, the result of a divine dispensation. From this perspective, the difficulties of the "unreal" life in exile are an inalienable part of a divine providence unfathomable to man. They are signs that indicate the Jewish people have been elected by the creator to assume the sufferings of the world and to receive and spread ultimate salvation. Since these ordeals are imposed by a superhuman power, they can be ended only by that same power. Every attempt to achieve this goal by merely human means must therefore be rejected as blasphemous and false. According to religious Zionism, the insolubility of the Jewish Question is the core of Jewish identity. The establishment of the state of Israel may seem to be the end, but it is, in fact, a continuation by other means of the *galut*, a relative solution to what is, in fact, an absolute problem.

Strauss's uncompromising view of political Zionism, then, proves to be matched by a no less radical understanding of religion. In his early writings, he repeatedly insists on their mutual incompatibility, while forcefully dismissing any attempt at synthesis and integration as jeopardizing the Zionist cause. For this reason, he criticizes not only cultural Zionism but also religious Zionism and even the anti-Zionism of Jewish neoorthodoxy. From the neoorthodox perspective, Zionists were apostates who had been unable to resist the temptations of modern European culture, and who had abandoned religious faith in divine providence for the sake of a secular trust in progress and human autonomy. In this way, neoorthodoxy argued, Zionism had surrendered Judaism to the power, the discretion and the mutual quarrels of the modern nation states and undermined Jewish resilience. In its view, the failure of assimilation proved that Jews could find salvation only in theocracy, faith, and obedience to the revealed Law. Instead of trying to find a place among the other nations, the Jews ought to remain in exile, since the latter could be truly ended only by the coming of the Messiah. The violence of the *goyim* or non-Jews had to be endured resignedly, in the knowledge that justice ultimately was on the side of the Jewish people.

Strauss forcefully dismisses these accusations as well as the view underlying them. In his rejoinder, he charges his opponents with dangerous political naïveté as well as with intellectual dishonesty. To begin with, he argues that neoorthodoxy's angry polemic against Zionism hardly contributes to alleviating the predicament of German Jews.[28] Second, its simplistic presentation of the relationship between the Jewish people and the other peoples as a matter of "justice against injustice" constitutes a serious obstacle to reaching a viable political balance of powers. Third, he objects to the fact that, in spite of its antipolitical discourse, neoorthodoxy nevertheless deploys a political strategy that is not devoid of demagoguery: its defense of theocracy mobilizes the fundamental religious premises primarily because of their political utility, not because of their meaning and content.

According to Strauss, religious neoorthodoxy deploys a purely consequentialist argument. It preaches faith and obedience to Mosaic law by systematically emphasizing their salutary consequences, such as national unity, social cohesion, the fulfillment of psychological needs, or the even force of habit. If the law is upheld for these reasons, it argues, faith in the fundamental religious dogmas is wont to follow. For Strauss, this view amounts to an outright reversal of priorities. The only valid reason for obedience to the law, he rejoins, is the existence of God and the authority of Mosaic revelation.[29] If the law is to be obeyed, it is to be obeyed because it is the will of God, revealed by him directly and miraculously to Moses, and not because obedience has salutary consequences. By giving precedence to human concerns over God and the Torah, neoorthodoxy forgets "that religion deals *first* with 'God' and *not* with the human being." The view that the deeper meaning of the law consists in its "therapeutic" effects nullifies the seriousness of faith, and culminates in rigid dogmatism. Strauss's dismissal is particularly scathing: "For the sake of such a 'deeper' meaning of the Law one swallows the dogmas whole, unchewed, like pills. One asserts that that without inspiration the Law would lose its binding force, and one forgets that one doesn't base it on inspiration at all."[30]

If neoorthodoxy were to be consistent, it would recognize that "the question of God and His revelation must be posed quite simple-mindedly and honestly, without regard to any actual disadvantages involved."[31] As a result, it would be compelled to reaffirm in all clarity the traditional Jewish theological dogmas. In its turn, political Zionism would be able to express its fundamental objections and reservations regarding the dogmas. At the same time, it would be able to show its loyalty to the great heritage of the Jewish past. Thus, it would finally come to light that political Zionism does not conduct "a battle against the rule of the Torah of God," as neoorthodoxy claims, but merely wants to maintain a critical distance with regard to religion, Strauss holds. This critical distance is ultimately rooted in "the fact that, as a result of the European critique, the dogmatic presuppositions of Orthodoxy have been recognized as questionable."[32] As a result, Strauss argues, political Zionism necessarily must embrace liberalism: "the Zionism I wish to characterize as primarily political Zionism is liberal, that is, it rejects the absolute submission to the Law and instead makes individual acceptance of traditional contents dependent on one's own deliberation."[33]

As Strauss himself observed: "when religious Zionism understands itself, it is in the first place Jewish faith and only secondarily Zionism."[34] Neoorthodoxy takes this argument one step further, asserting that putting Jewish faith first requires abandoning Zionism. As a result, it cannot regard the factual, historical establishment of the state of Israel as *tikkun*, but merely as a phase—albeit an important one—in the *galut*: "The establishment of the state of Israel is the most profound modification of the *galut* which has occurred, but it is not the end of the *galut*: in the religious sense, the state of Israel is a part of the *galut*."[35] Even more than for religious Zionism, for neoorthodoxy the Jewish Question is an absolute problem, a token of divine election. From this perspective, the establishment of the state of Israel can never be more than a relative solution that leaves intact the absolute character of the theological-political problem.

However, Strauss's effort to understand rigorously both political Zionism *and* Jewish religion reveals a profound tension. Although he cautions that the Jewish content endangers political Zionism, he nevertheless asserts that this content contains a specific ancestral legacy he wishes to hold on to "clearly and honestly," even while admitting that political Zionism cannot satisfy the claim to truth that inhabits this legacy. Underlying these concerns, a fundamental problem becomes visible. The process of returning to reality ultimately aims at a reversal of the specific relationship between conditions of existence and normality that characterizes life under *galut*. On the one hand, it strives toward a maximum of normality: the Jewish people must leave the ahistorical and apolitical isolation upheld by faith in a divine promise, and act as a people among other peoples. On the other hand, however, this means that the conditions of existence of the Jewish people as a specifically *Jewish* people are minimized. Normalization, understood as becoming historical and political, entails that certain distinctive characteristics of Jewish identity are relinquished, such as faith in divine election, in Mosaic revelation, and in the coming of the Messiah. The faith-based internal cohesion of the Jewish people is lost, and as a result the Jewish identity of the remaining individuals becomes deeply problematic. Differently stated: with the descent of the *Luftvolk* to the solid ground of historical and political normality, the survival of Judaism as Judaism is put at risk.[36]

Political Zionism, Strauss observes, does not counteract the "de-Judaizing" (*entjudende*) tendencies of assimilation—as Herzl hoped it would—but it actually sustains them.[37] As a result, political Zionism is faced with a dilemma. On the one hand, it derives its legitimacy from the conscious and radical break with the world of *galut* and with the religious foundations of the Jewish tradition. On the other hand, insofar as it claims the title of "Zionism," it cannot avoid referring to that same tradition. Precisely this claim to be *Zionism*—even if it is *political* Zionism—shows that Jewish nationalism has ties to traditional hopes that it can never completely sever without compromising its name.[38] Strauss formulates this dilemma concisely with reference to the process of returning to reality:

> This is precisely our present-day dilemma, namely, that . . . this path has deviated, and has had to deviate, from the content that alone could fulfill this reality; for the attitude that held this content together like an iron ring, the spirit that was alive in them, was the spirit of *galut*.[39]

Political Zionism's appeal to the "will" of the Jewish people ultimately proves to beg the question. Mere normalization, Strauss notes, is not enough: "'A people like all other peoples' cannot be the program of self-critical Zionism."[40] Clearly, this puts him in a very difficult position. On the one hand, the Jewish people cannot survive *without* politics: the closed world of faith and *galut* has been definitely and irretrievably destroyed by modern science and modern politics. On the other hand, it cannot survive with politics *alone*: its legacy continues to emit a claim that is constitutive of Jewish identity and thus cannot be ignored.[41] This claim, however, inevitably points back to religion, which, properly understood, is apolitical and even excludes politics. Jacob Klein, one of his oldest friends, aptly summed up the "theological-political predicament" in which the young Strauss found himself: "His primary interests were two questions: one, the question of God; and two, the question of politics."[42] As his early writings show, his vigorous attempts to keep the two questions separate only reveal a more profound interrelatedness. That Strauss was aware of this is borne out by the fact that in his early writings, he explores the possibilities of doing justice to both the principles of modern science and modern politics and the demands of the Jewish legacy, without resorting to halfhearted and inconsistent compromises or syntheses.

## Biblical Politics, Biblical Science, and the New Theology

Simply put, Strauss searches for ways of reading the Bible freed from traditional and dogmatic elements, and in conformity with the demands of modern science. This combination, he hopes, will enable political Zionism to relate to the great legacy of the Jewish past without compromising its secular and political orientation. This approach requires rejecting all the theological presuppositions traditionally involved in explaining the history of the Jewish people, Strauss asserts. In taking this position, he sides with the renowned historian Simon Dubnow, whose monumental history of Judaism appears in the course of the 1920s and 1930s.[43] Interpreting early Jewish history, Dubnow attempts to explain the events that are related in the Bible solely in terms of natural, political, economic, and cultural factors. Although he is very critical of many aspects of Dubnow's approach, Strauss generally agrees with the latter's sober, political perspective. To boot, he adds, the Bible itself can be seen to contain several natural, causal explanations that support this perspective:

> Thus, the biblical sources themselves give us the possibility of arriving at a—perhaps not deep, but nevertheless accurate—conception of the beginnings of our people. We are thereby urged to assume that the theological conception of these beginnings may derive from a time in which there was no longer any political life, and therefore also no longer any political understanding.[44]

In this pragmatic perspective, the traditional, theological reading of the Bible must be considered as the product of the particular conditions of *galut*, in which the Jewish people were cut off from historical and political reality. Therein lies the specific value of Dubnow's approach for political Zionism, Strauss points out. It is the means par excellence to promote the political awareness of modern Judaism. Moreover, by deriving this purely political account from the Bible itself, it disarms Zionism's opponents, who continue to appeal to the traditional reading.[45]

But, in that case, what happens to religion? According to Strauss, Dubnow's work is rooted in the modern critique of religion, and as such it is an indispensable aid for political Zionism. However, as he also notes, Dubnow's resistance to the traditional reading of the Bible is primarily aimed against what he holds to be the central Jewish dogma: the existence and providence of God in relationship to Jewish history. In Dubnow's reading, there is no place for God as a "real presence," as a provident, wrathful, and just creator: at the most, God is an object, a projection of human experience. Under what conditions, then, can political Zionism nevertheless address the question regarding God and revelation, as Strauss demands? And what happens to the recognition of the primacy of God that is at the core of the Jewish legacy? Isn't it simply excluded by Dubnow's purely pragmatic and causal approach to biblical history?

It seems we are back at the old clash between the critique of religion and science on the one hand and religion on the other. This, however, is not the case, Strauss holds. In his view, the relationship between the two has changed since the seventeenth century. Indeed, initially there was conflict: "There was a time, not so long ago, when the two powers, tradition and science, did not coexist peacefully on parallel planes, with no points of contact, but engaged in a life-and-death struggle for hegemony on the single plane of the 'truth.'"[46] As Strauss emphasizes again, this struggle was decided in favor of the critique of religion and of science. They confronted religion with the alternative: either adapt to the requirements of science and critique, or face ruin. However, he continues, the adaptation religion submitted to was not so much its own merit as the consequence of the fact that eventually the critique began to criticize itself. The Enlightenment's reflexive turn, which is associated with Immanuel Kant, set limits to reason, and thus created new space for religion.

The latter, nevertheless, paid a high price for this commodity: it was compelled to abandon its claim to transcendence and to truth. The place of transcendence was taken by the transcendental constitution of religious consciousness as a necessary postulate of reason. In the long run, however, it became apparent that "an idealistically reinterpreted religion may perhaps be the most amusing thing in the world, it can in any case no longer be religion."[47] Reduced to a mere postulate, religion could be related to various aspects of human experience, but without the claim to transcendence, it was cut off from the source that nourished and sustained it. At the end of this development, it became necessary to address this claim anew, this time with regard to the conditions that had been created by the critique of religion and its self-critique. "In a fundamentally different intellectual situation, the problem of theology had to be posed anew, as one that could be dealt with scientifically."[48]

In this way, Strauss brings to light the historical and intellectual background of the problem he himself is struggling with, as it was adumbrated earlier herein: how to do justice to the ancestral Jewish legacy *and* to the criteria of modernity. Meeting this challenge seems to depend on the possibility of developing a scientific approach to the problem of theology. As becomes apparent from Strauss's early writings, such an approach is, in fact, already available. Not without some enthusiasm, he discusses the so-called new theology that emerges in this period. Challenged by the reflexive turn of the Enlightenment, this new theology points to the shortcomings of the modern historical-critical reading of the Bible, and attempts to take the fundamental claims of religion seriously again. Protestant authors such as Karl Barth, Rudolf Bultmann, and Rudolf Otto integrate elements of neo-Kantianism, phenomenology, and existentialism in a postcritical exegesis of the Bible, in order to return to the roots of religion. In the case of Barth, this leads to the development of a form of neoorthodoxy, a reflexive return within the folds of tradition, reconnecting with the sources of religious experience.

In his autobiographical writings, Strauss discusses more amply the historical background of the "return movement" (*Rückkehrbewegung*) as it developed within Judaism. With its watchword *t'shuvah*, Hebrew for both "return" and "penitence," it addressed assimilated Jews alienated from the tradition by their upbringing and disappointed in the promises of liberal democracy. Its foundations were laid by Hermann Cohen, whose elaboration of neo-Kantianism had led him back to Judaism.[49] Cohen's impulse was taken up and developed by two of the most important Jewish thinkers of the twentieth century: Franz Rosenzweig and Martin Buber. Each in his way contributed to what the young Strauss calls "the reconstruction of traditional theology in a situation created by the critique of tradition."[50]

The new Jewish theology rejected the way in which the so-called moderate Jewish Enlightenment of the eighteenth century had tried to salvage Judaism after the attack of the first wave of the radical Enlightenment. The moderates, led by Moses Mendelssohn, had argued that although the radical Enlightenment was justified in refuting the *external* elements of faith in revelation—such as the authority of oral and written tradition, as well as miracles—this did not mean that its *internal* elements had also been refuted. The latter had retained their validity, and had proven impervious to the scientific and historical critique. Inspired by Kantianism and German Idealism, the moderate Enlightenment no longer understood the fundamental tenets of Judaism against the background of an external and material relationship between God and the world. Rather, it "internalized" these tenets as postulates of reason. Thus, revelation was no longer regarded as a factum brutum surpassing human reason, but it was transformed into a transcendental "religious a priori." Even God himself did not escape this reduction: his external power over the world vanished in favor of the authority of a regulative idea.

According to the return movement, this internalization did more harm than good to Judaism, allowing its contents to evaporate into shadowy precepts without any binding character. The idealist approach liquidated not only the externality of the tradition, but also the immediate human experience of God. With his philosophy of the "I and Thou" (Ich und Du), Buber attempted to restore this experience. Against the moderate Enlightenment, he argued that God and revelation are no mere ideas that guide human reason. On the contrary, the divine can only be experienced as an irruption of the absolute that is completely at odds with all human pursuits, expectations, and desires. It has the character of a compelling, anomalistic call, to which man must respond in an unconditional love for God in order to learn to recognize and love his fellow man.

Rosenzweig added to Buber's contribution by pointing out that the individual rediscovery of the immediate experience of God did not suffice to warrant a return to tradition. It was also necessary to be attentive to the traces of this experience that are to be found in the Bible. From his study Hegel and the State, Rosenzweig concluded that philosophy in its ultimate form—the Hegelian system—had failed.[51] All arguments the philosophic tradition had mustered against revelation had missed their mark. For this reason, he declared the "old thinking" bankrupt and advocated a "new thinking" (neues Denken). Rejecting the idealist quest for the conditions of possibility of experience, he advocated a "radical empiricism" based on the immediate and intuitive experience of three irreducible entities: God, man, and the world. Since it focused on experience, the new thinking was free of the prejudices and reductionisms of traditional philosophy, Rosenzweig argued. For this reason, it was well equipped to guide and accompany the return to Judaism.

According to the young Strauss, the new theology is able to realign science and religion in a way that allows both to assert themselves without compromise, and that permits a fertile interaction. In his early writings he appeals to Hermann Cohen and Rudolf Otto in particular. From Cohen, founder of Marburg neo-Kantianism, he borrows the notion that a rational and scientific critique of religion is already available in principle within religion itself. As Cohen argues, the founders of Jewish and Christian monotheism, the biblical prophets, waged a permanent battle against the folk religion of their times. They opposed the mythical belief in local deities, which was based on terror, by invoking the infinitely greater and more terrifying omnipotence of God. In opposing this mythical order, they evinced a critical rationalism that is akin to the philosophical critique of myth and religion. Theology, which transmits and interprets the legacy of the prophets, is thus faced with the task of conserving and keeping this critical rationality alive. In Strauss's words: "In the final analysis, scientific critique of religion is an *immanent* critique. It exists already where the term 'science' cannot yet be spoken of in the Scholastic sense. The theologians only continue what the prophets had begun."[52]

The latter holds no less for the new theology. The fact that it uses modern scientific and philosophic insights in no way signifies that it violates religion, Strauss argues together with Cohen. On the contrary, these insights support, conserve, and activate the critical potential inherent in religion. In this way, it also becomes possible to take seriously again the foundations of the Jewish religion: insofar as they too express the original rationalism of the prophets, they can be incorporated in a modern philosophical system without being deformed or evacuated. Cohen's achievement, moreover, is counterbalanced and complemented by the work of Rudolf Otto. In his groundbreaking study *The Holy*, Otto firmly rejects the science of religion of the Enlightenment and its Romantic heirs.[53] Against the naturalist account of religion as well as against the transcendental constitution of religious consciousness, he reminds theology of its proper name: its primary subject is not the world, nor man nor religious experience, but God in his transcendence.[54] Otto thus understands divine transcendence radically, independently of man and the world. The holy is the numen, the radically Other that in its mysterious strangeness instills fear because it escapes human control. It is Otto's great merit, Strauss argues, that he deliberately develops his thesis with a view to the modern context: "Otto operates with categories that are useful for the reconstruction of traditional theology in a situation created by the critique of tradition."[55] The specifically modern character of Otto's theology becomes apparent in his identification of the numinous with the irrational, as the central characteristic of the religious object:

> In an earlier day, in a world filled by the irrational moment of religion, it was necessary for theology to achieve recognition for the legitimacy

of the rational. Today, in a spiritual reality dominated by *ratio*, it is the office of theology to bring to life for our era "the irrational in the idea of the Divine" through the medium of the theoretical consciousness.[56]

The fact that transcendence is equated with the irrational does not preclude a rational, scientific theology, Strauss argues. Rather to the contrary: precisely because he draws attention to the irrational, Otto is compelled to reaffirm the place and the role of rationality. This he does by revisiting the medieval doctrine of attributes, the characteristics ascribed to God by man. By understanding the irrational as the bearer of rational attributes, Otto rehabilitates the inherent rationality of human speech about God. For this reason, Strauss stresses, his theology is particularly valuable for Judaism, especially with regard to an adequate relationship to its biblical and ritual tradition. This tradition, he argues, "makes available to us the most perfect expression that the substance of the religious object could possibly find 'in human language.'"[57] Otto's postcritical theology may thus enable modern Jews to read the Bible anew, as a testament of transcendence. Aided by the reconstituted doctrine of attributes, moreover, it allows them to trace the rationality underlying the traditional conception of God.

Just as Cohen's theology makes it possible to integrate traditional Jewish content within a modern philosophical and scientific framework, Otto's work enables us to honor the foundations of the Jewish religion without forsaking the legacy of the European critique of religion. In this sense, the new theology of Cohen and Otto is the necessary supplement to Dubnow's critical reading of biblical history, aimed at promoting the political awareness of modern Jews. Combined, they constitute the means by which political Zionism can relate to the Jewish tradition in a way that meets the criteria of modernity. Politics and theology each receive their due against a common postcritical background: this, we can infer, is the solution Strauss tries to develop in his first publications for the Jewish Question, understood as a theological-political problem.

Conspicuous in Strauss's youthful interest in the new theology is that it attaches far greater importance to Hermann Cohen than to either Franz Rosenzweig or Martin Buber, even though the latter two had eclipsed Cohen in the 1920s. Presumably, Strauss judged Cohen's thought to be more original and more akin to his own radical understanding of religion. This, at any rate, is what we can infer from his later autobiographical reminiscences. As he explains there, he found that none of the thinkers of *t'shuvah* truly succeeded in finding a way back: either there was no genuine return, or what was arrived at was not Jewish religion. The latter reproach is aimed especially against Buber's work. Because Buber gives priority to the immediate experience of God, biblical texts are no more than the human expression or interpretation of a divine call that is absolute, speechless, and literally "inhuman." Moreover, Buber generalizes this characteristic by regarding the various world religions as different interpretations or expressions of this experience. In his view, no interpretation is better than any other in capturing and expressing the experience of absolute alterity. As a result, Strauss observes, not only Buber's own philosophy of "I and Thou" but Judaism as well is reduced to being a mere interpretation. In this way, however, Buber loses sight of the specificity of Judaism. For instance, he one-sidedly emphasizes the *tremendum*-character of the experience of the divine. As a result, faith becomes an attitude characterized by the total absence of support, when expectation abides in "the opened abyss of the final insecurity," the terrifying moment of what Buber calls "the eclipse of God" (*Gottesfinsternis*).[58] Thus, he forgets that the Jewish prophets do not only express their experience of the divine in terrifying abyssal visions. They also offer comforting predictions of the ultimate victory of divine justice and messianic restoration, and thus an absolute certainty.

By concentrating exclusively on the experience of the divine, moreover, Buber neglects another aspect of Jewish tradition, Strauss finds. One of the central claims of traditional Judaism is that the fate of the Jews evinces a mysterious and privileged relationship to the absolute. This relationship is not regarded as one of many possible interpretations, but as the result of an indubitable divine promise. Buber was unable to take this claim seriously, at least any more seriously than similar claims of other religions. As a result of his single-minded focus on the experience of the divine, he refused to have his faith in revelation "tainted" by any orthodoxy, attempting to revive Judaism by concentrating on elements traditionally held to be secondary, such as Hasidic tales. Regarding the primary elements, he continued to harbor strong reservations.

According to Strauss, similar reservations attached to Rosenzweig's concept of *t'shuvah*. In his case as well, the medium of return proved to be more important than the destination. According to Rosenzweig, return to tradition by means of "a leap of faith" was both dangerous and bound to fail. On the basis of his radical empiricism, he argued that a successful attempt to return had to take as focal point the actual experience of the alienated modern Jew. Although Strauss agrees with this focus, he draws a different conclusion from it: if experience is indeed the starting point, the modern Jew has no other choice than to leap back into faith or, more precisely, into the revealed law:

[W]hen speaking of the Jewish experience, one must start from what is primary or authoritative for the Jewish consciousness, and not from what is the primary condition of possibility of the Jewish experience: one must start from God's Law, the Torah, and not from the Jewish nation.[59]

According to Strauss, Rosenzweig was unable to meet his own requirements. His concept of "experience" remained indebted to the modern concept of the individual, which originated in opposition to the traditional religious understanding. In the light of the latter, his distinction between immediate contemporary experience and what was handed down by tradition had little importance: from the point of view of orthodox faith, experience always takes place within a continuum sustained by the authority of the revealed law. An individual's biography cannot be dissociated from faith, since it derives its sense and meaning from faith. For Rosenzweig, however, the revealed law was secondary to the Jewish people: it is the product of the common descent of the Jewish people, as it were, a cultural densification of its turbulent history.

Yet tradition teaches the reverse, Strauss rejoins: according to the Pentateuch, the Jewish people were unified as the chosen people only as a result of the revelation of God's law. Upholding the primacy of experience therefore does not require the preliminary affirmation of the national sentiment or the national spirit, but obedience to the law in its entire traditional rigor. On this point, however, Rosenzweig had fundamental reservations. He conceived of law and tradition as a reservoir from which the individual could draw elements that would assist and guide his return. Strauss strongly objects to this approach: "The sacred law, as it were the public temple, which was a reality, thus becomes a potential, a quarry, or a store-house out of which each individual takes the materials for building his private shelter."[60] That this approach is based on an implicit denial of the divine origin is exemplified by the ambivalence of Rosenzweig's neoorthodoxy toward traditional orthodoxy— he always opposed the orthodox legalist approach to the law. In his view, the Torah was a mirror in which the individual's inner experience of God could recognize itself, just as it could recognize itself in other elements of tradition. Concurrently, in his reading of the Bible he emphasized commandments over the prohibitions that are central in the orthodox view. Similarly, Rosenzweig was very reluctant regarding the miracles reported in the Bible. His faith in miracles developed very slowly, always attended and tested by the "new thinking" and its focus on immediate experience. Within orthodoxy, this reluctance is absent, Strauss points out: an omnipotent and inscrutable creator is an undeniable guarantee for the authenticity of all recorded miracles. Every form of doubt is regarded as a weakness of faith, which should be independent of one's personal situation.

Rosenzweig's selective approach and his emphasis on the free individual intercourse with the tradition derived from a historicization of the Torah, conditioned by modern premises like individualism and liberalism. For this reason, Strauss argues, he was no more able than Buber to accept the rigorous externality of the revealed law as a whole. Although both thinkers opposed the "internalizations" of the moderate Jewish Enlightenment, in fact they carried out a similar transformation. They reconstituted the externality of revelation in the experience of the *tremendum*—bypassing the law—in order to reinternalize it as the object of a free individual quest. From the perspective of the latter, the law and other elements of tradition were only a sounding board at the disposal of the "homecomers" (*Heimkehrer*). This helps explain why, in his early writings, Strauss maintained a critical distance with regard to both Rosenzweig and Buber in his attempt to balance post-critical theology and political Zionism.

## Quaestio Iuris: The Legacy of Spinoza

The project, however, never gets past this first step, and is never systematically elaborated. After 1925, both Dubnow and the new theologians disappear completely from Strauss's writings, as does the attempt to do justice to both the Jewish content and political Zionism. What is more, political Zionism itself gradually recedes into the background. When Strauss broaches the subject again in writing in 1932, he can be seen to be taking leave of his youthful commitment, a process that is officially brought to a conclusion in 1935, as we will see. For all purposes, his initial enterprise seems to be a closed chapter.

Whence this remarkable change? Why does Strauss abandon his project even before it has begun to get off the ground? The most important reason is that gradually its fundamental presupposition has become doubtful. This presupposition, it will be remembered, was that the "European critique," the critique of religion, had effected a profound and irrevocable change in the situation of Judaism. Its success ushered in the end of *galut* and the beginning of emancipation and assimilation, initiating a process that eventually would lead to political Zionism on the one hand and the new theology on the other. In his contributions to the Zionist self-assessment of the 1920s, in his efforts to take religion seriously and in his debates with cultural and religious Zionism as well as with Jewish orthodoxy, Strauss never ceases to press this point: modern Judaism cannot ignore or escape the legacy of the critique of religion, modern science, and modern politics.

This does not mean, however, that he simply sides with "Europe." When he discusses the way in which Europe effectively and radically affected the closed world of *galut*, he does so with the intention of determining both the point and the scope of this impact as accurately as possible. In several of his early publications, he warns against the uncritical application of modern scientific theories to the problems of Judaism. Such attempts, he argues, can only further jeopardize the situation of modern Jews. Instead, one must time and again ask the question, with what right does one transfer elements from the European context to the Jewish context? Or, more emphatically, "Of what concern is Europe to us as Jews!" (*Was geht uns als Juden Europa an!*)[61] According to Strauss, this *Rechtsfrage* or *quaestio iuris*, the question regarding the legitimacy of contact between the two spheres, is nothing less than "the central problem of our spiritual situation."[62] Hence, his answer is actually intended to be restrictive: the success of the critique of religion is, in fact, the *only* point on which there has been any legitimate contact between Europe and Judaism.

An important implication of this restriction is that the legitimacy of political Zionism, like that of assimilation, is made essentially dependent on the pertinence and the legitimacy of the critique of religion, more specifically on the fact that "this critique *made an impact on* the Jewish context."[63] Precisely this "fact" becomes increasingly doubtful to Strauss in the course of the 1920s. Apparently, the tension underlying his uncompromising understanding of both political Zionism *and* Jewish religion became ever harder to uphold. To estimate the importance of this event, we do well to turn to the autobiographical preface to *Spinoza's Critique of Religion*. As he explains there, the problems attendant to both Zionism and the new theology and its qualified return to tradition proved to be of such a magnitude that he eventually came to wonder "whether an unqualified return to Jewish orthodoxy was not both possible and necessary—was not at the same time the solution to the problem of the Jew lost in the non-Jewish world and the only course compatible with sheer consistency or intellectual probity."[64] Similarly, in a lecture of 1932, he notes, "The possibility emerged that European reservations vis-à-vis the Jewish tradition were no longer at all possible and necessary: Judaism *in its entirety* (*das integrale Judentum*) appeared to become possible again."[65]

As the early writings show, however, the young Strauss is not prepared to make this momentous decision without further ado. Before taking this step, he considers it his first and foremost duty to revisit the one genuine obstacle to an unqualified return to orthodoxy, the obstacle that is at the same time the basis of his own youthful commitment: the critique of religion. What this entails can already be inferred from his very first publication, where he draws attention to "the role *Spinoza* plays in the formulation of the modern view of the world and the modern view of the state."[66] For how else could the critique of religion engage in a "life-and-death struggle for hegemony on the single plane of the 'truth'" other than with a *Tractatus Theologico-Politicus*, a theological-political treatise?[67] Spinoza was the first to attack the authority of revealed religion by offering a systematic and scientific analysis of the Bible in order to disengage theological claims to truth and political claims to power. His critique provided the groundwork for the antireligious attack of the Enlightenment, as well as for the development of modern biblical science.[68] More importantly, the critical shockwaves of the *Theological-Political Treatise* also affected the Jewish religion and the ancient vault of the *galut*.

This does not exhaust Spinoza's significance for Judaism, however. As Strauss points out, in the final chapters of the *Treatise* he designed a political model that is generally regarded as a prototype of modern liberal democracy, a secular society based on individual freedom.[69] In Spinoza's model, citizenship was open to all, and hence also to Jews. On the basis of his critique of the Bible, Spinoza had concluded that Mosaic Law was no longer effective. As a result, nothing could prevent the Jews from abandoning their old world and participating in European culture.[70] In this respect, Strauss argues, the *Theological-Political Treatise* can be regarded as the founding document of Jewish assimilation:

> When what mattered was the justification of the breakup of the Jewish tradition and the entry of the Jews into modern Europe, perhaps no better, but certainly no more convenient, reference offered itself than the appeal to Spinoza. Who was more suitable for undertaking the justification of modern Judaism before the tribunal of the Jewish tradition, on the one hand, and before the tribunal of modern Europe, on the other, than Spinoza, who, as was almost universally recognized, was a classical exponent of this Europe?[71]

But even this does not yet sufficiently capture Spinoza's importance for modern Judaism, Strauss warns. In the third chapter of the *Theological-Political Treatise*, Spinoza wrote of his orthodox Jewish contemporaries: "If the foundations of their religion did not effeminate their minds, I would certainly believe that they will some time, given the occasion—so changeable are human affairs—establish their state again, and that God may elect them again."[72] With irony bordering on sarcasm, Spinoza intimates that the possibility of a restoration of the Jewish state primarily depended on the readiness to forfeit the fundamental principles of Jewish religion, which he held responsible for the precarious isolation of Jews in the first place. The view that Jewish suffering under *galut* had a supernatural ground, and the strongly ritualized way of life based on it, reflected and consolidated a fatal lack of political organization. According to Spinoza, the Jews had to free themselves from the stranglehold of tradition by means of a sober, critical reading of the Bible.

Hence, Strauss observes, the *Theological-Political Treatise* is the birth certificate not only of assimilation, but also of political Zionism. In spite of—or perhaps owing to—his irony, Spinoza was the first to anticipate the possibility of a purely political solution of the Jewish Question.[73] He detached the restoration and self-preservation of the Jewish people from its traditional divine guarantee, and made it entirely dependent on a purely human, political effort.[74] As is well known, Spinoza paid a high price for his critical position. The orthodox Jewish community of Amsterdam pronounced a *herem*, a ruling of total excommunication, against him, after which he led a solitary and withdrawn existence.

The irony of history, however, seems to have followed that of the philosopher, who subsequently came to be known as one of the founders, not only of modernity, but also of Jewish modernity. All of the central characteristics of the modern Jewish condition point to Spinoza's work: not only the break with tradition and assimilation, but also political Zionism and modern theology ultimately derive their legitimacy from the success of his critique of religion. However, Strauss rejoins, the fact that a critique is successful does not yet mean that it is justified and well founded. Being victorious in a life-and-death struggle does not yet prove that victory was deserved. On the contrary, if on closer examination the critique should prove to be unfounded, to what extent can it be called successful? This question can be answered only by means of a careful investigation of the foundations and the effectiveness of Spinoza's critique of religion. Only such an investigation can answer the *quaestio iuris* and thus also the crucial question whether an unqualified return to Jewish orthodoxy is imperative. Strauss notes tersely in the autobiographical preface, "Orthodoxy could be returned to only if Spinoza was wrong in every respect."[75]

With this programmatic assertion, Strauss also indicates how far he had moved away from the return movement of Buber and Rosenzweig. The main reason for their inability to return unconditionally under the authority of the law is that they remained beholden to the basic premises of the Enlightenment, he submits. Rosenzweig's critique of traditional philosophy was mainly a rejection of Hegel's idealist synthesis between religion and Enlightenment. By rejecting this synthesis, he intended to clear the path for the "new thinking." According to Strauss, however, this reasoning was insufficient in order to justify a blanket farewell to the "old thinking," let alone a return to religion:

> It was believed that one could dismiss any direct and thematic discussion with the Enlightenment, since it was assumed—logically, in the sense of the "overcome" Hegelianism—that with the "overcoming" of Hegelianism one had simultaneously "overcome" the Enlightenment which Hegelianism had "transcended." In truth, however, the critique of Hegelianism had actually led, in the nature of the case, to a rehabilitation of the Enlightenment.[76]

In developing their new theology, the advocates of *t'shuvah* wrongly assumed that a dismissal of the Hegelian synthesis necessarily entails the rejection of its constitutive parts. Rather, Strauss argues, if one rejects the synthesis, both constitutive parts are actually restored and thus also the tension that existed between them before they were "sublated." This means that both religion and Enlightenment reappear in their "life-and-death struggle for hegemony on the one plane of the 'truth.'"[77] In this sense, Buber and Rosenzweig were too hasty. The main obstacle to be overcome in order to return to Jewish religion in its original sense is not the idealist internalization but the Enlightenment critique, which had been aimed exclusively against religion in its rigorous, external sense. For this reason, Strauss concludes that although "Jewish theology was resurrected from a deep slumber" by Rosenzweig, his one-sided identification of philosophy with Hegelianism prevented him from advancing to a deeper level, that of the original conflict between radical Enlightenment and revealed religion.[78] Had he done so, Strauss implies, he would have found that the avowed victory of the former and the defeat of the latter must be reconsidered. Why occupy oneself with a new theology beholden to Spinoza's critique of religion, when in fact this critique itself is in need of scrutiny? Thus, what began as a contribution to the self-reflection of postwar political Zionism now leads to an inquiry into the foundations of European and Jewish modernity. As a theological-political problem, the Jewish Question proves to possess a complexity that requires us to return to the origins of modernity.

# CHAPTER 2

# The Shadow of Spinoza

*Farewell here, no matter where. Conscripts of good will, we'll have a ferocious philosophy: ignorant of science, wily for comfort: let the world go hang. That's true progress. Forward—march!*

—Rimbaud, *Illuminations* ("Democracy")

## "A Humanly Incomprehensible Betrayal"

Reviled as a godless heretic in his own time, Spinoza was rehabilitated in the eighteenth century by German philosophy, exalted by nineteenth-century Romanticism, and finally received into the philosophical pantheon in the twentieth century as one of modernity's founders.[1] This process was not exclusively Western European; Spinoza's reputation became firmly established in the Jewish world as well. According to Strauss, however, the inviolability attendant to this almost canonical status led to a certain neutrality and even indifference, which constitutes the primary obstacle for any attempt at a critical reassessment. Fortunately, Strauss points out, this obstacle was already cleared away by Hermann Cohen. The founder of neo-Kantianism and the rejuvenator of Jewish theology was also the first to challenge the modern Jewish veneration of Spinoza.

In an essay of 1910 entitled "Spinoza On State and Religion, Judaism and Christianity" ("Spinoza über Staat und Religion, Judentum und Christentum"), Cohen launched an unusually fierce attack on Spinoza.[2] With the *Theological-Political Treatise*, he argued, Spinoza had written a tendentious political pamphlet in which he had given free rein to his feelings of hatred and revenge toward the Jews. As the title indicated, the text was a hybrid construct aimed at securing the writer's interests on two separate fronts: religion and politics. On the one hand, Spinoza put his talents as a political writer at

31

the service of the secular regime of the De Witt brothers, from which he had received a modest stipend. On the other hand, he had tried to placate the orthodox Christian establishment by discrediting Judaism, developing a critical reading of the Old Testament that denied Mosaic authority and reduced the old religion to the status of a mere political instrument. The fact that he was far less severe with regard to the New Testament, and that he declared his agreement with Paul's critique of Mosaic Law, was the proverbial last straw for Cohen. Speaking of "a humanly incomprehensible betrayal" of Judaism, he castigated Spinoza as a renegade who abused his exceptional intellectual gifts to bolster the anti-Jewish attitude of Christianity. In Cohen's view, the *herem* issued by the Amsterdam *sanhedrin* was fully justified.

This severe judgment marked a turning point in the Jewish reception of Spinoza.[3] In Germany as well as abroad, Cohen enjoyed a brilliant reputation as a philosopher, theologian, and Jewish thinker. That a leading light of modern Judaism castigated one of its "founding fathers" was a remarkable event. Precisely because of its contentious and untimely character, Strauss hails Cohen's attack as an excellent starting point for his own inquiry. This does not mean, however, that he adopts Cohen's view throughout. Rather, he develops his own approach in a critical reading of Cohen's essay. For, if he praises Cohen's courage in contesting the prevailing view, he also suggests that Cohen may have gone too far. In particular, his "biographical" reading of the *Theological-Political Treatise* leads to a misguided interpretation. Whether Spinoza was actually driven by anti-Jewish sentiments is without importance, Strauss insists. Both the purpose and the results of the *Treatise* can be sufficiently understood by a "dutiful" (*pflichtmäßig*), historical-critical reading, without the need for any reference to the historical or biographical details of Spinoza's relationship with Judaism.[4]

According to Cohen, the connection between politics and theology implied by the title of the *Treatise* is contingent, a mere reflection of Spinoza's contingent personal interests. Against this objection, Strauss argues that there is an intrinsic and coherent connection. As its title asserts, the *Treatise* intends to show "that the freedom to philosophize can not only be allowed with due regard to piety and peace in the state, but that it can only be suspended together with piety and peace in the state."[5] Thus, the connection becomes clearly visible when one looks at the declared purpose of the *Treatise*: to secure the freedom of philosophizing, which the earthly powers regarded as a threat to peace and stability, and which the religious powers regarded as a threat to piety. Religious piety and political peace, however, were anything but separated issues in Spinoza's time. Secular and spiritual powers were locked in a dogged struggle for political power, in which *both* parties invoked theological arguments. Hence, Strauss asks rhetorically, "Can one speak of an objective isolation from one another of the political and ecclesiastic-theological problems in the seventeenth century?"[6] Starting from modern premises, Cohen's critique erroneously takes this isolation for granted. As a result, it ignores the indications supplied by the *Treatise*'s subtitle.

When the purpose of the *Treatise* is taken seriously, Cohen's other objections equally lose their power. Thus, his allegation that Spinoza wrote the *Treatise* to take revenge on the Jews because of the *herem* amounts to a reversal of cause and effect, Strauss argues. Spinoza was excommunicated because he held the freedom of philosophizing and the autonomy of reason to be incompatible with faith and obedience to revealed law, and not the other way around. Similarly, Cohen's objection that the *Treatise*'s focus on the Old Testament reveals an anti-Jewish bias misinterprets the particular character of its approach. In Spinoza's time, the dominant interpretation of the Bible was protestant. According to Protestantism, the traditional, institutional reading of the Bible was responsible for the decay of Christianity.[7] In order to stop this decline, a return was necessary to the original and pure biblical teaching. Hence, principles of faith and religious doctrines could only be derived in direct confrontation with the biblical text, without appealing to external sources. For this reason, Strauss argues, Protestantism devoted relatively more attention to the Old Testament. Since Spinoza aimed to criticize the protestant spiritual powers of his time, he was compelled to imitate this procedure. Thus, he deliberately presented his critique as an attempt to restore the original and pure meaning of the biblical teaching. In reality, his exegesis was directed against that of Protestant orthodoxy: its aim was to show that the original biblical teaching had no cognitive value whatsoever and thus did not have any power over autonomous reason. Ostensibly a return to the source, the *Treatise* conceals a critique of the source itself.[8]

A similar observation can be made regarding Cohen's objection that the *Treatise* reduces the Jewish religion to a mere political instrument. On this point as well, Strauss argues, Spinoza emulates the strategy of protestant orthodoxy, which equally developed a politicizing reading of the Bible in order to support its political claims. Pointing to the separate but parallel existence of worldly and spiritual powers in the ancient Hebrew state, Protestantism wanted to assert its own power against the secular powers and to justify its interference in worldly affairs. A partisan to the cause of the Dutch republic, Spinoza used the same argument, only to turn it against protestant orthodoxy. In his view, the separation of powers in the Hebrew state had produced dire consequences: by proclaiming the revealed law, Moses had intended to subject religion to politics in the first place, in order to secure Jewish national unity. In this way, Spinoza argued ad hominem in favor of the cause of the Dutch regents, insofar as it concurred with the cause of philosophy. The stipend he received from the secular authorities did not play a significant role. In assigning the monopoly of power to the state rather than the church, he argued that only the state could guarantee the neutrality and the freedom of philosophy both against the church and against the state itself. By the same token, he denied the church any position of power.[9]

Hence, Strauss concludes, those elements of the *Theological-Political Treatise* Cohen disparages by tracing them to Spinoza's biography can be explained in much more plausible way by a "dutiful" *(pflichtmäßig)* interpretation that takes into account the historical and intellectual context. Cohen's "biographical" critique fails to appreciate the specific motive underlying the *Treatise*: the emancipation of philosophy as the autonomous application of human reason, or, in Spinoza's own words, the "natural light" *(lumen naturale)*.[10] Nevertheless, Strauss adds, Cohen's attack does have the merit of clearing the path for an adequate interpretation of the *Treatise*, precisely by calling attention to the motive of the author. For, regardless of whether the work was inspired by anti-Jewish sentiments, Spinoza did investigate the Bible with a specific intention, and this investigation had an undeniable impact on traditional Judaism. Therefore, it is of the utmost importance for modern Judaism to understand how this impact was possible:

> We are guided here by the interests of Judaism. These interests are affected in the gravest manner by the question of which image of the biblical world possesses the binding power of the truth. This is why Spinoza, who through his critique contributed more than anyone to the removal of the traditional image, is of interest to us.[11]

But if not Spinoza's intention, are not the method and the results of his biblical research necessarily anti-Jewish? According to Cohen, both exhibit a treacherous preference for Christianity. Here again, Strauss rejoins, the evidence adduced can be accounted for without this accusation. Admittedly, Spinoza opens the *Treatise* with an analysis of prophecy. Although this may create the impression that Spinoza singles out the Jewish tradition and spares Christianity, this approach is, in fact, predicated on Spinoza's effort to emancipate human reason. In order to argue the autonomy of rational knowledge, he is compelled first to determine the epistemological status as well as the cognitive value of prophecy. Only when it is demonstrated that reason alone can lead to true knowledge can Spinoza introduce analytical and critical distinctions. Contrary to what Cohen assumes, this does not involve a pro-Christian prejudice.

Even when Spinoza appears to side openly with Christianity there are pragmatic reasons, Strauss adds. Thus, when he espouses Paul's critique of the Jewish law, he does so because he regards charity as the only true biblical commandment and thus as the core of faith and piety. Of course, this "minimalist" conception of faith is anything but Pauline: it derives from Spinoza's view that biblical doctrine has no cognitive but only practical value. Already in the preface of the *Treatise*, Spinoza writes that his investigations taught him that "the authority of the prophets only carries weight in those matters that regard the practice of life and true virtue, and that otherwise their opinions hardly affect us."[12] The argument in support of this view is supplied in the thirteenth chapter, the title of which states that "Scripture teaches nothing if not very simple things and aims at nothing beyond obedience," and thus has no authority over autonomous reason.[13] The radical implications of this view, however, were hidden from view by the ostensibly pious references to Paul.[14]

While this counters Cohen's objections to Spinoza's method, there remains the matter of the results of his investigations. These, however, cannot be said to be more critical with regard to Judaism than regarding other revealed religions, Strauss holds. Even where they focus on the Old Testament, they are concerned with biblical elements that were controversial within Jewish orthodoxy as well. The question of the corporality of God, for example, had been a bone of contention among Jewish theologians long before Spinoza uttered his criticisms. The same holds for the tension between national or particular elements and universal elements that permeates the Pentateuch, and which Spinoza takes to task. The Bible contains both passages that refer to the divine election of the Jewish nation and passages that proclaim the love of God for all nations. Hence, the fact that Spinoza rejects divine election as religious particularism and appeals to the universal elements cannot be attributed to an inadmissible reading of the Bible, nor to a politicizing interpretation of biblical history. These and other observations lead Strauss to the conclusion that "the essential conclusions of Spinoza's Bible science are sufficiently motivated by the actual nature of the object of this science."[15]

According to Strauss, Spinoza was compelled to *defend* the autonomy of reason and the freedom of philosophy against the worldly and the spiritual powers. For this reason, he had to adapt and accommodate his modus operandi to their theological-political discourse. Cohen, for whom the legitimacy of the Enlightenment is a matter of course, incorrectly interprets Spinoza's political and historical accommodations as a pointed attack against Judaism. The emergence of biblical science, however, should be regarded as a *European* event, Strauss asserts: Spinoza's efforts to emancipate reason were not primarily aimed against Judaism, but against all forms of revealed religion insofar as they denied the autonomy of human reason. This more general orientation made Spinoza a founder of the Enlightenment. Hence, there is no reason to speak of a "humanly incomprehensible betrayal."[16]

Nevertheless, Cohen's errors are instructive because they help us to more accurately raise the question regarding the significance of Spinoza's biblical science for Judaism. If the motives underlying the *Theological-Political Treatise* can be made sufficiently clear by means of a "dutiful" reading, without invoking Spinoza's personal relationship to Judaism, how can its undeniable historical effect on Judaism be explained? How did a general critique of revealed religion succeed in profoundly affecting the traditional Jewish world? Differently stated: if Spinoza's motives are explicable without referring to his personal background, what is their relevance for the interests of Judaism? The customary answer is that Spinoza's reading of the Bible is more sober and honest than its traditional counterpart. Strauss, it should be remembered, initially shared this judgment when he appealed to the historical work of Dubnow. The following passage shows that he has come to question this view:

> From our standpoint, however, it must be asked in all seriousness how this "honesty" relates to possible higher needs of Judaism, whether it bestows a right to destroy the beautiful world of tradition? What does the struggle for the autonomy of science and the state have to do with the interest of Judaism? What interest can Judaism have in knowing what the dawn of its history was *really (wirklich)* like?[17]

Underneath these questions, we can discern the *Rechtsfrage*, the *quaestio iuris* already discussed in the previous chapter: of what concern is Europe to Judaism, and with what right has Europe penetrated and altered the world of tradition? Was the contact between the two worlds legitimate? Did Judaism have—and does it still have—an interest in being enlightened about its origins, and if so, what is that interest? The radicalism with which Cohen summons Spinoza before the tribunal of Judaism fortifies Strauss in his view that a renewed confrontation with the *Theological-Political Treatise* is in order. In the next section, we will see how he stages this confrontation.

## Before the Tribunal:
## Biblical Science and the Critique of Religion

Strauss's debate with Cohen is the catalyst for his own investigations, not only in the theoretical sense, but also in the material and practical sense. By the strength and quality of his article, he is appointed as a researcher at the Academy for the Science of Judaism (Akademie für die Wissenschaft des Judentums), under the supervision of Julius Guttmann. An interesting coincidence: the academy had been founded shortly after the First World War through a collaboration between Franz Rosenzweig and Hermann Cohen.[18] Strauss's official research assignment is to investigate the biblical science of Spinoza and some of his predecessors.[19]

When one compares the original assignment with the result, however, a discrepancy leaps to the eye. The book that presents the fruits of Strauss's research bears the full title *Spinoza's Critique of Religion as the Basis of His Biblical Science: Investigations into Spinoza's Theological-Political Treatise*. Apparently, the focus originally assigned (Spinoza's biblical science) has changed to his critique of religion, which is now identified as its basis to boot. This is remarkable, considering the fact that it runs counter to the reigning view, according to which the relationship is exactly the reverse: biblical science as the basis of the critique of religion. In fact, it runs counter to Spinoza's own assertion. As he claims in the *Theological-Political Treatise*, his critique of the Bible is based on an impartial, scientific reading of Scripture. This is the claim—the claim to greater "honesty" mentioned earlier—with which, after Spinoza, biblical science developed into one of the most important tools of the Enlightenment, if not the most important.

Why this striking reversal? Strauss provides the following motivation. In the course of his research, it became apparent that the focus had to be shifted to the critique of religion as a *condition of possibility* for biblical science.[20] To begin with, he points to the method of biblical science, which Spinoza explicitly models on natural science. This becomes apparent from the set of basic rules Spinoza formulates in the seventh chapter of the *Theological-Political Treatise*, entitled "Of the Interpretation of Scripture." First, the Bible may be explained only by means of the Bible itself.[21] Second, the text may be judged only by its literal meaning, for only the latter is the true meaning which as such is accessible to both the believer and the nonbeliever.[22] Third, the reconstruction of the true meaning must proceed from the general to the specific, or from the universal to the particular. This means that one has to determine first what the Bible teaches everywhere in a univocal, clear, and unambiguous way with regard to universal themes. Once this has been done, less general elements can be interpreted in the light of what has been established.[23]

As we saw, Strauss argues that this modus operandi largely mirrors the "purist" approach of contemporary protestant scholars. However, he also points out that Spinoza's restoration of the Bible's original teaching by returning to the uncorrupt, authentic text serves an entirely different purpose. His biblical science is rooted in a hermeneutical decision to understand the Bible as a literary text and to subject it to literary criticism, following criteria that apply to the interpretation of texts in general.[24] The fundamental presupposition of this decision is that the Bible is a document written by human beings. As Strauss succinctly puts it, "The Bible is a human book—in this one sentence we can sum up all the presuppositions of Spinoza's Bible science."[25]

Although this presupposition warrants the possibility of a scientific approach, it is far from obvious that it has a sufficient scientific foundation itself, Strauss continues. From a religious point of view, to say the least, it is unacceptable. For a believer, the Bible derives its specific authority from its nonhuman, divine origin: its contents were revealed by God himself and subsequently written down by man. This premise, of course, leads to an entirely different exegesis. Hence, when Spinoza posits the basic assumption of his scientific hermeneutics, he first has to confront a rival hermeneutics. If he wants to see his interpretation accepted, he is first compelled to subvert the traditional reading of the Bible. In other words, he must successfully refute the rival point of view before he can go on to found biblical science.

Moreover, there is a second argument that shows the priority of the critique of religion over biblical science. This becomes apparent when one looks at the relationship between the *Treatise* and Spinoza's other great work, the *Ethics*. From the central teaching of the *Ethics*, the impossibility of revelation follows logically. When God is identified with the unchangeable and intelligible order of nature, every supernatural and inscrutable intervention is excluded, such as revelation or creation ex nihilo.[26] The only divine laws are the eternal and immutable laws of nature, and God's activity coincides with the reign of causal necessity, understood as logical necessity. For God to violate his own laws by declaring his will in a miraculous way would amount to a logical contradiction.[27] The same holds for man: to act against divine will or natural necessity is impossible. According to Spinoza, the unity of will and understanding of God or nature are operative in everything that is, including human action. Carrying this doctrine of "predestination" to its extreme, he denies the existence of sin.[28]

On the most fundamental level, then, Spinoza's critique of revealed religion is identical to the closed system of the *Ethics*, Strauss argues.[29] When one accepts the basic premises of this system, it automatically follows that the biblical assertions about God and the prophets are based on errors. What is more, it follows that there is no place for the inscrutable and omnipotent biblical God within the totality of beings. But if revelation is so carefully excluded from the bulwark of the *Ethics*, whence the need to venture outside and attack existing revealed religion by means of its most authoritative text? Why undertake a critique of religion at all? The explanation, Strauss argues, requires us to turn once again to the historical context of the *Theological-Political Treatise* and its purpose: to secure the freedom of philosophizing in combination with political and religious stability. In the seventeenth century, this freedom is threatened by a theological-political conflict. While the legitimacy of philosophy and the right of reason to judge autonomously are beyond question for Spinoza, he sees religious orthodoxy expand its tutelage in ever more violent ways, and in an escalating conflict with secular powers. In writing the *Treatise*, Spinoza responds to this situation by pursuing a twofold goal.

To begin with, he wishes to defuse the theological-political powder keg by presenting an interpretation of the Bible less prone to producing controversy and compatible with the freedom of philosophizing. It should be noted that Spinoza does not intend to eradicate religion root and branch. Although he regards religion as a kind of superstition, he also indicates that its errors and prejudices are rooted in human nature and thus possess a natural necessity.[30] Superstition originates when the human striving for self-preservation attaches itself to transitory objects and becomes entangled in the web of the passions. Man attributes his misfortunes, his powerlessness and despair to the anger of a higher power, which he subsequently tries to appease by means of rituals. In this way, he subjects himself to a projection of his own fear, trying to avert illusory dangers with illusory measures. Escape from this vicious circle is possible only when the striving for self-preservation is directed toward the eternal, when man discovers the eternal within the self-determining activity of the mind. In the theoretical or philosophical life, man learns to know and love the eternal, and his striving for self-preservation finds its highest fulfillment.[31] Nevertheless, only few are capable of liberating themselves from the domination of the passions, Spinoza holds. The large majority remain irretrievably caught in the temporal, are incapable of "governing their affairs in accordance with a fixed plan," and fall prey to superstition.[32]

Nevertheless, in the form of religion, superstition can play a useful social role, on the condition that its doctrines and commandments are coordinated as much as possible. As we have seen, Spinoza makes clever use of the "purism" of protestant exegesis. In his "purified" reading, the principles of the biblical teaching approximate as far as possible those of a minimal rational morality. To this end, ostensibly appealing to Paul, he accords a central place to the commandment of charity, although in fact he merely attributes a practical significance to it. In this way, he allows a "disarmed" Bible to retain its function as a support and guide for whoever is incapable of leading a philosophical life, as opposed to the philosopher, whose autonomy is the correlate of his theoretical activity.

This brings us to the second and most important goal of the *Treatise*, which is to secure the survival of philosophy. The theological-political conflicts of the age, Spinoza observes, prevent the few capable of philosophizing from detaching themselves from the authority of Scripture. Caught in the prejudices and superstitions forced on them by the theologians, they lack confidence in the legitimacy and the power of their own reason. Hence, Strauss argues, the program of the *Treatise* is aimed at reawakening their confidence in reason by challenging the claims of theology. The scientific reconstruction and interpretation of the Bible is intended to show that its *sole* purpose is to promote pious obedience to the commandments of justice and charity. In this, it differs fundamentally from philosophy, the sole purpose of which is the discovery of the truth through reason. Thus, the domain of theology is closely circumscribed and strictly distinguished from that of philosophy. According to Spinoza, the theologians' sole task is to oversee the following of the biblical teaching, nothing more. They have no right to place philosophy under their tutelage, let alone to persecute the philosophers.

In order to rekindle confidence in reason, however, Spinoza cannot appeal to the *Ethics*, since the latter already presupposes the legitimacy of reason. Before he can initiate his readers into his philosophical system, they must be liberated from the prejudice that reason cannot operate autonomously because it is subject to revealed religion. To this end, an impartial and scientific determination of the biblical teaching is required. Only when this determination has been completed can the question be raised whether the biblical doctrine is true, and can the prejudice be critically refuted. Hence, Strauss argues, the scientific design of the *Treatise* is essentially propaedeutic: the book aims to liberate the reader toward philosophy—Spinoza's philosophy—but it is itself prephilosophic or pretheoretic. It does not address philosophic or theoretic reason, but only reason as such, in order to release reason from the hold of revealed religion.[33]

According to Strauss, however, this presentation is somewhat misleading: if we are to believe Spinoza, we first have to ascertain what the Bible teaches *de facto*, in order to subsequently judge whether this teaching is also valid *de iure*.[34] This obscures the fact that the very first step is possible only on the basis of a preliminary critique of the orthodox interpretation. For, as we saw earlier on, the hermeneutical basic rules of Spinoza's biblical science imply that the Bible is a human product, and this implication in its turn presupposes the successful refutation of the opposing view: "The mere fact that Spinoza's Bible science *ought to be* (*sein soll*) the foundation of a critique of revelation proves that in truth the critique of revelation *is* the precondition of Bible science."[35] The requirement that a scientific inquiry into the Bible be the basis of a critique can be fulfilled only when the hermeneutic position of the opponent has *already* been subjected to critique and rejected.

This sequence becomes apparent in the structure of the *Theological-Political Treatise*, Strauss observes. The basis of biblical science is laid only in the seventh chapter, "On the Interpretation of Scripture." In the preceding chapters, Spinoza criticizes various aspects of the traditional interpretation of the Bible, in particular prophetic revelation, divine providence, the authority of tradition, and miracles. The critique developed in these chapters is intended to be radical, principled, and universal: Spinoza contests both the possibility and the intelligibility of revelation in general, and thus aims at all religions that claim to be revealed and claim to have universal validity.[36]

The two purposes of the *Theological-Political Treatise* thus require a new scientific exegesis of the Bible, which is capable, on the one hand, of mitigating the theological-political conflict because it is generally acceptable and, on the other hand, of referring theology within its proper boundaries, so that potential philosophers can be shown the way toward philosophy. In both cases, however, a *critique* of the principles of the traditional exegesis is the necessary prerequisite. Only when the position of the opponent has been refuted convincingly is Spinoza able to deploy his own hermeneutical principles, and can biblical science proceed. The foundation of the latter must therefore be sought in the critique of religion.

But is the critique itself scientific? Spinoza, at any rate, answers in the affirmative. In his view, it is purely theoretical and free of any presuppositions. According to Strauss, however, there is reason for doubt. In his view, it is possible and even necessary to ask whether indeed there are no presuppositions at play. In fact, the possibility of raising this question is contained in the very priority of the critique of religion over biblical science he has uncovered:

However, when Spinoza reaches beyond the context of his own life and thought and when he embarks on the critique of another context, he is subject to a norm other than the one immanent to him. By undertaking this critique he subjects himself to the judgment implicit in the question (*das Gericht der Frage*) of whether he hit or missed the criticized context.

Only when this question is posed do the specific presuppositions of his critique emerge.[37]

With his critique of religion, Strauss explains, Spinoza leaves the seclusion of his philosophical system in order to assail the legitimacy of a different, alien order. By taking this step, it becomes possible for a third party to ascertain whether the critique attains its goal, and on what grounds. Strauss's use of the word "tribunal" (*Gericht*) in the original German passage is striking. For where else could a *Rechtsfrage* be addressed? His choice of words shows how his original question continues to guide his current research and has become more focused. From the Zionist dilemma through the general confrontation between Europe and Judaism, we have now arrived at the point where Spinoza reaches beyond his philosophical system and prepares to strike out at revealed religion. The passage quoted, however, adds a number of other important elements. First, the presuppositions of Spinoza's critique of religion come to the surface only when it is viewed "in action," at the moment when it actually confronts its opponent. This requires, second, that the latter's position is also brought within the range of inquiry and taken into account, as the setting of a tribunal requires:

> We cannot hope for a decision on this point and thus on the answer to the question regarding the condition of possibility of radical critique of religion until we have investigated the critique of religion in its act or exercise (*in ihrem Vollzug*). It does not suffice to consider the position of the attacker only. For critique of religion transcends that position. Hence the position under attack must be seen as it is by itself. Furthermore, we must observe which assumptions come into play on both sides by virtue of the conflict (*Aus-einander-Setzung*).[38]

Strauss's analysis of the opponents' respective positions will be discussed in the following section. Still, a question remains. Who or what is the tribunal that is to judge the legitimacy and the effectiveness of Spinoza's venture? Under what "law" shall it be judged? And is it at all possible to take such an impartial perspective? Clearly, Strauss casts himself in the role of the adjudicator, but unfortunately he fails to clarify this issue.

## Spinoza's Twofold Strategy

What then, does an examination of the critique of religion "in its act or exercise" show us? One of Strauss's most important and most interesting insights is that, in fact, Spinoza deploys *two* different forms of critique, which, however, he fails to distinguish explicitly. This becomes apparent from a more or less conspicuous contradiction in the *Theological-Political Treatise*. In the preface, Spinoza writes, "No wonder, then, that of the ancient religion nothing remains but its outward cult."[39] This remark echoes the characteristic complaint of Protestantism, which viewed the present as a decline from the perfect beginning. Emulating this complaint, Spinoza ostensibly undertakes to counter the decay by returning to the origins of the "old religion," to the literal sense of the biblical text, determined "to assert nothing regarding it nor to admit anything as its doctrine, but what I can clearly derive from it."[40] In the fifteenth chapter, however, when Spinoza argues for the separation of philosophy and theology, the tone has altered markedly: referring to the origins of the "old religion," he calls them "prejudices of the ancient people" (*antiqui vulgi praejudicia*). Subsequently, he forcefully declares the primacy of reason, lashing out at the theologians who want to subject it to "the dead letter."[41]

Thus, Spinoza's central hermeneutic procedure—the return to the pure and authentic meaning of the Bible—conceals a twofold strategy, Strauss claims. While the first of these ostensibly submits to the literal meaning of the Bible in opposition to traditional Christian theology, the second radically calls into question the veracity of this literal meaning.[42] Although both strategies serve the general purpose of the *Treatise*—to encourage the philosophical reader to detach himself from the authority of the Bible—they apply different criteria.[43] While the first strategy argues exclusively on the basis of the Bible itself, the second acknowledges reason as its sole criterion. Hence, Spinoza's critique of religion is composed of two parts: on the one hand, a critique of the traditional theological interpretation of the Bible and, on the other hand, a critique of the Bible on the basis of reason. Combined, the two strategies constitute a powerful weapon in the battle against revealed religion. When each is considered separately, however, both ultimately prove to fail, Strauss finds.

The principal characteristics of the first strategy were already outlined in the previous section: acceptance in principle of the authority of the text in its literal meaning, and reconstruction of the original biblical doctrine by focusing on its universal elements.[44] Although Spinoza seemingly emulates the protestant exegesis, in reality his reading is pointedly antibiblical, aiming to show that the Bible in its original meaning cannot pose an obstacle to philosophy. The presuppositions underlying this covert attack, however, are deeply problematic, Strauss finds. Spinoza determines the contents of the biblical doctrine using the criterion of consensus: only those elements that are proclaimed everywhere and univocally, those elements on which the

Bible is in accordance with itself, may be regarded as constitutive of biblical doctrine.[45] An important corollary of this approach is that the Old and the New Testament are regarded as perfectly equal parts of a single whole. Thus, Spinoza discovers the same elements of biblical doctrine in such diverse figures as Moses, the old prophets, King Solomon, Jesus, and Paul. The precepts he thus distills from the text, however, are hardly distinguishable from basic moral precepts that can be discovered by human reason without recourse to revelation. For Spinoza, the principles of this "rational morality," which constitutes the true and original content of the Bible, reflect and reinforce the philosophical truth.[46]

The *Theological-Political Treatise*, however, aims to strictly distinguish the purpose of the Bible from that of philosophy. To this end, Spinoza distinguishes between the philosophical and the nonphilosophical parts of the biblical text, while regarding the nonphilosophical parts as a popular reflection of the philosophical parts, adapted to the understanding of the many. The philosophical elements can be disclosed only by a reading that, as Spinoza puts it, is more "spiritual" than the orthodox reading. According to Strauss, however, the "spirit" to which he refers is nothing other than reason, and the "spiritual" exegete is none other than the philosopher. The latter, moreover, is capable of understanding the rational principles by himself, without the help of the Bible. As a result, the purpose of the Bible comes to be defined entirely by means of its nonphilosophical parts: to preserve and promote obedience to God and to practice charity. Exclusively practical, this content can in no way thwart the purpose of philosophy, the attainment of knowledge. Thus, the criterion of univocality and consensus proves in fact to be used to sidetrack the biblical doctrine.

This becomes even more visible when Spinoza's exegetical principle is understood in its negative sense, Strauss explains. If the Bible only teaches when it is univocal and in accordance with itself, it does not teach anything when it contradicts itself. In this way, its range is severely restricted, and it becomes fairly easy for Spinoza to point out all kinds of contradictions throughout the Bible—especially as regards issues on which it disagrees with philosophy—giving free rein to reason regarding everything the Bible does not teach. The only elements of biblical doctrine that remain are the general principles of obedience and charity, both aimed at securing the salvation of the soul. They constitute the *unum necessarium*, the "one thing needful," by which the believer must abide. Strictly speaking, biblical doctrine does not extend beyond this requirement: all further dogmatics developed by orthodox theology can be rejected as incoherent on the basis of the principle of contradiction.[47]

In this way, however, Spinoza's project encounters a major difficulty, Strauss observes: the primary condition for the "purist" critique is the acceptance, even provisionally, of the authority of the literal biblical text. One cannot have the cake and eat it: if Spinoza wants to uphold his own exegetical principle, he too is bound by the *unum necessarium* of obedience. As a result, his efforts to liberate philosophy are inadmissible. On closer inspection, the requirement of literalness proves to be the weakest point of Spinoza's first strategy, the refutation of the orthodox interpretation of the Bible. As we have seen, his main presupposition is that the literal meaning must be the point of departure for this refutation, since it is accessible to believer and nonbeliever alike. As Strauss points out, however, for a believer a correct understanding of even the literal meaning of the Bible is impossible without the aid of divine light, without the belief that it has been revealed by an inscrutable creator. By the same token, the fact that the Bible contradicts itself and does not offer a univocal doctrine is no refutation, but rather a confirmation of the mysterious and divine character of revelation. This basic assumption, however, is ignored *a priori* by Spinoza's requirement of equal accessibility. Hence, his reading of the Bible already presupposes the refutation of the orthodox point of view. In other words, Spinoza commits what is called a petitio principii: he presupposes what he sets out to prove. "The critique of orthodoxy stands or falls by resolutely keeping the opponent to the literal meaning of the text of Scripture. . . . Since his opponents do not recognize as their authority the merely literal meaning of Scripture, the whole of Spinoza's critique of orthodoxy, in so far as that critique seeks to refute orthodoxy, rests on a *petitio principii*."[48] In this respect, and contrary to Spinoza's own claim, his "purist" reading is neither purely immanent nor free from presuppositions.

If the very point of departure of Spinoza's first strategy rests on a petitio principii, and if its results do not exempt him from obedience, one can only conclude that it ultimately fails, according to Strauss: "Thus it is not on the basis of Scripture that Spinoza can bring about the liberation of philosophizing—his real aim."[49] This means that the success of the *Theological-Political Treatise* comes to depend on the success of the second strategy, the critique on the basis of reason. Here again, Spinoza starts from an element he considers to be equally accessible to believer and nonbeliever. Even when religious orthodoxy insists that divine assistance is indispensable for a correct understanding of the Bible, he argues, this does not do away with the fact that the text also tries to convince unbelievers of the religious truths by referring to *miracles*, held to be perceptible to believers and nonbelievers alike. A classic example, often invoked by Strauss, is the well-known biblical contest between the prophet Elijah and the prophets of Baal on Mount Carmel.[50] As opposed to the altar devoted to Baal, the altar erected by Elijah in praise of Jehovah caught fire; this event could be witnessed and recognized as a miracle by both parties.

As Strauss points out, miracles are directly related to the foundations of revealed religion. According to orthodoxy, they occur when the creator intervenes in his creation, and as such they bear witness to the miraculous origins of man and the world. An omnipotent, provident, and inscrutable God who created the world also possesses the power and the freedom to intervene in it, either by revealing himself in words or by intervening in the workings of nature.[51] This explains why the protestant return to biblical sources in the seventeenth century was accompanied by a renewed interest in the subject. By appealing to miracles, the protestant orthodoxy of Spinoza's time attempted to provide an empirical and experiential basis for its theological and political claims.[52] Small wonder, then, that this interest found a critical echo in the *Theological-Political Treatise*: the seventh chapter on the interpretation of the Bible is prepared by six chapters that offer an incisive critique of prophecy, revelation, and miracles in general.[53]

At first sight, we may wonder why Spinoza takes so many pains, Strauss remarks. After all, doesn't the *Ethics* provide a comprehensive and profoundly rational critique of miracles? From the identification of God and nature, it follows that miracles, including creation out of nothing and revelation, are impossible. As we saw in the previous section, Spinoza's critique of religion is essentially contained in this philosophical or "metaphysical" critique. At the same time, however, this begs the question: insofar as the metaphysical critique derives from the system of the *Ethics*, it already presupposes the constitution and thus the legitimacy of philosophy that the *Theological-Political Treatise* seeks to establish. Hence, Spinoza cannot appeal to the metaphysical critique in order to convince the potential philosophers among his readers: he is compelled to refute the biblical accounts of miracles on a prephilosophical level.

On this level, Spinoza's most obvious point of departure is experience, to which orthodoxy also refers. As a "positive" religion claiming an empirical foundation, revealed religion becomes susceptible to a critique that equally invokes experience in order to combat these claims. Hence, what Strauss calls Spinoza's "positive critique" raises the question whether God can be known through the experience of miracles, or, more formally, whether it is possible to deduce the existence of God from experience, as the orthodox theologians contend.[54] Moreover, Spinoza gives an additional reason to proceed in this manner: traditional orthodox theology connects its empirical foundation to a concept of miracles not to be found as such in the Bible. When it understands the miracle as a divine disruption of the laws of the natural order, it uses a concept of nature derivative from Greek philosophy and thus alien to the Bible. Insofar as it accepts and uses this concept, theology acknowledges the legitimacy of philosophy and reason.[55] This does not yet amount to an affirmation that unassisted reason is able to fathom God and the world, as Spinoza tries to demonstrate. Theology recognizes the right of reason, but not its autonomy. It regards reason as essentially limited and in need of revelation. Even this limited leeway, however, is sufficient for the critique of miracles, based on experience, to be able to appeal to reason.

At first, Spinoza appears to proceed very cautiously. He indicates that he intends to use his rational capacities only to test the theological propositions, without saying anything as to their truth.[56] Subsequently, he turns to theology, which attributes demonstrative power to miracles as supernatural events, accessible to both the faithful believer and the nonbeliever who only uses unassisted reason. At this point, however, Spinoza introduces a crucial proviso: he states that unprejudiced reason cannot regard a miracle as a supernatural phenomenon, since it cannot claim to know the limits of the power of nature. From the perspective of unprejudiced reason, what theology calls a miracle is at most a problem that cannot be explained on the basis of current knowledge of nature.[57] In a letter to his friend Henry Oldenburg, Spinoza expresses this condition in a succinct manner:

> I venture to ask you whether we petty men possess sufficient knowledge of nature to be able to lay down the limits of its force and power, or to say that a given thing surpasses its power? No one could go so far without arrogance. We may, therefore, without presumption explain miracles as far as possible by natural causes. When we cannot explain them, nor even prove their impossibility, we may well suspend our judgment about them and establish religion, as I have said, solely by the wisdom of its doctrines.[58]

By means of this "deferral," Spinoza's positive critique deploys a silent but deadly power, Strauss points out. Even in its limited form, the right of reason is the basis for the legitimate expectation of progress in our knowledge of the limits of nature. In the light of this expectation, the experience of miracles—recorded and situated in the past—loses its demonstrative power. The fact that in biblical times an event was held inexplicable and thus attributed to divine intervention does not imply that it must remain unexplained. Critical scientific observation and analysis of the event, combined with historical research, may eventually yield a purely natural explanation. Until such an explanation has been found, however, to deduce without further ado the existence of an omnipotent God from the current knowledge of nature is inadmissible. From this perspective, the biblical accounts are indeed nothing more than "prejudices of the ancient people," the fruit of the primitive and associative mode of thinking Spinoza deems characteristic of the Bible as a whole.[59]

As long as the limits of nature are insufficiently known, unprejudiced "positive" reason cannot recognize any phenomenon as a miracle. However, the reverse also holds: all that reason can successfully claim against theology is the postponement of judgment and additional research. As long as no definitive result is available, the possibility remains that the biblical events related as miracles will prove to be miracles after all. Therefore, the positive critique must be buttressed by further investigation into the reliability and credibility of biblical miracle stories. Strauss calls this supplementary critique "philological-historical," as it assesses the Bible's literary and historical consistency and examines biblical authorship.[60]

Spinoza's philological-historical critique focuses on the orthodox conviction that Moses is the author of the Pentateuch, and thus aims at the heart of orthodoxy. According to tradition, Moses was directly and personally inspired by God in the Sinai desert to write the Pentateuch. Subsequently, moreover, the text was handed down in a continuous and uninterrupted process, without even the minutest change. Against this claim, Spinoza adduces a variety of arguments aimed to prove that the Pentateuch was written much later by someone else with far less talent and authority, and who presented events from his time as the fulfillment of earlier prophecies. No single human being, Spinoza holds, could have performed the many miracles attributed to Moses, just as it is impossible that the story, if at all reliable, survived intact through the ages.[61]

Ultimately, the philological-historical arguments are merely intended to support the positive critique. The latter is the principal weapon with which Spinoza seeks to free reason from orthodox theology's tutelage. Since reason can legitimately postpone judgment on miracles, it is also able to bracket the authority of theology. No more is needed for the addressees of the *Treatise* to clear the way toward Spinoza's philosophy, to the metaphysical system of the *Ethics* in which there is no place for an inscrutable God or for miracles. As soon as the reader enters this system, the propaedeutic endeavor of both the critique based on the Bible and the positive critique becomes superfluous.

As Strauss remarks, Spinoza presents both phases in the trajectory as if the former is founded in the latter: the positive critique, he maintains, is based on the principle of the unlimited power of nature, which underlies the metaphysical critique. If this relation holds, nothing seems to stand in the way of the refutation of revealed religion and religious orthodoxy. According to Strauss, however, there is no such relation. The positive critique and its corollaries are no more capable of refuting revelation than the critique based on Scripture. Take, to begin with, the philological-historical critique, which argues that the events, actions, and prophecies recorded in the Bible are improbable and implausible, both in themselves and as a result of the process of tradition. For a believer, however, this is not a valid argument. The philological-historical critique only proves that miracles are improbable or even impossible from a human point of view, and this is something a believer will not deny. On the contrary, he will contend that this proves the superhuman, divine character of miracles, just like the improbability of an unbroken line of tradition is a sign of the workings of divine providence. In neither of the two cases does the philological-historical critique disprove the possibility that a divine agent miraculously intervenes in the order of things and communicates his will to an elect human being with superhuman powers. Spinoza is only able to deploy his standard of judgment within certain limits, Strauss asserts: "But what is Spinoza actually proving? In fact, nothing more than that it is not *humanly* possible that Moses wrote the Pentateuch, and that the text of a book should come down to us through the centuries without any corruption of the text at any single passage."[62]

This brings us to the positive critique itself. Contrary to Spinoza's claim, there is no foundational relationship between the metaphysical and the positive critique, Strauss holds. The positive critique, which aims to demonstrate that miracles cannot be known by reason, is based on the recognition that we are ignorant of the power of nature, and that it would be presumptuous to limit this power by referring to divine intervention. This claim, however, differs fundamentally from the more sweeping contention of the metaphysical critique that the power of nature *is* unlimited, from which it follows that divine intervention is impossible.[63] Hence, the positive critique can never go as far as the metaphysical critique: it can only submit that miracles cannot be known to scientific reason, not that they are impossible. The positive critique, Strauss argues, "merely proves that miracles are not recognizable as such by the truly unbelieving mind which does not openly assume—or surreptitiously smuggle in—an element of faith. Reason devoid of faith, engaged in the pursuit of scientific inquiry, shows itself as immune to miracles."[64]

As Strauss explains, positive reason can only maintain that miracles cannot be known because it is essentially immune to the demonstrative power the believer attributes to them. Immunity, however, does not yet constitute a refutation, so that the argument from unknowability has only relative validity. Since a final judgment is postponed to an indefinite future, the knowability of miracles remains an open question. The foundational relationship argued by Spinoza does not provide a solution, on the contrary: if the power of nature is indeed unlimited, progress in human knowledge can never come to an end, so that a conclusive explanation of miracles remains outstanding.[65] Thus, the positive critique based on reason runs aground on its own presuppositions. In Strauss's view, however, this does not necessarily constitute a complete failure. As he goes on to show, positive reason puts its immunity to effective critical use. It does so by presenting its openness as the sign of a higher, more advanced, and more reflective consciousness. From this vantage point, it can then denounce belief in miracles as a primitive, prescientific and hence lower form of consciousness.[66] The distance thus created acquires the character of an unbridgeable progress. In this context, Strauss makes an observation that will prove to be crucial to his philosophical trajectory:

> On the basis of this *essentially historical* self-awareness (*wesentlich historisches Selbstbewusstsein*), the positive mind finds itself—independently of all secondary, inconclusive philological and historical criticism applied to miracles and which, in principle, leave the question open—unmovable (*unerreichbar*) by all reports on miracles, and therefore all experience of miracles. To the positive mind it is plain that the prophets and the apostles did not view and analyze the events which they report with the same sobriety and severity which that mind brings to bear on events observed.[67]

The mainspring of the "positive spirit" is the will to investigate and judge, in total freedom, that which is immediately given. This sole intention is understood as a progress with regard to other positions that do not begin with immediate experience. The latter are branded "prejudices" and thus are compelled to substantiate and justify their claims regarding what transcends immediate experience.[68] Hence, the concept of "prejudice" is essentially a *historical* category, Strauss emphasizes: it is not so much the result as the *expression* of the "essentially historical self-consciousness."[69] It posits a caesura in time between a dark past characterized by ignorance, superstition, and submission on the one hand, and an enlightened future of knowledge and freedom on the other. With the concept of prejudice, the positive spirit denotes the enemy it combats: initially, it is revealed religion; later on it encompasses all claims to knowledge of the past. The fight against prejudice thus takes the form of a historical project, a campaign the final result of which is already encapsulated in the self-declared "advancedness" (*Fortgeschrittenheit*) of the positive spirit.

In this way, Strauss points to the effective core of Spinoza's critique of religion and his biblical science, but also to what he considers to be the essence of the Enlightenment and modernity in general. For unprejudiced reason and the positive spirit operate independently from both the philological-historical and the metaphysical critique. In fact, they precede them: "The authority of Scripture was shaken prior to all historical and philological criticism, but also prior to all metaphysics, through the establishment of the positive mind, through the disenchantment of the world and through the self-awareness of the disenchanting mind."[70] The critique of religion as the foundation of biblical science is not exclusively linked to Spinoza's philosophical system. As Strauss puts it, one need not be a Spinozist to conduct biblical science.[71] The positive spirit is the starting point of the early, radical Enlightenment as such, in its attempt to dismantle revealed religion once and for all and to liberate itself from all prejudice. Prejudice, according to Strauss, is "the unambiguous polemical correlate of the all too ambiguous term 'freedom.'"[72] The freedom claimed by the positive spirit is a negative freedom, a "freedom-from" rather than a "freedom-to." It only manifests itself in bringing to light, investigating and rejecting prejudices.[73]

This approach did not originate with Spinoza, Strauss points out, but with René Descartes. Cartesian methodical doubt attempted to liberate itself from all prejudices at one fell swoop, in order to find an unshakable foundation for science. In Descartes's view, the realm of prejudice included the traditional Aristotelian analysis of the visible world, which had been adopted by Christian scholasticism. This analysis interpreted the order of the world as a causal chain that ultimately points to God as the first unmoved mover. According to Descartes, however, the traditional investigation of the causal chain could only lead to the recognition of the imperfection of human understanding, not to knowledge of God. Divine existence could be ascertained only through self-knowledge: man had to free himself from the causal chain in order to discover the immediate cause of his existence. In this way, the immediate or the present became the focal point of Cartesian metaphysics. Likewise, Spinoza rejected traditional philosophy's starting point and concentrated on the immediately given.[74]

But how effective is reason's declaration of independence against a position that claims to be based on something that precedes all human judgment? According to Strauss, the critique based on experience and reason misses its target, not only because positive reason postpones judgment, but also because it fails to do justice to an important principle of revealed religion. The positive spirit is characterized by a "will to immediacy" that aims to stay as close as possible to present experience and that refuses any other guidance.[75] Viewed from this perspective, the tradition of revelation is based on something located in a remote past and hence a prejudice under suspicion. Since tradition and presence are mutually exclusive, the former can only throw a misleading veil over the latter. This presupposition, however, ignores the fact that, for a believer, mediation by a tradition is an essential condition for the presence of revelation. From a religious point of view, immediately hearing and seeing revelation in a direct confrontation with God is deadly for man.[76] Only a prophet with superhuman powers is able to endure the *tremendum*, the terror that attends the presence of God.[77] Prophetic mediation, which creates a safe distance with regard to the "inhuman" character of revelation, is the source of tradition's authority, Strauss argues. By permanently representing revelation, it answers to the "will to mediacy" of the God-fearing believer, whose pious obedience is based on the recognition that the tradition continually reveals and expresses God's will. This principle of continuous mediation thus allows revelation to be experienced by all believers as a covenant that is continually renewed:

> If the will to mediated hearing of revelation is grounded in actual hearing of revelation, then the tradition of revealed religion, and with this the obedience to the tradition and the fidelity to that tradition is grounded in the actual hearing of the present revelation. Then all critique of prejudice, and even more, all critique of the "rigidity" (*Starrheit*) of the tradition from the point of view of "experience," cannot touch the seriousness and the depth of the will, grounded in immediate hearing, to mediacy.[78]

In Strauss's analysis, then, the believer's "will to mediacy" appears as an equal opponent of the positive spirit's "will to immediacy." The consequences of this equality, moreover, do apply not only to revelation, but also to miracles in general. The positive critique, it is true, asserts that miracles are unknowable to unbelieving reason, so that an impartial, scientific determination is impossible.[79] However, Strauss asks, isn't the mere intention to ascertain scientifically itself based on a blind and premature dismissal of the specific doubt and expectation that attend the experience of miracles? Even the followers of Baal, for example, did not experience the events on Mount Carmel as scientific observers, but with doubt, expectation, and the readiness to see a miracle that would decide between Jehovah and Baal. It is only because of this disposition that they were able to recognize the miraculous ignition of Elijah's altar as a sign of the God of Israel and convert. Miracles, Strauss stresses, cannot create faith, but they presuppose a principal readiness to believing in a higher power.[80] From this perspective, the position of the positive spirit is at least as problematic, he argues:

> Just as the assertion of miracles is called in question by the positive mind, positive critique of miracles is called in question by the mind that waits in faith or in doubt for the coming of the miracles. The weapon which the positive mind believes it has discovered in the fact that the assertion of miracles is relative to the pre-scientific stage of mankind, is taken away from the positive mind by the observation that this fact permits the opposite interpretation. Is the will to "establish," which needs only to have become victorious for experience of miracles to become impossible, itself something to be taken for granted? Does not man come to his most weighty and impelling insight when he is startled out of the composure of observation by which facts are "established," when he finds himself in the condition of excitation, in which alone miracles become perceptible at all?[81]

While the positive spirit may have developed sufficient power to explain the historical success of the critique of religion, its position is no more or no less legitimate than that of religious orthodoxy. The historical results of the positive, scientific approach to the Bible are only valid within the charmed circle of confidence in autonomous reason with regard to what is immediately given. However, just this confidence is lacking in religious orthodoxy. It regards reason as constitutionally incapable of discovering the truth by its own lights, and thus in need of completion and perfection by revelation. The latter, however, is never accessible without the aid of divine light, so that an appeal to tradition is always required.

Thus, Spinoza's conflict with revealed religion remains essentially undecided, Strauss observes: both parties are in a deadlock. Even if Spinoza is able to defend his position against the claims of religious orthodoxy within certain bounds, he remains incapable of *refuting* these claims. For this reason, the inquiry regarding the conditions and limits of the critique of religion must focus on what, at least for Spinoza, is at stake in the conflict: the autonomy, competence, and authority of reason. For this reason, Strauss devotes a large portion of his book to Spinoza's debate with two orthodox opponents on this issue. In the fifteenth chapter of the *Treatise*, which discusses the relationship between theology and reason, Spinoza distinguishes between a "dogmatic" and a "skeptical" position: while the former acknowledges the right and the competence of reason, the latter altogether denies "the certitude of reason" and makes it subservient to the authority of Scripture.[82] As the main representative of the "dogmatic" position, Spinoza refers to Moses Maimonides, the great medieval Jewish thinker, while he attributes the "skeptical" position to a contemporary and opponent of Maimonides, "a certain Rabbi Jehudah Alphakar."[83] According to Strauss, however, Alphakar's view as Spinoza presents it is hardly distinguishable from the orthodox Calvinist view of his time. Hence, Spinoza's critique of the "skeptical" position can also be interpreted as a covert debate with Calvin.

## Maimonides: The Limits of Reason and the Interest in Revelation

Moses Maimonides (1135–1204) broke with the profound distrust of Jewish orthodoxy with regard to philosophy. In his great work, *Guide of the Perplexed*, he tried to reconcile reason and revelation by integrating the central articles of Jewish faith within a philosophical, more specifically Aristotelian framework. Although his attempt was eyed with suspicion and disapproval, he succeeded in defending his position to such a degree that he came to be regarded as one of the greatest thinkers of Judaism. His fame even extended beyond his religious community: Thomas Aquinas, with whom he is often compared, cites his work as an important influence. Precisely because of its appeal to reason and philosophy, Maimonides's position becomes susceptible to Spinoza's critique, Strauss argues. However, this critique cannot proceed on the basis of the biblical text itself, for reasons that will sound familiar:

> Spinoza's critique of Maimonides on the basis of Scripture presupposes that the literal meaning is the true meaning of Scripture. This presupposition is however rejected in principle by Maimonides since it would lead to conclusions that would contradict the revealed character of Scripture. Therefore, before argument can be taken up against Maimonides on the basis of Scripture, his hermeneutics must be called into question.[84]

In the seventh chapter of the *Theological-Political Treatise*, Spinoza summarizes the basic tenets of Maimonides's hermeneutics as follows. The Bible contains many passages that appear to contradict reason. In such cases, Maimonides asserts, the exegete is allowed to interpret the passages in question allegorically and assume that the literal, outer meaning hides an inner meaning that is in agreement with reason.[85] For Spinoza, this approach is unacceptable. He is astonished that Maimonides, who pretends to offer a rational exegesis, in fact simply adapts the biblical text to his personal views.[86] Moreover, he adds, the possibility of an allegorical interpretation of the Bible implies that the truth is predetermined, and this is merely a prejudice. If Maimonides had envisaged a truly scientific, rational, and philosophical approach to the Bible, he should have focused exclusively on the literal meaning, studying Scripture in accordance with the positive and rational principles mentioned in the previous section. This truly scientific approach would have revealed that the Bible has no epistemological value whatsoever. As Strauss argues, however, these arguments are based on Spinoza's biblical science. Since the latter presupposes the successful refutation of Maimonides's hermeneutics, once again we are caught in a petitio principii: Spinoza starts from the legitimacy of the positive-scientific approach in order to argue that same legitimacy.[87]

Spinoza raises several other objections against allegorical exegesis. These, however, equally fail, according to Strauss, since they misinterpret Maimonides's intention and design. The distinction between an inner and an outer meaning is part of Maimonides's teaching on prophecy, or, as Strauss calls it, "prophetology."[88] This term is particularly apposite, since it reflects the attempt to integrate a central element of religious tradition within a philosophical framework. According to prophetology, revelation is an emanation of the divine intellect, by which the prophet is enlightened in direct contact with God. Because of the instantaneous, overwhelming, and superhuman character of this event, the prophet must transmit the divine message to the faithful in figurative terms, by means of similes and images. This he is able to do because his reason and imagination are perfectly developed and act in perfect cooperation. Reason, which receives the emanation, uses images derived from the concrete, physical, and material world in order to make understandable what is, in fact, abstract, immaterial, and purely intelligible. The principle of allegorical exegesis is rooted in this collaboration: it discloses the inner and purely rational meaning of the text behind the imagery that constitutes the outer meaning.

However, even if the principle of allegorical exegesis itself can be justified, its purpose remains problematic: to harmonize the biblical teaching and the rational truth. In Spinoza's view, this endeavor is absurd, since the truth is not fixed in advance but has to be discovered by means of scientific investigation. In his dismissal, however, Spinoza overlooks a fundamental difference between his open concept of truth, knowledge, and science, and Maimonides's closed concept. For Maimonides, the truth is indeed fixed: the scope of reason has been definitely circumscribed by Aristotle. Whereas

for Spinoza theoretical reason is autonomous and sovereign, for Maimonides it is delimited and transcended by the "suprarationality" of revelation on the one hand, and by the apex of theoretical reason, Aristotle's
philosophical teaching, on the other. This latter concept of science, of
course, is far better equipped to integrate reason and revelation than Spinoza's open concept.[89]

A similar misunderstanding occurs in Spinoza's critique of prophetology. According to Spinoza, reason and imagination are fundamentally opposed, so that the exceptional cooperation argued by Maimonides is *eo ipso*
impossible. Even if Maimonides concedes that in general the imagination
is an obstacle to reason, his Aristotelian concept of knowledge enables him
to make a decisive exception: reason can be committed to the truth to such
an extent that it exerts a positive influence on the imagination and subjects
the latter without suppressing it. Spinoza, who views the imagination in
Cartesian terms, is unable to make this exception. This, Strauss argues,
shows that his critique of prophetology presupposes the constitution of
modern philosophy and thus the preliminary rejection of revelation.[90]
Since the *Theological-Political Treatise* operates on a prephilosophical level,
however, Spinoza's objections are not valid.

The difference between the two philosophical paradigms becomes
visible again with regard to biblical miracles. As we saw, Spinoza's positive
critique views miracles as merely unsolved problems against the background of scientific progress. Maimonides, on his part, attempts to accommodate miracles, including creation, within the Aristotelian framework. In
doing so, however, he departs from the traditional view. Although he acknowledges the reality and the possibility of miracles, he downplays their
importance with regard to faith, emphasizing the natural order and its laws.
In his view, miracles are no infraction of God into his own order, but only
an unusual and temporary change within the sublunary sphere, which is
characterized by transience. In relation to the unchangeable heavenly
order, miracles deserve to be given less significance than they are traditionally accorded. Still, a problem remains, according to Strauss. When
creation is structured with the aid of Aristotelian physics, miracles are an
anomaly that detracts from its divine perfection. Maimonides solves this
problem by arguing that an inscrutable God who creates the world is also
capable of intervening in his creation. As opposed to Spinoza, he does not
deny the possibility of miracles, but he downplays their interest for human
reason. Their demonstrative power, to which tradition attaches great importance, dwindles when one is able to understand creation theoretically
after the manner of Aristotle.[91]

Besides the critique based on Scripture and the positive critique, Spinoza also deploys his metaphysical critique against Maimonides. In the *Ethics*, divine understanding and divine will are identical, so that it is impossible for God to trespass on the natural order by revealing a law that can be broken by man. Maimonides likewise emphasizes divine unity, but he does so for a different reason. Strictly speaking, he suggests, it is inadmissible to ascribe to God any positive attributes whatsoever, for he is one and indivisible, and any distinctions or attributions diminish this unity. Hence, human speech about God is always figurative. For Maimonides as opposed to Spinoza, God's unity is inscrutable and transcends human comprehension. By appealing to the inevitably figurative character of speech, he limits the scope of reason and thus of theoretical-philosophical analysis. The authority of reason and theory does not extend beyond the sublunary sphere: everything that surpasses this sphere also surpasses the power of reason. This holds for the question regarding divine understanding and will, but also for the question whether the world has been created or is eternal. According to Maimonides, reason can do no more than deduce the greater probability of creation. Hence, it must be assisted by revelation. The latter does not contradict reason, but completes it and transcends its limits. Spinoza's metaphysical critique takes the radically opposed viewpoint that reason is autonomous and sovereign. Its radius encompasses the infinite realm of nature, which is identical with God. Man's philosophical investigation of the natural order is therefore equivalent to understanding the one divine substance. *Theoria* or philosophical speculation is the only way to attaining human perfection and felicity: intellectual love of God (*amor intellectualis Dei*). According to Spinoza, *theoria* is the highest human interest or concern, to which all other concerns are secondary.

This "radicalization of the theoretical interest," as Strauss calls it, determines not only the theological, but also the political aspects of Spinoza's critique of Maimonides.[92] For Spinoza, the theoretical life is an individual matter, reserved for the few sufficiently gifted. The majority of people is largely driven by passions and pursues other interests than the theoretical. For this reason, the majority of nonphilosophers require the authority of religion, in the purified and rationalized form advocated by Spinoza. This religion of piety and charity mainly fulfills a practical, political purpose: it ensures social cohesion and stability, and thus also the minimal conditions for the theoretical life.[93]

An important implication of this view is that politics does not possess a specific rationality distinguishable from the rationality inherent in the unchangeable workings of nature.[94] On this issue, Strauss points to the marked difference between Spinoza and another founder of modern political thought, Thomas Hobbes. For the latter, uncovering the specific rationality of the political may be said to be the cornerstone of his work. In contrast with Hobbes, Strauss observes, Spinoza's political thought does not begin with what is proper to human nature, but with nature as an encompassing whole. This difference becomes apparent with regard to the concept of natural law. Hobbes derives natural law from the human pursuit of self-preservation, which he considers to be a rational pursuit. For Spinoza, by contrast, the *summum naturale ius*, the highest natural law, is founded in the one and indivisible substance, in which rationality, right, and power coincide.[95] Viewed from this cosmic perspective, the existence of all beings coincides with their rationality and their power. Both the individual human being and the state are mere units of power within the economy of nature.[96] The rationale of the state resides entirely in its function, the extent to which it succeeds in developing enough power to regulate and harmonize the explosive amalgam of individual passions and strivings into a durable whole.[97] In this process, religion can play an important role. However, between the rationality of the philosopher, who is free of passions, and that of the state, a profound qualitative difference remains. The philosopher is beyond the state, even though he realizes that the stability of the state is important to his survival as well. Because of this sober view, Spinoza's political doctrine is often typified as a "political realism," influenced by Niccolò Machiavelli, the opponent of "imaginary principalities" and thinker of the raison d'état. Strauss firmly rejects this characterization: Spinoza's so-called realism is, in fact, prepolitical, since it is based on a completely apolitical, philosophical account of the passions.[98] For this reason, his anti-utopianism differs fundamentally from that of Machiavelli. While the Florentine rejects utopia as an obstacle for a realistic understanding of politics, for Spinoza it is primarily an obstacle on the kingly road toward the perfection of theoretical understanding, the highest human interest.[99]

Maimonides, by contrast, does not subject the interests of politics to the interests of theory. In his view, both equally receive their due from revelation, which in Judaism takes the form of *law*. The purpose of the Torah is to regulate all aspects of human life in accordance with divine will, so that all those who obey its commandments may attain happiness. According to Maimonides, the purpose of the law includes theory: as distinguished from merely human law, which only looks after the well-being of the body, the divine law also envisages the perfection of the soul.[100] This is borne out by the fact that the Bible calls on man to understand the creator by studying creation. Maimonides interprets this exhortation as an authorization and even an imperative to engage in theory after the manner of Aristotle. The latter, he points out, also regards the theoretical life as the endeavor to acquire knowledge of God, and hence as the way to attaining the perfection of the soul. In this way, Maimonides lets the highest goal of the revealed law coincide with that of philosophy: the theoretical life is the most pious life, the perfect realization of the law.

This does not do away with the fact that for Maimonides, too, the theoretical life is primarily a solitary activity for the talented few. Unlike Spinoza, however, he does not put society at the service of the speculative life. The goal of the Torah is that *all* members of the community shall know the truth and live in accordance with it. After all, revelation is a crucial moment within general divine providence, God's care for man.[101] According to Maimonides, providence is linked to the emanation of the divine intellect in this way, that the higher human intellect is developed, the more it shares in the workings of providence.[102] While this accords a privileged place to theory within the purpose of the law, it adds a social-political dimension: those whose rationality is most developed are also responsible for supervising obedience to the law. In this way, revelation establishes a social hierarchy in which intellectual development and rationality are inextricably connected with political responsibility. This connection is exemplified by the prophet, who thereby surpasses both the philosopher and the lawgiver as such.

In Maimonides's view, the divine law connects the pursuit of theoretical knowledge of God to the care for society. Spinoza, by contrast, rejects this connection by drawing a sharp distinction between *lex humana*, the human law, and *lex divina*, the divine law. The latter, he argues, only enjoins the perfection of the individual human being: its purpose has no bearing whatsoever on society. As a result, the Mosaic Law, which is directed at the Jewish people as a collective, cannot be a divine law. Its elaborate code of commandments and prohibitions has only a political significance, and compliance has no immediate relevance to the welfare of the soul. The organization of society only plays a marginal and utilitarian role in fulfilling the divine law. Politics only pertains to the choice of the means used to satisfy the basic requirements of life, which are of little importance from the point of view of *lex divina*. However, Strauss rejoins, this means that there is no intrinsic reason to reject Mosaic Law in favor of another law. In a utilitarian view of politics, the Torah could just as well meet the elementary conditions set by Spinoza. What, then, is the actual reason for his dismissal? One possible explanation was already mentioned earlier: seventeenth-century orthodox Protestantism justified its claims to power by invoking the example of Mosaic Law. Spinoza perceived these claims as a threat to both social stability and

the freedom of philosophy.[103] In order to avert this danger, he felt compelled
to disarm orthodoxy by calling into question the authority of Mosaic Law.

Convinced of the legitimacy and sovereignty of reason, Spinoza ele-
vates the interests of philosophy above all other interests, including those
of Judaism. His relationship to Judaism thus proves to be an important aspect of his dispute with Maimonides, Strauss observes. According to Maimonides, faith and obedience to Torah necessarily precede theoretical
activity. In integrating Aristotelian philosophy and the Jewish tradition, and
by using philosophy to buttress the main articles of faith, he aims to restore
to Jewish life its ancient splendor and strength. Thus, the interests of theory
converge with the encompassing interest of the revealed law, Strauss asserts:
"[Maimonides's] argumentation takes its course, his disputes take place,
*within* the context of Jewish life, and *for* that context. . . . Maimonides's philosophy is based in principle and throughout on Judaism (*vollzieht sich in
grundsätzlicher und stetiger Orientierung am Judentum*)."[104]

For Spinoza this orientation is based on a prejudice that needs to be
tested by positive reason which has liberated itself from all prejudices. As a
result, he does not feel obliged to justify his position against Judaism. On the
contrary, he reverses the burden of proof and challenges Judaism to justify itself before the impartial tribunal of reason. Hence, his trust in autonomous
and sovereign reason proves to be conditioned throughout by a "radical and
continuing distance from Judaism."[105] According to Strauss, this distance is
characteristic of Spinoza's critique of Maimonides in general: his rejection of
Mosaic Law as well as of the intrinsic connection between theory and politics, of prophetology, and of allegorical exegesis. In each case, the critique is
based on a "self-empowerment" of positive reason and the new concept of
science that attends it, and thus on the basic immunity toward revelation and
miracles in general. This shows that the separation of philosophy and theology the *Theological-Political Treatise* aims at has in fact been carried through
already before Spinoza has developed a single argument.

Underlying the difference in their relationship toward Judaism is a
fundamental disagreement concerning the power of reason and the human
interest in revelation. For Maimonides, reason is limited on two accounts.
On one account, its scope has been exhaustively circumscribed by the *cor-
pus aristotelicum*, which is a catalog of all available knowledge of the sublunary world. On the second account, it is limited by certain questions it
cannot answer independently since they surpass the sublunary sphere, like
the question regarding creation or eternity. These questions are so crucial
that man is unable to live without knowing the answers to them. Even in its

most perfected form, however, reason alone is unable to discover them. Hence, the "insufficiency" of reason is inextricably related to "man's inadequacy for the guidance of his own life."[106] Man has a vital interest in revelation, which alone can supply the truth. Hence, the interest in revelation *precedes* faith in revelation: this, according to Strauss, is the fundamental postulate of Maimonides's position. This assertion is worth keeping in mind; as we will see, Strauss will thoroughly revise this interpretation in the light of further research.

Conversely, Spinoza's ultimate presupposition is the fundamental adequacy or "sufficiency" of reason and man's capacity to lead his own life. This postulate is decisive for his entire design in the *Theological-Political Treatise*: before he can mobilize reason in a critique of revelation and the Bible, he is compelled to counter the "insufficiency thesis" that underlies it. As Strauss observes, in fact Spinoza does so already in the rhetorical conditional sentence that opens the *Treatise*, "*If* men could govern all their affairs in accordance with a fixed plan."[107] For this reason, Strauss summarizes the conflict between Maimonides and Spinoza in the formula "insufficiency of man—sufficiency of man," emphasizing that this applies both on the intellectual and the ethical and political level.

From his analysis, Strauss draws the following conclusions. The most important one has already been mentioned: Spinoza's attack on Maimonides is based on a petitio principii, and thus fails to hit the mark. Even though Spinoza may appear to get an argumentative hold on Maimonides because of the latter's appeal to philosophy, the core of Maimonides's position remains intact. Spinoza is unable to refute the insufficiency thesis without already presupposing the sufficiency of reason. All he is able to do is counter the claims raised on behalf of religion against the sovereignty of reason, by insisting on the ignorance and the openness of the positive spirit. This, however, does not do away with the fact that the positive spirit acquires its immunity by imposing itself on its own authority. In this respect, it does not differ from faith in revelation, Strauss remarks: "Thus the free mind becomes free. It becomes what it is. It brings its potential into actuality. It presupposes itself, as faith presupposes itself."[108] Thus, what began as an attempt to refute culminates in a status quo: both opposing parties appeal to a premise that is founded in itself, and which as such is "believed in." Thus, the opposition between Spinoza and Maimonides amounts to "the antithesis of belief in sufficiency and belief in insufficiency." This antithesis becomes even more pointed when Spinoza faces his "skeptical" opponent, John Calvin.

## Calvin: "Like Clay in the Potter's Hand"

For Calvin, as for Maimonides, the highest human felicity consists in attaining knowledge of God. Although this knowledge is present in each human being in a very imperfect form, however, man is incapable of perfecting it by his own lights. To this end, he needs additional guidance from the Bible, which confirms and supplements the inner knowledge. In order to become amenable to the divine message, however, he must subject himself to divine authority. In Calvin's view, true knowledge of God cannot be separated from *pietas* or obedient piety, which is a combination of fear, awareness of one's sinfulness and the experience of one's insignificance compared to divine omnipotence.

In his *Institutes of the Christian Religion*, Calvin rejects philosophy and theory wholesale. The view that human reason is capable of judging autonomously and free from prejudice is itself fraught with prejudice, he argues. It is rooted in disobedience and displays a disturbing lack of self-knowledge. Instead of providing knowledge of God, theory leads man away from the one thing needful, and as such it is a source of pernicious errors. As Strauss puts it, "Theory, stripped of prejudices and presuppositions, theory which seeks first of all to examine cautiously and suspiciously, is thus viewed as in actual fact full of presuppositions: in the place of the fear of God, which is the beginning of wisdom, it puts disobedience."[109] Whoever takes as his point of departure the complete and unconditional trust in his own rational capacities thereby reveals himself to be unwilling and insusceptible to the shock of conscience that is the precondition for divine grace, without which no correct understanding of Scripture is possible. Blinded by self-love, pride, and complacency, he surrenders to the temptations of the flesh, which for Calvin is the root of all evil.[110]

Because Calvin radically understands both the insufficiency of reason and the inscrutability and omnipotence of God, every common ground disappears and his position becomes unassailable for Spinoza's attempts at refutation. To begin with, his critique based on Scripture fails: an impartial, immanent critique has no demonstrative power whatsoever, since Calvin accepts neither the criterion nor the method used by Spinoza. Thus, his principle of general accessibility of the biblical text founders on the petitio principii, Strauss observes:

> It is a *petitio principii* if the critic takes as his point of departure that he is applying his critique to the teachings of human beings, that the character which he shares with his opponent, "what is common to all men," is the only possible ground for the critique. Still less may the

critic invoke Scripture. For Scripture cannot be divested of that operation of grace by "the Holy Spirit" without which there can be no genuine understanding of Scripture.[111]

Piety is an atheoretical and even antitheoretical attitude, which as such cannot be refuted by theoretical arguments. The latter presuppose that reason is competent to judge independently, and this Calvin radically denies. The same holds for the fundamental question of whether man has an intellectual, moral, and political interest in what is revealed by the Bible. In Spinoza's view, what the believer calls "interest" is nothing but the relationship of human fear to its own projections. If the fear is removed, the "interest" disappears, and submission is replaced by the freedom of the intellectual love of God.[112] Aside from the fact that the theoretical attitude includes the rejection of any such preliminary interest, the argument on this point is inadequate, Strauss finds. By opposing fear and love, Spinoza overlooks the crucial distinction that Calvinism makes between profane or superstitious fear and the true fear of God. The latter is no slavish fear of danger or punishment, but is the basis for the pious love of God, which is able to inspire exceptional courage.

The fact that Spinoza ignores this crucial difference proves that the experience of fear of God and awareness of sin are completely alien to him, Strauss observes.[113] As a philosopher, he is compelled to deny the reality of sin: if God or nature is operative in all human actions, as the *Ethics* asserts, no action can be sinful. In this context, Strauss quotes a letter in which Spinoza cites the words of the prophet Jeremiah: "Behold, as the clay is in the potter's hand, so are ye in mine hand."[114] In the same letter, Spinoza argues that his strict determinism merely brings the Calvinist doctrine of predestination to its logical conclusion. This assertion is ironic, of course: it obscures the fact that Spinoza's understanding of man's relationship to God is fundamentally opposed to the Calvinist understanding. In Spinoza's view, this relationship is not characterized by sin, weakness, and insufficiency, but by man's transience as a part of the eternal substance. Like all arguments against orthodoxy, the denial of sin is based on the assertion of the autonomy of reason and the denial of any vital human interest in a revealed truth.

A similar fate befalls Spinoza's critique on the basis of reason, in particular his positive critique of miracles. Where the legitimacy of theory is denied outright, there is no place whatsoever for a philosophical concept of nature. Unlike Maimonides, Calvin rejects the scholastic distinction between the ordinary natural order and the exceptional, supernatural intervention of God. Since Calvin extends the latter over the whole of creation, the former is wholly absent. In his understanding, there is no sublunary sphere with a proper regularity intelligible to unassisted human reason. For Calvin, creation is characterized by irregularity and unpredictability, which show that God continually rules and guides his creation. As a result, the difference between miracles and the ordinary course of the world disappears: every instance in the existence of creation is due to divine providence.[115] By the same token, Calvin does not regard miracles as special events meant to engender or support faith. Man learns to perceive the permanence of God's power and providence in creation only when divine grace has allowed his inner light to develop into unconditional faith and submission.[116]

Because Calvin does not distinguish between the miraculous and the natural, Spinoza is unable to drive a critical wedge between the two and play them off against each other, Strauss explains: "Trust in God, obedience to Him, discerns in each cosmic process . . . the hand of God at work. This attitude sees no reason to discriminate between 'miracles' and 'nature.' It is not bound to concede this distinction to the scientific mind."[117] Unlike Maimonides, Calvin does not defend revelation from a cosmological viewpoint, but from an anthropological perspective according to which faith and piety radically exclude theory as a legitimate human activity. His position thus becomes immune to any argumentation based on scientific and theoretical grounds. Moreover, it enables Calvin to undermine the foundation of Spinoza's entire undertaking, Strauss observes: "Even if all the reasoning adduced by Spinoza were compelling, nothing would have been proven. Only this much would have been proven: that on the basis of unbelieving science one could not but arrive at Spinoza's results. But would this basis itself thus be justified?"[118] This pivotal remark should be kept in mind, as we will return to it in the next chapter.

Still, Spinoza is able to reverse this question and maintain that the Calvinist rejection of theory is premature and unjustified. In support, he can point to the discord within the orthodox camp, between the "dogmatists" and the "skeptics." But does this mean that he is able to tackle and decisively refute the underlying premise of an almighty, inscrutable, vengeful, and provident God? At most, Strauss holds, a positive critique can argue that this premise is improbable and illogical, and that biblical evidence supporting it is implausible.[119] In addition, Spinoza can invoke the rule of noncontradiction and argue that the Bible contradicts itself. However, the philosopher is deprived even of this ultimate weapon, Strauss argues, for orthodoxy can respond that an inscrutable creator cannot communicate his will to man other than by means of contradictory speech.[120]

The only way in which Spinoza would be able to definitely refute the fundamental premise of orthodoxy is by proving "that in the universe of beings there is no place for an unfathomable God."[121] Such a proof is possible only in the form of a conclusive philosophical system in which everything is accounted for without recourse to an inscrutable God. This system would also provide the tailpiece for the positive critique, ensuring that its arguments no longer have to be hypothetical. According to Spinoza, the *Ethics* aims to be just that: if, as it argues, God coincides with nature, the whole indeed becomes fully intelligible.[122] On closer inspection, however, this claim proves to be deeply problematic. Indeed, the intelligibility of God or nature and the concomitant impossibility of revelation and miracles follow logically from the fundamental principles of the *Ethics*. But it does not mean that these principles themselves are immediately obvious and acceptable. In fact, they are completely arbitrary, Strauss finds. Their meaning consists entirely in their function: they determine the conditions that must be satisfied for the whole or the cosmos to be intelligible. Their obviousness is only the result of the fulfillment of these conditions. Whether Spinoza actually succeeds in fulfilling them, however, is moot. Are the basic principles of the *Ethics* clear and conclusive? Strauss asks. And if they are, are they necessarily true? Or are they only clear and conclusive because they leave out of consideration certain elements of the whole? As Strauss suggests, Spinoza may be guilty of a certain reductionism in order to make the cosmos appear as a transparent and intelligible whole. At any rate, he fails to raise his account beyond the level of the merely hypothetical and conditional. What is more, fulfillment of the conditions presupposes the acceptance of the independence and autonomy of reason.[123]

This, Strauss concludes, shows that Spinoza's position itself turns out to be based on a kind of faith, faith in the authority and sufficiency of reason, and the belief that the theoretical life is the one thing needful. As a result, Spinoza is compelled to combat the Calvinist assertion of reason's insufficiency by all possible means. Of course, the reverse also holds: inspired by its faith, Calvinism cannot leave the theoretical life undisturbed. At the end of his reconstruction of their debate, Strauss encounters two implacable opponents, each of whom radically denies the other any right to exist:

> Thus Spinoza's position and that of Calvin stand directly opposed to each other, without being able to arrive at agreement or even at mutual toleration. These positions are not defensive positions, impregnable by virtue of a fundamental circle and on that very account inadequate for attack. Rather, the passionate faith in the justice and truth of his cause compels each of the two opponents—it could indeed not be otherwise—to the attack: to the opponent's position *every* right is denied. One is not yet satisfied by a smooth and clear-cut severance

of religion from theory. But revealed religion and theory fight, on the same plane of the one and eternal truth, their life and death combat.[124]

Ultimately, the conflict between Spinoza and Calvin is a conflict of interests, the stakes of which are not only epistemological but also and primarily *moral*, Strauss adds: what human way of life is in accordance with the truth?[125] The "passionate faith" in the rightness of their cause makes both opponents unwilling to even try to understand the other's position. As a result, each tends to combat a caricature of his opponent. When Calvin anathemizes theory as a pretext for indulging in carnal lust, he forgets that philosophers predicate their activity on overcoming their desires and passions, even if they admit that few actually succeed in doing so.[126] Conversely, Spinoza ignores a number of features crucial to the self-understanding of revealed religion, like the distinction between profane fear and genuine fear of God, but also the "will to mediacy" characteristic of faith in revelation. Likewise, he takes no notice of the fact that these features derive their meaning from fundamental premises that remain impervious to his critique.

However, if Spinoza's critique of religion ultimately fails to reach, let alone affect its target, how can its historical success be explained? Strauss asks. The effect of his attack on the power and the authority of revealed religion is undeniable. The arguments and criticisms proffered in the *Treatise* eventually came to form the basic vocabulary of successive generations of *Aufklärer*. As we saw in the previous chapter, even the young Strauss invokes the success of Spinoza's critique of religion as an indisputable and irreversible accomplishment in his debate with the opponents of political Zionism. Nevertheless, the upshot of his present analysis is that the critique did not really succeed in refuting the core of revelation. Hence, he now concludes, the key to its success must necessarily be sought *outside* of theory.

## Happiness and Ridicule: The Epicurean Connection

When Spinoza attempts to penetrate the core of revealed religion, his own position becomes problematic. Faith in revelation, understood as *pietas*, has a foundation impenetrable to theoretical scrutiny, from which it is able to call its opponent into question. More particularly, it is able to raise the question regarding the *motive* that underlies theory.[127] When Strauss attempts to explain the historical success of the critique of religion, this becomes the focus of his inquiry. In this way, he rejoins his debate with Hermann Cohen, whose intensely critical reading of the *Theological-Political Treatise* also pointed to Spinoza's ulterior motives. Although

Strauss praised Cohen for asking the right questions, he did not share his answers. As he argued, a "dutiful" historical interpretation suffices to show that the *Treatise* is not exclusively nor primarily directed against Judaism, but against revealed religion as such, and that it aims at emancipating philosophy from the hold of theology. Nevertheless, Cohen's initial question remains valid: what is the motive underlying the attempt to emancipate philosophy by attacking revealed religion? To answer this question, Strauss suggested, a different approach was needed from the biographical speculations proffered by Cohen.

In *Spinoza's Critique of Religion*, Strauss develops this alternative approach. Access to Spinoza's motive, he argues, can be found through the principal blind spot of his critique of Calvinism: the crucial distinction between profane and numinous fear, and the concomitant vital interest in revelation posited by religious orthodoxy. By ignoring this difference, Spinoza is able to combat religion as a projection of profane fear that perpetuates human subjugation by leaving man in the grasp of passions and desires. By the same token, liberation of the reader toward philosophy, the *Theological-Political Treatise*'s principal goal, is first and foremost liberation from the fear of an unpredictable and wrathful higher power, Strauss infers. Spinoza's primary means to achieve this goal is scientific or theoretical knowledge of the true causes that underlie fear-inspiring phenomena like miracles and the experience of death. Such knowledge takes away the immediate fear, but it also alleviates the more general human disquietude by showing that the cosmos is characterized by a perfectly intelligible regularity. In this way, Spinoza's ultimate interest, and hence the motive that informs his efforts against revealed religion, becomes visible: *foelicitas* or happiness as a condition of rest in which the soul contemplates the unchangeable order of nature. In Spinoza's perspective, religion is a disturber of the peace who keeps the philosophically talented from pursuing and attaining true happiness, and who therefore must be kept in check.

If such is the mainspring of Spinoza's critique, however, his approach is not entirely novel. As Strauss points out, there is an ancient philosophic tradition that aims to allay the fear of gods with a rational account of the cosmos: the *Epicurean* tradition. For Epicurus as for Spinoza, science is a means to attaining a condition of serenity: knowledge of the true causes of events is in the service of the purity of happiness or *eudaimonia*. Similarly, both thinkers reject religious belief as ignorance of the true causes, and religion as a source of fear and unrest. Ultimately, Strauss argues, the Epicurean motive points to the desire to experience the world as a stable and unchangeable order independent of divine will and power.[128]

Clearly, this opposition recurs, albeit in an intensified form, in the "life-and-death struggle" discussed in the previous section. Spinoza's philosophic worldview is aimed against religious orthodoxy's radical denial of causality, which regards every instance in the existence of the world as a divine dispensation. Because of this relation, uncovering this Epicurean connection is an important moment in Strauss's inquiry. While it marks a breakthrough in his analysis of Spinoza's critique of religion, it also enables him to pinpoint an essential characteristic of the Enlightenment: "Interest in security and in alleviation of the ills of life may be called the interest characteristic of the Enlightenment in general."[129] Of course, unlike Epicurus, Spinoza and his followers do not face an ancient state religion, but a revealed religion with much more far-reaching claims. Because it appeals to a radical fear, this religion exercises an infinitely stronger hold on human thought, as well as on social and political life. Still, the early Enlightenment thinkers systematically remain attached to the traditional opposition between science and superstition. This means that Spinoza's blind spot actually becomes the point of departure for their struggle, Strauss argues:

> The Epicurean critique of religion continued effective during the period dominated by revealed religion. This was possible because the distinction asserted in revealed religion between superstitious and genuine fear of God was denied or overlooked. Revealed religion itself came to be contested as mere superstition.[130]

Nevertheless, compared to the Epicurean critique of religion, its modern counterpart does make its distinctive points. To begin with, the original apolitical, even antipolitical concern for the peace of the individual soul is now replaced by a concern for social and political peace. Concurrently, revealed religion is actively contested as a source of social and political instability and held responsible for repression, intolerance and discord, inquisition, the persecution of other faiths, and bloody religious wars. The second difference, related to the first, involves the exact point of attack. While Epicurus rejects the belief in higher powers because of its frightening and disturbing effects, the Enlightenment critique of religion mainly turns against its illusory character. Religion, it argues, covers reality with a veil of fancy, prejudice, and vain hope that puts happiness beyond man's reach. The critique of religion, therefore, helps man liberate himself from all illusions that prevent him from seeking and finding happiness in the present, Strauss notes: "whereas the Epicureanism of antiquity turns against religion as against a fearsome illusion, in the modern evolution of atheism what predominates is the struggle against illusionary happiness for the sake of real happiness."[131] In this way, the critique of religion becomes a struggle of science against illusion that runs parallel with the political struggle against those who perpetuate illusion in order to protect their power and further their own interests.

This brings us to a third aspect highlighted by Strauss. The view of religion as an obstacle on the way to human happiness is attended by a rejection of the biblical doctrine of man's original perfection and subsequent fall. When independent reason posits itself as a higher self-consciousness over against a primitive and imperfect past, this "essentially historical opposition" implies that perfection and happiness are no longer located in a remote past, but in a future that is within man's reach. The premise of original imperfection creates a historical space in which man has to rely on his own efforts to attain happiness, by cultivating and developing his natural powers, aided by a scientific method: "The specific cast of mind of the modern centuries, the belief in method, in culture—let us not forget that 'culture' means 'culture of nature'—implies directedness towards the future, belief that perfection is to be sought in the future, the denial of perfection as lost forever, as not to be recovered by human striving."[132]

In its struggle, the modern critique of religion politicizes and historicizes the Epicurean motive, Strauss argues, leading to an increase in scale that reflects the power and the influence of the "superstition" it combats. The radical interest in revelation, postulated by Calvinist orthodoxy, requires an equally radical counterposition: intellectually as well as morally and politically, man is not dependent on a divine truth to attain perfection. Although his beginnings are imperfect, he is able to use his capacities to create the social and political conditions for his happiness. Culture, labor, and science project a world in which illusion, fear, and disquiet lose their rationale, and thus relinquish their grip on man. In this world, the Epicurean maxim "live covertly" (lathè biôsas) loses its meaning: in the modern critique of religion, the Epicurean "will to happiness" becomes the engine of a political struggle against religion, superstition, and prejudice, in the name of freedom. Twenty-three years after Spinoza's Critique of Religion, he will epitomize the result of this transformation as "political hedonism, a doctrine which has revolutionized human life everywhere on a scale never yet approached by any other teaching."[133] As Strauss repeatedly stresses, the Epicurean motive precedes the rise of modern science, and guides its development. Undeniably, many Enlightenment thinkers explicitly referred to Epicurean atomism and naturalism as an inspiration for their scientific theories. However, their interest was determined by a preliminary striving for human happiness. In other words, it is *because* they recognized their own antireligious motives in Epicurus's work that they became interested in the Epicurean doctrine of nature. Even after the web of fear, superstition, and prejudice had been ruptured, and science had triumphed over religion, the Epicurean motive remained part and parcel of scientific progress.[134]

Combined, the two chief results of Strauss's inquiry lead to the following conclusion: the historical success of Spinoza's critique of religion does not derive from the strength of his scientific arguments, but from the motive that inspires it, based on a specific interpretation of the human need for serenity and stability. In Strauss's analysis, each of Spinoza's offensive arguments proves to be based on the petitio principii of the sufficiency of reason. With regard to revealed religion, therefore, only a *defensive* position is possible: unassisted reason can successfully ward off religious reference to miracles by invoking immediate experience and the openness of independent reason. Mere defense does not suffice, however, since this would amount to recognizing and acknowledging the opponent. The latter must be defeated and eradicated, in the name of genuine human happiness. But how is this possible if theoretical arguments based on reason cannot get a hold? What other strategy, what other weaponry is available to Spinoza and his followers?

Strauss's answer is remarkable, perhaps even surprising. In his view, the critique of religion's most important weapon consists in *ridiculing* revealed religion, such as by pointing out the contrast between its fundamental premises and the evidence adduced in the Bible. When, for example, the Bible relates how God foretold the future name of a city to Moses, and when religious orthodoxy regards this as a demonstration of divine omnipotence, the critique of religion can mock and deride this as a grotesque triviality. The fact that orthodoxy asserts a necessary connection between the fundamental premises of religion and every detail of the Bible is thus turned into an argument against orthodoxy. As Strauss remarks, the example above can easily be multiplied, and the critique of religion did so gratefully and successfully. Nonetheless, he points out, ridicule only pertains to the consequences of principles; it does not affect the principles themselves. As a result, its validity is limited:

> This critique has a prospect of success, not by direct argumentation, but only by virtue of the mockery that lends spice to the arguments, and lodges them firmly in the hearer's mind. Reason must turn into "esprit" (*Geist*) if reason is to experience her more than royal freedom, her unshakable sovereignty, and to realize it in action. Through laughter and mockery, reason overleaps the barriers that she was not able to

overcome when she proceeded pace by pace in formal argumentation. But all the self-consciousness of the Enlightenment cannot conceal the fact that this critique, peculiar to the Enlightenment—historically effective as it was—does not reach the core of revealed religion, but is only a critique of certain consequences and is therefore questionable.[135]

Although Strauss does not make the connection explicitly, we may surmise that ridicule also plays an important role in the "essentially historical consciousness" of positive reason. The latter can only differentiate itself from religious faith by degrading it to superstition or a lower form of consciousness. Since it cannot do so by directly attacking the foundations of religion, it can only succeed by mocking secondary elements of the Bible as the products of a primitive, prescientific consciousness, as "prejudices of the ancient people." In this way, reason's leap over its own fundamental limitations becomes a "progress" that renders it immune to miracle reports and that makes the past appear as the realm of prejudice. By the same token, the offensive power of ridicule compensates the merely defensive capacities of the critique of religion.

## Farewell to Spinoza

After this long philosophical, theological, and historical excursion, let us return to the *quaestio iuris* that initiated and guided Strauss's inquiry into Spinoza's critique of religion. Did the critique really reach its target? Did Spinoza effectively refute or have an impact on revealed religion in general, and Jewish religion in particular? Were modern Jews justified in breaking through their isolation, entering historical reality and opening themselves to contact and exchange with Europe? From an analysis of the main argument of his book, we may conclude that, according to Strauss, the answer to these questions is, on the whole, negative. The critique of religion missed the core of its target and left religious orthodoxy largely intact in its faithful obedience to the revealed law of an inscrutable creator. All Spinoza could legitimately do was strike a purely defensive attitude based on belief in the sufficiency and autonomy of reason. Since no effective theoretical, philosophical, and scientific arguments were available to stage an offensive, he had to resort to rhetorical means, excoriating and mocking his opponent. Motivating this endeavor was the Epicurean motive, which opened the prospect of an ultimate victory: the scientific construction of a disenchanted world.

If this conclusion is correct, however, what is the significance of Spinoza's critique of religion for the interests of Judaism? Strauss asks. Spinoza's claim to "greater honesty" in his reading of the Bible, showing the real Jewish past, is based on the problematic assumption that the Bible is of human origin, and that unassisted reason is competent and authorized to study it. These assumptions, however, can be fundamentally challenged and countered by Jewish religious orthodoxy. In the latter's view, to understand and determine what is "honest" and "real" is possible only from a condition of faith and submission. Hence, the "reality" in which Judaism had an interest throughout its long past differs fundamentally from the "reality" Spinoza's biblical science claims to lay bare. Between the two conceptions yawns the same chasm that separates the world of the believer from that of the unbeliever. The "greater honesty" of Spinoza's scientific method consists in the willingness to ignore what for the orthodox reading is a *conditio sine qua non*. This willingness, however, is based on presuppositions that are no less problematic than those of orthodox piety.

Against the basic principles of orthodox exegesis, Spinoza can muster no conclusive theoretical argument without committing a petitio principii. Hence, it is difficult to imagine in what way the results of his positive biblical science could ever affect, let alone promote, the interests and priorities of Judaism. From a religious perspective, the world of tradition has no immediate need to be enlightened, let alone dismantled, from without. Moreover, as Strauss repeatedly underlines, the theological dimension is inevitably connected to the political dimension. Strictly speaking, he argues, Spinoza's struggle for the autonomy of science and the state had nothing to do with the Jewish interest. His attempt to revive his readers' confidence in reason was based on a preliminary distancing with regard to Judaism, which could not be bridged subsequently. Both in its basic principles and in its goals, the *Theological-Political Treatise* passed by the core of Judaism without so much as grazing it. As a result, the solution to the Jewish Question as a theological-political problem it offered was bound to fail.

Without doubt, Strauss's findings profoundly change his perception of the process of *Einwirklichung*, the end of Jewish exile and the reentry into history. This holds, to begin with, for his view on the process of emancipation and assimilation. Initially, we may recall, he hailed the success of the critique of religion as "the decisive cause of what is known as assimilation, which therefore is Jewishly legitimate also from this perspective."[136] In the light of his inquiry, this "Jewish legitimacy" has become deeply questionable. In 1932, two years after *Spinoza's Critique of Religion*, Strauss publishes an article entitled "The Testament of Spinoza."[137] In this article, he concludes that the arguments modern Jews borrowed from Spinoza in order to justify their emancipation and assimilation to the European tradition have lost their force. In this way, it has become apparent that Spinoza's critique has no intrinsic relationship with, and thus no relevance for, the Jewish context, since there is nothing particularly Jewish about his philosophy.

However, Strauss emphasizes, this not only applies to assimilation, but also to the movement that evolved from it as both a continuation and a corrective. As Strauss goes on to explain, political Zionism equally lacks an intrinsic connection with Judaism. When Spinoza discusses the possibility of a restoration of the Jewish state in the third chapter of the *Treatise*, he does so in a markedly detached and noncommittal way:

> Spinoza does not actually wish for or demand the restoration of the Jewish state: he merely discusses it. As if condescending from the height of his philosophical neutrality, he leaves it to the Jews to liberate themselves from their religion and thus to obtain for themselves the possibility of reconstituting their state.[138]

Neutrality, Strauss argues, is the key to Spinoza's testament. Though born a Jew, he addressed the problems of Judaism as an outsider and a philosopher, from the perspective of a modern, political-hedonistic concept of the human interest. From that same perspective, he suggested—as it were in passing—a solution that was no more than an afterthought in the margins of his critique of religion. Like the latter, however, this solution presupposes the distance with regard to Jewish interests, and as such, it has no intrinsic bearing on these interests. Like the process of assimilation, it comes from the outside and leads back to the outside. Based on a preliminary break with Judaism, it requires a similar break from the addressee, who must relinquish his Jewish identity. Hence, Strauss concludes, there is no sense in continuing to venerate Spinoza either as a great Jew or as the father of Jewish emancipation, assimilation, and political Zionism. Like his perception of the Jewish Question as a theological-political problem, strictly speaking the solutions he proposed are of no use to the Jews as Jews.[139]

Small wonder, then, that in "The Testament of Spinoza" Strauss begins to bid farewell, not so much to Spinoza as to his legacy, biblical science, and political Zionism. This event, however, is all but clamorous. As mentioned in the previous chapter, only in 1935 does Strauss hint at the fact that he has taken final leave of his youthful political commitment. And only in his autobiographical writings of the 1960s does he spell out the reasons in more detail. On this occasion, he points to the fact that political Zionism conceived of the difficult situation of modern Judaism as a problem capable of receiving a definite solution. The "Jewish Question," he argues, is a specifically modern concept, one of the many abstractions that circulated in the nineteenth century. Like the "Social Question" and the "Labor Question," it was part of an understanding of history as something man can create, direct, and purify of its contradictions and turbulences. As a result, political Zionism approached the Jewish problem primarily as a general human problem, and only secondarily—if at all—as a specifically Jewish problem.[140] This approach, however, ran counter to the Jewish religious tradition, according to which the restoration of the Jewish nation was dependent on the coming of the Messiah, sent by God to liberate, redeem, and restore. As Strauss observes in retrospect, the goals of political Zionism had become possible through a break with this messianic hope: "This project implied a profound modification of the traditional Jewish hopes—a modification arrived at through a break with these hopes."[141] While expressing great admiration for the accomplishments of the Zionist project, the older Strauss leaves no doubt that he eventually came to regard political Zionism as fundamentally insufficient because of this break. Its solution was predicated on a complete redefinition of the Jewish Question within a modern, purely political and thus alien framework. In this way, the core issue was avoided and left intact: political Zionism "could not solve the Jewish problem because of the narrowness of its original conception, however noble."[142]

The young Strauss, however, remains reticent about the consequences to be drawn from his study of Spinoza. Thus, some important questions remain unanswered. If, as he concludes, Judaism is not even the addressee of Spinoza's testament, and if neither political Zionism nor the new theology offer a solution to the Jewish Question as a theological-political problem, how should one attend to the Jewish interests in modernity? To the extent that his inquiry answers the *quaestio iuris* in the negative, doesn't it point to an unqualified return to Jewish orthodoxy and the old theology as "the only course compatible with sheer consistency or intellectual probity"?[143] We should not forget that in the book Strauss tacitly retracts the accusation he had thrown at the orthodox opponents of political Zionism. By placing Spinoza in the Epicurean tradition, he admits that the orthodox censure of assimilation and political Zionism as *apikorsuth* or Epicureanism was, in fact, justified.

On a number of occasions, however, Strauss makes clear that this was by no means his intention. The most important reason is that he holds himself to be incapable of an unqualified return in the first place. Shortly after *Spinoza's Critique of Religion* is published, he writes a letter to his colleague and kindred spirit Gerhard Krüger, then a professor of philosophy in Marburg, in which he explains with particular frankness the personal motives that led him to his inquiry:

To me, only one thing was clear: that I *cannot* believe in God. I put
this to myself in the following way: there is an *idea Dei innata, omnibus
hominis communis* [innate idea of God, common to all men]; to this
*idea* I can give or refuse my *assensus* [assent]; I believed that I had to
refuse it; I had to make clear to myself: Why? I had to justify myself
before the tribunal (*Forum*) of the Jewish tradition; and without any
philosophical-historical reflection (*geschichtsphilosophische Reflexion*),
simply because I would not have considered it defensible to give
up, out of frivolousness and convenience, a cause for the sake of
which my ancestors took upon themselves everything conceivable
(*alles nur Denkbare*).[144]

Seeking to justify his unbelief as a political Zionist, and out of loyalty
to his Jewish heritage, Strauss felt compelled to revisit the conflict between
modern philosophy and religious orthodoxy in its most radical and most
fundamental form. As he goes on to explain to Krüger, the result of his inquiry was that on the whole, Jewish orthodoxy was indeed correct in casti-
gating the unbeliever as an Epicurean. Nevertheless, he significantly adds
that not every kind of unbelief is necessarily of Epicurean origin. Even if
the success of the critique of religion and of the Enlightenment as a whole
was chiefly due to its tactics of ridicule, the principle of the defensive critique seemed to hold its own against orthodoxy. If Spinoza's unbelieving
rationalism proves to be untenable, this does not yet mean that every form
of unbelieving rationalism is untenable. Hence, further scrutiny is necessary. Moreover, in the autobiographical preface to the Spinoza book he
mentions another important impediment to an unqualified return. Since
Spinoza's critique of religion was aimed against revealed religion as such,
demonstrating its ultimate failure implies that orthodoxy based on revelation *as such* emerges unbeaten:

The victory of orthodoxy through the self-destruction of rational
philosophy was not an unmitigated blessing, for it was a victory not of
Jewish orthodoxy but of any orthodoxy, and Jewish orthodoxy based
its claim to superiority to other religions from the beginning on its
superior rationality.[145]

Thus, even from the perspective of religious orthodoxy, a leap of
faith cannot solve the problem of the Jewish individual who specifically
wishes to remain loyal to his ancestral legacy, as there is no intrinsic compelling reason why he should return to his own tradition rather than another. To say the least, the study of Spinoza showed that the original battle

between unbelieving Enlightenment and believing orthodoxy is essentially undecided. At the same time, rejecting an unqualified return to orthodoxy seems to amount to siding with unbelieving reason. This consequence is anything but unproblematic: Strauss repeatedly suggests that the self-confidence of positive reason is based on a form of faith. The principal claim of radical Enlightenment, however, was that it was based on true knowledge, not on faith. This problem makes further investigation of the conflict all the more pressing. Thus, the book on Spinoza in no way signifies the end of Strauss's grappling with the theological-political problem. In the next chapter, we will see that his search takes a surprising and decisive turn.

# CHAPTER 3

# The Second Cave

> *. . . there was never anything so deerly bought,*
> *as these Western parts have bought the*
> *learning of the Greek and Latine tongues.*
>
> —Hobbes, *Leviathan*

## The Crisis of the Enlightenment:
## Jacobi, Mendelssohn, and the Pantheism Controversy

In *Spinoza's Critique of Religion*, Strauss concludes, "Even if all the reasoning adduced by Spinoza were compelling, nothing would have been proven. Only this much would have been proven: that on the basis of unbelieving science one could not but arrive at Spinoza's results. But would this basis itself thus be justified?"[1] As we saw, the book raises serious doubts on this point. What is more, Strauss subsequently informs the reader that the crucial question was already raised in an exemplary manner by someone else: "It was Friedrich Heinrich Jacobi who posed this question and by so doing lifted the interpretation of Spinoza—or what amounts to the same thing, the critique of Spinoza—on to its proper plane."[2] The announcement is singular, both in the literal and in the figurative sense: while Strauss indicates that Jacobi's critique of Spinoza is nothing less than a model as well as a yardstick for his own investigation, it is the only reference to Jacobi in the whole work.

Today, Friedrich Heinrich Jacobi (1743–1819) is mostly remembered as a literary critic and author who paved the way for Romanticism and the Sturm und Drang movement. In his day, however, he was also a renowned philosophical opponent of the Enlightenment. In the genesis of Strauss's work, he is more or less the connecting piece between what precedes and what follows the Spinoza book. In 1921, Strauss obtained a doctorate in philosophy with a dissertation on Jacobi's critique of Enlightenment rationalism.[3] As we will see, his findings did play an important role in his subsequent approach to Spinoza's *Theological-Political Treatise*. After the publication of the Spinoza book in 1931, the Akademie assigns Strauss as a coeditor to the jubilee edition of the collected works of Moses Mendelssohn, the great Jewish thinker and leader of the moderate Enlightenment.[4] Strauss's most extensive and most interesting contribution consists in an incisive and insightful investigation into the so-called Pantheism Controversy, a polemic between Mendelssohn and Jacobi that shook the intellectual world of eighteenth-century Germany. At the heart of the controversy was the legitimacy of the Enlightenment, disputed by Jacobi and defended by Mendelssohn. Interestingly enough, the debate's main focus was the philosophy of Spinoza. For this reason, a closer look at Strauss's writings on Jacobi and Mendelssohn is indispensable in order to understand how he continues his research after the Spinoza book.

In his dissertation, Strauss shows how Jacobi attacks the foundations of Enlightenment rationalism on two separate, albeit closely related, accounts: knowledge, on the one hand, and morality and politics on the other. On the level of knowledge, his critique is directed against Descartes's method of universal doubt, the core of modern rationalism. In Jacobi's view, the Cartesian method attempts to secure the reality of Being by reducing it to its indubitable conditions of possibility, from which point it subsequently tries to reconstruct Being rationally. According to Jacobi, this operation amounts to nothing less than a systematic reduction of Being to non-Being or Nothingness, a procedure for which he coined the term "Nihilism." All that is left is the pure thinking subject, which thereby becomes the source of reality and the sole guarantor of the knowability of reality. Strauss paraphrases this view of the Cartesian project as follows: "We can only understand what we can produce. The philosopher who wants to understand the world must therefore become creator of the world."[5]

Moreover, according to Jacobi the Cartesian procedure is deliberately selective: it filters out those aspects of the object that resist reduction and rational reconstruction. In this way, it ignores and even destroys certain vital elements that it can never replace or reconstruct. These elements point to what he calls "natural certainties" (*natürliche Gewissheiten*), which are known prior to any attempt at rational knowledge and therefore constitute the possibility of such knowledge. From this point of view, both the source of knowledge (human understanding) and its object (reality) are "irrational" or, rather, "suprarational" (*überrational*). They come to light in propositions that are grasped with intuitive immediacy and therefore cannot be the object of subsequent rational proof, such as "I am" and "There is a world outside of me," but also "There is a God."[6] As a result, Jacobi rejects Kant's notion of God as a regulative idea of reason. The latter, he argues, reverses the original primacy of God with regard to reason, and thus is devoid of any content, both theoretically and ethically useless.[7]

Because of its deliberate negation of these natural certainties as limits of knowledge, Cartesian rationalism and the modern sciences based on it can be no more than "the organization of ignorance," Jacobi holds. For if the method of rational demonstration exerts its power within a domain limited by irrational and transcendent certainties, a strict determinism can apply only within those same bounds. Unable to fully justify the precedence of radical doubt over natural certainty, it can never attain to the truth, since it is based on an initial surrender of the truth. Rationalism sacrifices theory or contemplation in order to radically exclude irrationality. In Strauss's words, "Doubt is the renunciation of the theoretical life (truth) for the sake of the theoretical evil (irrationality) that is necessarily related to it."[8]

On the level of ethics and politics, Jacobi's argument runs closely parallel to his epistemological critique. In this case, his polemic is aimed against the idea of autonomy at the heart of the moral and political program of the Enlightenment. In his dissertation, Strauss summarizes the main contention as follows:

> Autonomism is the ethical form of general doubt, of the principle of modern culture, which invokes the autonomy of religious conscience, of scientific reason and of moral legislation (*sola* fides, *sola* ratio, "*only* a good will"). In opposition, Jacobi emphasizes that, in ethical matters, it is simply unnecessary for the acting subject to understand the norm and to affirm it out of its own insight. It is not the case that insight precedes and obedience follows, but precisely the reverse: only out of obedience, as a result of following the norm, from the penetration of the norm into the center of our lives as a consequence of obedience, does moral insight emerge.[9]

Just as the principle of radical doubt and belief in proof and demonstration express a refusal to submit to the transcendence of reality, so does the concept of autonomy disclose a rejection of the ethical norms inherent in this reality, incited by man's proud desire to be the sole source of morality. Correspondingly, just as it leads to organized ignorance and determinism on the level of knowledge, so does rationalism lead to atheism and fatalism on the level of morality and politics, Jacobi asserts. Its claim to the contrary, rationalism is incapable of replacing what it has destroyed, unable to establish morality on purely immanent grounds.

The intrinsic relationship between epistemology, ethics, and politics postulated by Jacobi explains why his opposition to the Enlightenment takes the form of a critical discussion of Spinoza. The latter, in Jacobi's view, exemplifies the defiance of Cartesian rationalism in the face of transcendence. In his introduction to Mendelssohn's contributions to the Pantheism Controversy, Strauss recalls how Jacobi locates the root of rationalism in "the tendency to prove everything and to accept nothing as given; if one follows this tendency honestly, i.e., without compunction, it leads to Spinozism, i.e., to atheism and fatalism . . . the origin of the tendency to prove everything is the will of man not to be dependent on a truth that transcends him, the will 'not to obey the truth, but to command it,' pride, vanity."[10] With unrivaled clarity, Jacobi argues, Spinoza's thought shows that the common root of the Enlightenment's philosophy and politics is a rebellious and revolutionary effort to liberate man from the authority of transcendence. As Strauss goes on to note, Jacobi was "still too closely tied to the theistic tradition not to be compelled to see in atheism (and 'Spinozism is atheism') a result of anti-theism, of the revolt against God."[11]

According to Jacobi, however, the motive underlying this revolt proved to be at least as tyrannical as that of its putative opponent: Descartes and Spinoza heralded a new metaphysical despotism of autonomous demonstrative reason, which found its political complement in the new political despotism of Hobbes's *Leviathan*. His objections notwithstanding, Jacobi respected both Spinoza and Hobbes for the consistency and rigor of their thinking. In fact, he preferred these "classics of despotism" to the German *Aufklärer* of his time. What he perceived as their halfhearted rationalism and their readiness to compromise with autocratic regimes provoked his aversion to such an extent that he went so far as to defend the ideal of a liberal state.[12] Nevertheless, he remained intensely critical of rationalism, because of the lack of justification and the "nihilism" of Cartesian doubt.

Claiming at least equal justification, Jacobi's own philosophic doctrine takes precisely this deficit as its point of departure. His procedure is first to pursue rationalism to its ultimate consequences, up to the point where its fatalism, atheism, and nihilism become apparent, as well as its rootedness in ignorance. The knowledge of this ignorance (*Wissen des Nicht-Wissens*) then becomes the basis for a *salto mortale*: a leap out of rationalism and nihilism into faith or *Glaube*, motivated by the willingness and the courage to take the risk of believing reality instead of doubting it. As Strauss emphasizes, the concept of *Glaube* at the heart of Jacobi's doctrine is not primarily religious: it comprises both "faith" and "belief" in the Humean sense, according to which human knowledge is ultimately based on indemonstrable beliefs. In this respect, it proved to be a most powerful weapon in Jacobi's polemic against the Enlightenment, for it enabled him to argue that even the choice for rationalism and demonstration rests on a primary belief, an initial act of faith.[13]

In Jacobi's view, *Glaube* is not only an epistemological but also, and even primarily, an ethical category: affirmation of the transcendence of reality is the basic prerequisite for true virtue (*Tugend*), which in its turn is the necessary condition for true knowledge. Without the recognition of his heteronomy and of the necessity of loving obedience to God's commands, man can never hope to attain true knowledge. In fact, Jacobi goes so far as to equate virtue and knowledge: the Platonic character of this identification, far from being accidental, actually points to the foundations of his thought, Strauss emphasizes. According to Jacobi, the history of philosophy is determined by the predominance of one of two typical theoretical attitudes, whereby each type is rooted in a more general type of intellectual and moral attitude. The first, which Jacobi dubs "Platonic," is characterized by nobility, audacity, confidence, faith, and love, and is therefore able to gain access to truth and virtue.[14]

The other type, called "non-Platonic," displays the opposite qualities: baseness, apprehension, diffidence, distrust, disbelief, doubt, and pride, and accordingly the inability to attain truth and virtue. According to Jacobi, the non-Platonic attitude has become dominant in modern philosophy, and this decline has reached its nadir in the age of the Enlightenment. The latter, in spite of its earthly accomplishments, is animated by a Cartesian fear of the immediacy of transcendent reality, and characterized by the subsequent attempt to circumvent its claims. Faced with what he perceives to be the dire consequences of this refusal, Jacobi's doctrine of *Glaube* is an emphatic attempt to restore the Platonic attitude. Through a change in morality, it seeks to reaffirm the transcendence of reality, with a view to reinstating what has been lost and thus accomplishing a renewal of philosophy.[15]

Although Strauss's dissertation is largely a technical analysis of Jacobi's position, a number of elements characteristic of his approach prove to be influential in his ulterior investigations. The first of these concerns the critique of Cartesian methodical doubt. Very likely, Jacobi's challenging the legitimacy of radical doubt informs Strauss's question in *Spinoza's Critique of Religion*, mentioned at the beginning, whether "the basis of unbelieving science" underlying Spinoza's philosophy is justified. For, as he argues in the same book, it is precisely with an appeal to Cartesian doubt that Spinoza excludes both the possibility of miracles in general and of prophecy in particular (as a miraculous collaboration of reason and imagination).[16] In the same

context, Jacobi's comment on the selective character of methodical doubt
may very well lie at the basis of a crucial question concerning the *Ethics*,
which the later Strauss articulates as follows: "But is Spinoza's account clear
and distinct? . . . Is its clarity and distinctness not due to the fact that Spinoza abstracts from those elements of the whole which are not clear and distinct and which can never be rendered clear and distinct?"[17] In one of his
best-known works, *Natural Right and History* (1953), he seems to answer this
question in the affirmative, when criticizing modern philosophy's "dogmatic disregard of everything that cannot become an object, that is, an object for the knowing subject, or the dogmatic disregard of everything that
cannot be mastered by the subject."[18]

Second, among the elements of transcendent reality that are not and
cannot be rendered clear and distinct under the auspices of rational demonstration, Jacobi gives pride of place to the existence of God. Against Kant,
he argues that, as Strauss puts it in his dissertation, "The [philosophical] system must accommodate itself to the existence and meaning (*Sinn*) of God;
the fundamental religious phenomenon may not be twisted (*umgebogen*) for
the sake of the system."[19] Interestingly enough, we see Strauss himself making frequent use of a similar argument in his various discussions with cultural Zionism, Jewish orthodoxy, and the so-called return movement.[20]

This brings us to what may be called the "theological-political"
dimension of Jacobi's position. As we have seen, he subordinates the epistemological question to the moral and political question, and focuses his critique on the underlying ethical-intellectual attitude of Enlightenment
rationalism. This approach is akin to Strauss's approach in *Spinoza's Critique
of Religion*: like Jacobi, he concentrates on the motive that animates Spinoza's attack on revealed religion. Thus, he points out that Spinoza's theoretical critique, according to its own view of religion as based on obedience
and faith, necessarily presupposes disobedience and unbelief. As a result, a
critical reading of Spinoza must concentrate on "the 'Why?' of theory as the
'Why?' of disobedience and unbelief. This 'Why?' precedes all theory.
Rather than a theoretical insight or conviction, it is a motive."[21] Subsequently, Strauss traces this motive to the Epicurean tradition and its attempt
to relieve the human condition by liberating man from fear of the gods, the
cause of the greatest unrest and the gravest crimes. On the basis of this connection, he argues, "Interest in security and in alleviation of the ills of life
may be called the interest characteristic of the Enlightenment in general."[22]
As such, it animates Spinoza's construction of a world in which there is no
place for an inscrutable God, nor for a revealed law teaching man what is
good and what is evil.

Like Jacobi, Strauss argues that this concern, though justified and powerful, makes modern rationalism selective, in that it necessarily abandons or represses certain elements in order to be able to uphold itself. Thus, he finds, Spinoza ignores the crucial distinction between profane, superstitious fear and the genuine fear of God that is a precondition for the love of God and obedience to the revealed law. Driven by a Cartesian "will to immediacy," he is incapable of understanding the "will to mediacy" of the faithful, as a response to the enormity of revelation that inspires obedience and loyalty to tradition. Spinoza's success in mobilizing the "will to immediacy" in his critique of religion distracts our attention from the fact that it is animated by a motive that is no less problematic than that of revealed religion.

On these and other points, Strauss appears to have undergone the influence of Jacobi's thought. For both, the inquest into the motive of the Enlightenment points to a revolutionary antitheism animated by proud human reason and self-postulating, and therefore deeply problematic. In his dissertation, Strauss even goes so far as to subscribe to Jacobi's typological characterization of modernity as an age of fear, distrust, and pride:

> In any case, it seems to us that a specific moment of modern culture is viewed here for the first time in such a comprehensive manner. How little one has reason to regard—and to disregard—this expression as a mere circumstance of Jacobian sentiment, is made evident most clearly by the fundamental agreement in which it finds itself with the results of the research of contemporary sociologists (such as Troeltsch, Sombart, Max Weber, Scheler).[23]

However, Strauss immediately goes on to qualify his assent by adding that this does not mean he also shares the strong evaluative judgment (*Bewertung*) Jacobi appends to it. At this early stage, Strauss is less dismissive regarding the claims of modern rationalism, even if in many ways he shares Jacobi's insight into its flaws. Thus, he makes the critical remark that, although Jacobi is fundamentally aware of the scope of Cartesianism as "a general philosophic principle of method," he fails to do justice to "its profound practical legitimacy (*tiefes sachliches Recht*)."[24] As a critical response to Cartesian doubt, the foundation of Jacobi's doctrine of *Glaube* seems to be at least as questionable as that of its opponent. Accordingly, in *Spinoza's Critique of Religion*, though viewed with an increasingly critical eye, rationalism is still treated with more impartiality than is meted out by Jacobi.[25]

In a different form, this reservation is also visible on the ethical-political level. Commenting on Jacobi's defense of heteronomy, Strauss notes that it is basically the expression of the principle of traditionalism or, to be more exact, conservatism: "The *principle* of tradition—which doesn't mean the recognition of a *particular* tradition. Rather, one should say: principle of conservatism."[26] To the extent that the "leap of faith" implies the espousal of the principle of traditionalism, it leaves undetermined *what* particular tradition is embraced. Nevertheless, Jacobi insists that the leap of faith necessarily requires an espousal of the Christian tradition. Even though he justifies this view by equating the principle of Christianity with the absolute principle of religion as such, this cannot hide the fact that, as Strauss puts it, "the difficult problem of the specification (*Besonderung*) of the highest moral norm does not exist as a theoretical problem for Jacobi."[27] As a result, the leap of faith bears the mark of decisionism, in its attempt to affirm what, according to Jacobi's own doctrine, is in no need of affirmation. In exposing the act of faith at the basis of rationalism, the Jacobian option against Cartesian doubt succeeds in restoring the balance, but it fails to do better than its opponent.

These and other considerations suggest that Jacobi's influence on Strauss's early thinking, though certainly not negligible, is neither as decisive nor as univocal as it appears to be. Although Jacobi put him on the track of the crucial question regarding the "basis of unbelieving science," Jacobi's answer to this question did not satisfy him. In order to see how Strauss found his bearings in this quandary, we must take a closer look at his introductions to Moses Mendelssohn's collected works. Written between 1931 and 1937, they are of particular interest, not only because they reveal a profound knowledge of Mendelssohn's thought, but also because they focus on his dispute with Jacobi, which came to be known as the Pantheism Controversy. Above all, they suggest that Strauss had begun to find a way out of the quandary in which he found himself. Since both the Pantheism Controversy and its aftermath have been amply and excellently documented from a variety of perspectives by different authors, the discussion herein will be limited to such aspects and features as are salient in Strauss's analysis.[28]

The beginning of the Pantheism Controversy is well known. In 1783, Jacobi informed Mendelssohn, by way of a mutual acquaintance, that, "in his last days, Lessing had been a committed Spinozist."[29] For Mendelssohn, this disclosure amounted to nothing less than sheer slander. At that time, the German intelligentsia revered Lessing as a champion of the Enlightenment, while it denounced Spinozism as a heretical, atheistic, and anarchistic doctrine. By the same token, Jacobi cast a shadow over Mendelssohn's long-standing friendship with Lessing. With his declaration, Jacobi wanted to buttress his contention that the Enlightenment and its rationalism as such ultimately led to atheism and fatalism. Lessing, he claimed, had reached the same conclusion and had consistently embraced its radical consequences. By making this publicly known, Jacobi intended to force on the *Aufklärer* the dilemma of either following in the footsteps of Lessing and accepting the destructive effects of rationalism, or rejecting rationalism in favor of his own doctrine of *Glaube*. As a result, Mendelssohn was compelled to defend not only the memory of his friend, but also his own position as a protagonist of the moderate Enlightenment.

As Strauss argues, Jacobi's attack struck home because he and Mendelssohn found themselves on common ground. Both faced the same problem: "the final crisis of modern metaphysics of Cartesian-Leibnizian stamp."[30] More particularly, they both grappled with "the knowledge that the attempt of modern metaphysics to found the concept of God particular to faith by means of unbelieving speculation had failed."[31] The result of this attempt, generally known as natural theology or natural religion, had become increasingly problematic as the radical premises of "unbelieving speculation" had come to the surface and demanded a hearing. As we have seen, Jacobi responded to this crisis by a wholesale repudiation of modern metaphysics and the attempt to return to traditional faith. For Mendelssohn, this solution was out of the question. Refusing to abandon the moderate wing of the Enlightenment, he held on to the idea of a natural religion and to the possibility of harmonizing religion and reason, not least because it provided the cornerstone of his defense of Judaism as a religion of reason.[32]

In the course of his introductions, Strauss critically discusses several key elements of Mendelssohn's natural theology, showing how it became increasingly embattled by the atheism of radical Enlightenment on the one hand, and by the Jacobian return to faith on the other. For the present inquiry, these are relevant only to the extent that they enable Strauss to single out general characteristics and general problems. In this perspective, the most important point in his treatment is his observation that Mendelssohn systematically privileges goodness as the primary attribute of God. This, Strauss holds, is a central characteristic of the Enlightenment:

> The whole of Enlightenment, insofar as it implicitly or explicitly preserves a relationship with the tradition rooted in the Bible, is characterized by the fact that it combats the traditional doctrines and convictions by having recourse to the goodness of God. More precisely, proper to the Enlightenment is the unequivocal priority it accords to God's goodness over his power, his honour and his punishing wrath; for the Enlightenment, God is not primarily the demanding, summoning God, but rather the benevolent God."[33]

The priority of goodness over the other divine attributes determines almost all of the distinctive tenets of Mendelssohn's natural theology, Strauss maintains. It provides the basis for his demonstration of the immortality of the soul, of human perfectibility and freedom; his concomitant rejection of eternal punishment; and his denial of revelation. A good and benevolent God, Mendelssohn holds, does not need to make himself known by revelation, but enables man to acquire knowledge of his design by studying the perfect order of creation. Moreover, a benevolent God could not have created man but with a view to happiness, so that man must be infinitely perfectible. As a consequence, Mendelssohn rejects the ceaseless suffering of eternal damnation, for it contradicts human perfectibility as well as the perfection of creation. In addition, human perfectibility also implies that every individual possesses both an irreducible existence and certain inalienable rights that not even God can violate. This can never lead to difficulties, Mendelssohn assures, for any conflict between the rights of man and those of God is excluded.[34]

According to Strauss, however, giving priority to divine goodness does not express "a theological concern of any kind, but instead the concern for the substantiality, the independence, the autonomy, and the proper right of the Ego (*das Ich*): the unconditional goodness of God is given priority because it is in accord with the claims of the autonomous Ego."[35] In other words, Mendelssohn's natural theology proves to be ultimately guided by and accommodated to interests particular to modern philosophy.[36] This is rendered manifest by several observations. Thus, for Mendelssohn, one of the principal tasks of modern metaphysics consists in securing human happiness and individual progress by liberating man from the fear of death and divine wrath. Not surprisingly, he once referred to his natural theology as to a "rather Epicurean" theism.[37]

This modern character also becomes apparent in Mendelssohn's attempts to "correct" the doctrines concerning the immortality of the soul of two of his revered predecessors: Plato and Gottfried Wilhelm Leibniz. As Strauss shows, *Phädon*, Mendelssohn's translation of Plato's *Phaedo*, contains many alterations and emendations with the effect of mitigating and moderating the original teaching and its exigencies. In a typical manner, for example, Mendelssohn's Socrates emphasizes the consoling effect of the idea of immortality of the soul, whereas Plato's Socrates does not regard this as a valid argument but instead considers it an obstacle to philosophizing. A similar approach marks Mendelssohn's *Sache Gottes, oder die gerettete Vorsehung*, ostensibly an elaboration of Leibniz's *Causa Dei*. Whereas Leibniz argues for divine providence by asserting that God's justice is his goodness guided and limited by his wisdom, Mendelssohn reverses the order of wisdom and goodness. As a result, he must reject eternal punishment and suffering, which Leibniz could still justify as a necessary component of the best of all possible worlds.

However, although it was intended as a defense of the orthodox religious view of providence, Leibniz's concept of divine justice implied a radical break with the tradition, since it no longer allowed divine justice to be distinguished from divine goodness and divine wisdom. In this way, Strauss argues, Leibniz prepared the momentous transition from the old notion of law to the modern notion of right: "by dissolving the classical concept of justice which had preserved the original meaning of justice as obedience with regard to the law, he had considerably precipitated the process that aimed at the eradication of law understood as obligation in favor of right understood as claim."[38]

Mendelssohn, a self-confessed follower of Leibniz, could not but accept this result and adapt his natural theology in accordance with it. However, his edifice started to topple when his faith in the power and the authority of demonstration was decisively shaken in acrimonious disputes with critics who attacked his natural theology: "Compelled to defend his Judaism and his rationalism at the same time, he had to present Judaism as a purely rational religion. In any case, however, the teaching of the Bible is not demonstrative . . . Saving Judaism was only possible for him in this way, that he severely restricted the right and the significance of demonstration."[39] This restriction found its expression in Mendelssohn's introduction of the notion of "common sense" or "plain human understanding" (*gesundes Menschenverstand*), a specific human capacity to grasp intuitively and with full clarity certain essential truths that speculative reason alone cannot demonstrate. In Mendelssohn's view, since common sense alone could provide a basis for agreement among men, it had to guide and supplement reason, which he had come to regard as insufficient.

Not surprisingly, Strauss is critical of this move. First, he notes that this new configuration of reason and common sense is merely a reiteration of the traditional religious notion of revelation as a necessary guide for insufficient reason. Confronted with the failure of Cartesian-Leibnizian metaphysics as a substitute for traditional faith, natural theology could do no more than seek refuge on "the neutral isle of common sense," while the realm of speculation was invaded by the radical atheist metaphysics of Spinozism.[40] As Mendelssohn himself admitted, this move did not differ essentially from Jacobi's leap of faith out of speculation and demonstration. In both cases, the appeal to a faculty beyond speculation proved to be the only way of saving theology and teleology.

In addition, Strauss challenges Mendelssohn's judgment—foreshadowing the current view—that Jacobi's doctrine of *Glaube* threatens philosophical speculation and leads to irrational "enthusiasm" (*Schwärmerey*). On the contrary, he argues, it is precisely common sense that endangers speculation: "For common sense lets the animating conviction appear as self-evident, whereas [Jacobi's] admission that this conviction is merely believed, implies or may imply the knowledge of ignorance and therewith an impulse to speculation."[41] Differently stated, Jacobi's teaching preserves unexplored latitude for philosophical speculation, which is altogether excluded by Mendelssohn's notion of common sense.

Third, Strauss argues that the notion of common sense merely compounds the predicament it seeks to escape from. Cartesian philosophy, he explains, was motivated by the view that traditional philosophy had relied too much on everyday language. As a result, it called for a distinct and purely scientific language. This demand, however, could not be brought in agreement with the equally important requirement that the new philosophy enlighten humanity in general by supplanting the old popular beliefs, for:

> especially in its "language," this philosophy was further removed from the language of common sense than the earlier philosophy; it tended to extreme unpopularity. However, it thus became entirely incapable of replacing the "popular system," and therewith of fulfilling one of its most important functions, that of "Enlightenment." Small wonder, then, that "enthusiasm" reared its head anew. However, small wonder, as well, that common sense, which had allowed itself to be enlightened to the best of its abilities by modern metaphysics, when it perceived that it could expect a new "obscurantism" from the "subtleties" of this metaphysics, dismissed its nurse without further ado and declared itself mature.[42]

It did so, however, in the illusion that it could now freely marshal clear and distinct metaphysical truths, since it regarded the latter as having been assimilated within everyday language. Hence, although it was introduced to remedy the shortcomings of Cartesian philosophy, the notion of common sense remained within the horizon established by modern philosophy's estrangement from everyday language. As a result, it did not lead to a serious reconsideration of "earlier philosophy" in relation to premodern, "nonenlightened" common sense. As Strauss points out, Mendelssohn was convinced that premodern metaphysics had been definitely surpassed by modern metaphysics. He therefore persistently identified metaphysics with modern metaphysics, and thus proved incapable of understanding premodern thought as it understood itself. One example of this failure is his distorting appropriation of the Platonic teaching concerning immortality.[43]

According to Strauss, however, this general critique applies with equal force to Jacobi. The latter, in spite of his sweeping repudiation of modern metaphysics, also remains decisively bound to its presuppositions and exhibits a similar blindness to premodern thought. This becomes apparent in a central ambiguity of his critique of Spinoza. One of Jacobi's main objections against Spinozism is that it gives priority to action over thinking, whereby the latter is merely regarded as "the act in continuation" (*die Handlung im Fortgang*). However, he himself adopts precisely this very proposition in his polemic against the Enlightenment when he asks, rhetorically and polemically, "Can philosophy ever be anything more than history?" and when he asserts that "every age has its own truth, just as it has its own living philosophy, which describes the predominant manner of acting of the age in question in its continuation (*in ihrem Fortgange*)."[44] These assertions show that Jacobi's irrationalism and traditionalism, according to which true knowledge can only result from virtuous action motivated by obedience to transcendent reality, are actually rooted in historicism. This accounts for the decisionism characteristic of his leap of faith, as well as for his attempt to bring about a renewal of philosophy through a change in morality. In essence, his doctrine is an early example of how, after the first wave of the Enlightenment, modern thought turns against itself by becoming historical.

In spite of his efforts, Jacobi remained equally captive to the horizon of modern—historical—thought, Strauss concludes: "Persisting in his critique of Spinoza to the end, he would not have been able to appeal to history against the Enlightenment, nor to faith (*Glaube*) understood within the horizon of the concept of history."[45] The implications of this terse remark deserve our attention. A sustained critique of Spinoza, it seems, would have called into question "the concept of history" and, perhaps, opened the possibility of a nonhistorical approach to both Enlightenment and faith. It is hard to disregard the impression that, in this remark, Strauss is thinking of his own undertaking in *Spinoza's Critique of Religion*. There, it may be recalled, Strauss locates the origin of historical consciousness in the concept of "prejudice" introduced by Descartes and adopted by Spinoza. As a "historical category," this concept proved to be a powerful weapon that allowed Spinoza to deny the revealed character of the Bible and to disparage its contents as "prejudices of the ancient people." Subsequent attempts by Mendelssohn and the moderate Enlightenment to restore religion were based on this initial denial. An adequate critique of Spinoza, Strauss maintains, has to revisit the concept of prejudice and to reconsider the possibility of revelation, and thus to return to the original conflict between philosophy and orthodoxy.

Neither Mendelssohn nor Jacobi was prepared to go this far. Instead of leading to a revision of the foundations of modern philosophy, their resistance against radical Enlightenment only helped the latter to spread. With his announcement about Lessing, Jacobi aimed to discredit Spinozism and the Enlightenment. Instead, the Pantheism Controversy had the opposite effect: by being associated with the widely respected name of Lessing, Spinozism lost its ill repute and gradually came to be publicly accepted, respected, and even revered. As we saw in the previous chapter, this widespread admiration was called into question by Hermann Cohen, whose critique eventually inspired the young Strauss's research on Spinoza.

How can we assess the importance of Jacobi before and after *Spinoza's Critique of Religion* from Strauss's own perspective? As regards the time preceding the book, at the beginning of this chapter we saw that Jacobi set off the critique of Spinoza on the right foot, by questioning the legitimacy of "the basis of unbelieving science." The way in which he did so in his works as well as by dint of his role in the Pantheism Controversy probably exerted some influence on the young Strauss's general philosophical outlook, as well as on his subsequent research on Spinoza. Concerning the time following the book, Strauss's investigations into the Pantheism Controversy clearly reveal that his appreciation of Jacobi became more critical in the light of his encounter with Spinoza. More particularly, he finds that Jacobi did not go far enough in his critique of modern philosophy, because on crucial points he remained too strongly attached to its premises. An adequate critique, Strauss suggests, must go beyond Jacobi. Although it is not entirely clear to what extent he thought *Spinoza's Critique of Religion* fulfilled this requirement, his subsequent research on the Pantheism Controversy shows that in the meantime he had reached remarkable conclusions regarding "the basis of unbelieving science."

## Atheism, Intellectual Probity, and the Love of Truth

In 1935, Strauss publishes *Philosophy and Law* (*Philosophie und Gesetz*), a book that will be discussed in further detail in the following chapter. In the introduction, he summarizes the most important findings of his Spinoza book, including the connection between the modern Enlightenment and ancient Epicureanism.[46] However, Strauss is now conspicuously more critical than before, especially as regards the differences between the two. To begin with, he focuses on his earlier conclusion that the modern critique of religion no longer regards the attainment of happiness as a private and individual matter, but as a public and political project. As we saw, the "political hedonism" of the Enlightenment opened the perspective of a civilized world in which man creates the conditions for realizing happiness by subjecting nature through the use of labor and science.

On this point, Strauss sharpens his former analysis, pointing out that the Enlightenment thus tries to achieve with practical—political, economical, and technological—means what it cannot prove theoretically: that there is no place in the world for an inscrutable, omnipotent, and vengeful God, that all phenomena are explicable without him, and that man is capable of finding happiness without his assistance. The world anticipated by political hedonism is presumed to be the concrete realization of the completed metaphysical system of modern philosophy and thus the indirect, material refutation of revealed religion. In this respect, the effect of the Enlightenment's strategy of ridicule is not only consolidated but also justified retroactively by the success of political hedonism. That the basic premise of religious orthodoxy has, in fact, survived unscathed, and that the closed system is thus anything but waterproof, is something to be made entirely unimportant and insignificant by the sheer success of the enterprise. For this reason, Strauss calls the Enlightenment's strategy "Napoleonic":

> Animated by the hope of being able to "overcome" orthodoxy through the perfection of a system, and hence hardly noticing the failure of its actual attack on orthodoxy, the Enlightenment, striving for victory with truly Napoleonic strategy, left the impregnable fortress of orthodoxy in the rear, telling itself that the enemy would not and could not venture any sally. Renouncing the impossible direct refutation of orthodoxy, it devoted itself to its own proper work, the civilization of the world and man."[47]

With the expression "in the rear," Strauss stresses once again that the Enlightenment derives its main strength from a historical antithesis, using mockery to consign orthodoxy to a primitive and underdeveloped past. Even if it succeeded with flying colors, this does not do away with the fact that it can maintain itself only within this antithesis. In a perspicacious review of *Spinoza's Critique of Religion*, Gerhard Krüger summarized this assessment by stating that the Enlightenment was founded in "an unfoundable negative existential decision" against revealed religion.[48] Precisely because this decision cannot be founded theoretically, it forever bears the mark of the possibility of revelation, and the Enlightenment is forced to armor it with the accomplishments of modern science. However, Strauss asks—almost rhetorically—

can an armor be anything more than an instrument of defense, and does it have any raison d'être whatsoever without an enemy?

> Is it not, ultimately, the very intention of defending oneself radically against miracles which is the basis of the concept of science that guides modern natural science? Was not the "unique" "world-construction" (*Weltdeutung*) of modern natural science, according to which miracles are of course unknowable, devised expressly for the very purpose that miracles *be* unknowable, and thus that man be defended against the grip of the omnipotent God?[49]

The modern scientific worldview and world-construction as a defense shield against the possible invasion of divine omnipotence: this, according to Strauss, is the ultimate expression of the neo-Epicurean will to happiness, which first deployed its wide-ranging ambition in Spinoza's critique of religion. As his analysis points out, however, the thickness of the shield—like the intensity of the ridicule, perhaps—betrays the extent of the threat that continues to emanate from the "impregnable fortress" of religious orthodoxy. In other words, the positive spirit of modern science did not so much disenchant the world as originate a new kind of magic with which it could counteract but not exorcise the old magic. Even if it has proven to be extremely successful in doing so, however, it can only maintain itself as long as the threat of the enemy continues to exist.

Strauss goes on to expand and augment his original analysis with a second observation. In the Spinoza book, he observed that whereas original Epicureanism rejected belief in higher powers as illusory because of its terrifying and disturbing effects, the Enlightenment's political hedonism particularly objects to the illusory character itself, regardless of whether it is terrifying or comforting. On this point as well, Strauss adds a new element, arguing that this shift in focus eventually turned against the Enlightenment itself. In due course, the Enlightenment came to "enlighten" itself, exposing its own ideals of autonomy, individualism, culture, and civilization as illusions concealing the desolation of human existence. Following its offensive against transcendence, modern philosophy came to undermine its own immanent foundations. An early portent of this evolution was already mentioned in the previous section: the Pantheism Controversy, in which Jacobi—with his frontal attack against rationalism and his doctrine of belief—and Mendelssohn—with his "rather Epicurean theism" and his doctrine of common sense—confronted the Enlightenment with its own limits. Though an effort by thinkers like Kant was required to reestablish these limits, their precariousness had definitively been brought to light.

The Pantheism Controversy, however, was only the beginning. Since the nineteenth century, Strauss now argues, the process of self-undermining has continued and challenged all the putative accomplishments of the Enlightenment. At the end of this trajectory, facing a religious orthodoxy still intact, is an atheism that rejects all comforting illusions—including those of the Enlightenment—and confronts the desolation undaunted. This "new kind of fortitude" is based on what Strauss calls "intellectual probity" (*intellektuelle Redlichkeit*), which, as he further explains, is "the ultimate and purest ground (*Rechtsgrund*) for the rebellion against the tradition of revelation."[50] Although Strauss fails to append names explicitly, it is not difficult for the attentive reader to surmise that he is referring to thinkers such as Friedrich Nietzsche, Max Weber, and Martin Heidegger.[51] The latter deepened and expanded the Enlightenment's self-critique into a wholesale dismantlement of Western culture, including its Judeo-Christian and Greek roots. Their ruthless examination placed man in a world of will to power, disenchantment, and "thrownness" (*Geworfenheit*).

For Strauss, however, the obstinacy of this "atheism from probity" raises serious questions. Reverting once more to his study of Spinoza, he adds a third element: what distinguishes the late modern atheism from its classical, Epicurean predecessor is the conscientiousness and the moral seriousness with which it rejects orthodox biblical faith in God. Such characteristics, Strauss argues, suggest that it never succeeded in completely detaching itself from this faith. The uprightness and the zeal with which modern atheism rejects the illusion for the sake of the illusion prove to be descendants of biblical morality. Although it opposes revealed religion more than ever before, its dependency on the latter is apparent more than ever before. Strauss elucidates this contention in a long and dense passage worth quoting at length:

> Thus it becomes clear that this atheism, compared not only with the original Epicureanism but also with the generally "radical" atheism of the age of Enlightenment, is a descendant of the tradition grounded in the Bible: it accepts the thesis, the negation of the Enlightenment, on the basis of a way of thinking which became possible only through the Bible. Although it refuses, since it is unwilling to disguise its unbelief in any way, to represent itself as a "synthesis" of the Enlightenment and orthodoxy, yet it itself is the latest, most radical, most unassailable harmonization of these opposed positions. This atheism, the heir and judge of the belief in revelation, of the centuries-old, millennia-old struggle between belief and unbelief, and finally of the short-lived but by no means therefore inconsequential romantic

longing for the lost belief, confronting orthodoxy in complex sophis-
tication formed out of gratitude, rebellion, longing and indifference,
and also in simple probity, is according to its own claim as capable of
an original understanding of the human roots of the belief in God as
no earlier, no less complex-simple philosophy ever was. The last
word and the ultimate justification of the Enlightenment is the atheism stemming from probity, which overcomes orthodoxy radically by
understanding it radically, free of both the polemical bitterness of the
Enlightenment and the equivocal reverence of romanticism."[52]

The significance of this observation for the development of Strauss's
thought can hardly be overestimated. Strauss himself, at least, judged it sufficiently important to reproduce it in its entirety thirty-five years later, in
the autobiographical preface to the English edition of *Spinoza's Critique of
Religion*.[53] In this preface, moreover, he supplies a number of valuable clari-
fications. Thus, he explicitly connects the "atheism from probity" with the
names of Nietzsche and Heidegger.[54] The former, Strauss affirms, was initially an important source of inspiration: Nietzsche was the first to suggest
that both the Enlightenment and its self-destruction are the result of the
persistent urge to veracity and righteousness characteristic of biblical morality. In Strauss's judgment, however, this same urge animated Nietzsche's
own attempt to liberate himself from biblical morality, which explains why
he ultimately remained entangled in it.[55] Moreover, Heidegger's position
evinces a similar problem, Strauss argues: trying to purify philosophy from
every theological residue, the vocabulary of his own new thinking is interspersed with notions and concepts that are beholden to the Bible, such as
"anxiety" (*Angst*) and "thrownness" (*Geworfenheit*). As a result Strauss concludes, "The efforts of the new thinking to escape from the evidence of the
biblical understanding, i.e., from biblical morality, have failed. And, as we
have learned from Nietzsche, biblical morality demands the biblical God."[56]
Thus, the autobiographical preface reveals in all clarity what still remains
implicit in *Philosophy and Law*.[57]

For Strauss, this conclusion is the occasion for a farewell to the atheism from probity, and thus to his own youthful commitment to modern
philosophy. Having reiterated the passage from *Philosophy and Law* about
the "last word" of the atheism from probity in the autobiographical preface, he now adds, significantly, "Yet this claim, however eloquently raised,
cannot deceive one about the fact that its basis is an act of will, of belief,
and that being based on belief is fatal to any philosophy."[58] In its ultimate
form, modern philosophy reveals its foundation in an act of belief, and
thereby it disqualifies itself as unbelieving science or philosophy.

Looking back at the trajectory covered in the previous chapters, it becomes clear that the passage in *Philosophy and Law* reflects a crucial moment in Strauss's thinking. When he calls the atheism from probity "the ultimate and purest ground (*Rechtsgrund*) for the rebellion against the tradition of revelation," he appears to have found an answer to the question that sparked his analysis of the *Theological-Political Treatise*: the *quaestio iuris*, the question regarding the legitimacy of Spinoza's attack, but also the question regarding the "basis of unbelieving science" that he gratefully traced to Jacobi. Both questions, he now finds, point to the atheism from probity that proves to be rooted in an act of belief inherited from biblical faith. As a result, he seems to face a dilemma. On the one hand, an untenable atheism from probity proves to be "the ultimate and purest ground" for the entry of Judaism into history by means of assimilation and political Zionism. On the other hand, the only obstacle for a return to orthodoxy disappears, for the same probity also proves to be "the ultimate and purest ground" of unbelieving science. What initially appeared to be the only alternative to orthodox biblical faith now turns out to be another form of belief indebted to biblical faith. In *Philosophy and Law*, Strauss formulates the dilemma as follows:

> The situation thus formed, the present situation, appears to be insoluble for the Jew who cannot be orthodox and who must consider purely political Zionism, the only "solution to the Jewish problem" possible on the basis of atheism, as a resolution that is indeed highly honorable but not, in the long run, adequate."[59]

Undoubtedly, Strauss is referring to himself. In a letter of 1932 to Gerhard Krüger, he leaves no doubt that, even in the wake of his study of Spinoza, the way back to faith remained closed to him: "Our difference is rooted in this, that I cannot *believe*, and that therefore I search for a possibility to *live* without faith."[60] At the same time, his study of Spinoza did compel him to take leave of political Zionism, which was based on the questionable atheism of modern philosophy. The situation, thus, indeed appears to be insoluble for a Jew incapable of living in faith—either that of Jewish orthodoxy or that of atheism from probity—but compelled to justify his life and his unbelief in the shadow of the impregnable fortress of orthodoxy.

However, we should not fail to notice and appreciate Strauss's subtlety. Indeed, he writes that the present situation "*appears* to be insoluble," thus implying that the situation is not necessarily hopeless. In *Philosophy and Law*, Strauss confirms this impression with two further considerations, the full bearing of which will be clarified later on. Immediately after formulating the dilemma, he suggests that the present situation "not only appears insoluble but actually is so, as long as one clings to the modern premises": as long, that is, as one clings to the view that Enlightenment necessarily means *modern* Enlightenment, or that unbelieving science is necessarily *modern* unbelieving science.[61] In the next section, we will see that according to Strauss this view is problematic, to say the least. The second consideration is equally enigmatic, buried as it is in an inconspicuous footnote added to Strauss's observation on the atheism from probity, and which asserts that probity "is something very different from the old love of truth (*alte Wahrheitsliebe*)."[62] Taken together, both considerations suggest that in the meantime Strauss has discovered—or, rather, rediscovered—a possible alternative to the hopeless dilemma of orthodoxy and modern atheism. At the beginning of this rediscovery is the question whether the old has indeed been surpassed and eliminated by the new.

## The Socratic Question and the Fate of Philosophy

A recurrent observation in Strauss's commentary on the Pantheism Controversy is that the attempts of Mendelssohn and Jacobi to find a way out of the crisis of modern metaphysics run aground on their conviction that it has definitively superseded premodern philosophy. For Strauss, however, this conviction becomes increasingly doubtful. Can modern philosophy legitimately claim to have made irreversible progress on its predecessor? As we saw in the previous chapter, like "prejudice" and "freedom," "progress" is an expression of the historical self-consciousness of the modern spirit. Although the relationship between modern and premodern philosophy is not the main focus of *Spinoza's Critique of Religion*, Strauss does raise the subject. Thus, having defined the concept of prejudice as a historical category, he adds significantly, "This precisely constitutes the difference between the struggle of the Enlightenment against prejudices and the struggle against appearance and opinion with which philosophy began its secular journey."[63]

Modern philosophy, Strauss goes on to explain, construed this difference in a variety of ways. First, it regarded its struggle against prejudice as a renewal of the old "struggle against appearance and opinion" or, as the implicit reference to the Greek root of both terms shows, as a return to ancient philosophy's battle against *doxa*. At the same time, it understood this return as an essential advance and an improvement on its predecessor. Unlike *doxa*, it claimed, the concept of prejudice had a universal scope and validity, since it was based on radical methodical doubt. As a result of this radicalization, it came to regard the difference as a general opposition, whereby prejudice came to include not only revealed religion but also premodern philosophy. In chapter 2, the Cartesian critique of the scholastic use of Aristotelianism was already mentioned in passing: for Descartes, the traditional philosophical approach was an obstacle that prevented reason from focusing on what is immediately given. Strauss's research on the Pantheism Controversy provides additional elucidation on this point: while traditional philosophy focused on and was guided by ordinary language, in which opinion or *doxa* found its expression, Descartes rejected this orientation as an impediment to the general liberation from prejudice and the attainment of purely demonstrative knowledge. Philosophy's turn toward what is immediately given was therefore accompanied by the radical dismissal of the old orientation toward ordinary language and the construction of a scientific language destined to end what it perceived to be the reigning confusion.

When the Cartesian project entered a crisis, the validity of the critique of religion became doubtful, as Jacobi's attack and Mendelssohn's defense illustrated. The validity of the critique of premodern philosophy, however, was not called into question, even though it too had become problematic. Both Jacobi and Mendelssohn nevertheless remained attached to it: while the former did not succeed in abandoning Spinozism, the latter remained loyal to the modern project of a natural theology. Because of their belief in progress, neither was capable of approaching premodern philosophy without modern preconceptions.

Jacobi's and Mendelssohn's omission becomes a self-assigned task for Strauss following his farewell to political Zionism and modern atheism from probity: to critically revisit the Enlightenment's campaign against the prejudices of premodern philosophy, the so-called quarrel between the ancients and the moderns (*la querelle des anciens et des modernes*). This inquiry starts in the present, since the deeply rooted conviction of Jacobi and Mendelssohn does not differ essentially from the contemporary view. At the beginning of the 1930s, concurrent with his research on the Pantheism Controversy, Strauss writes a number of reviews and lectures in which he reappraises the quarrel in order to understand what he calls the "situation of the present" (*die Lage der Gegenwart*).[64] If the departure from his youthful commitment has compelled him to find new bearings, it has by no means put an end to his investigations. In these writings, Strauss finds that the campaign against prejudice has culminated in the wholesale destruction of all traditions. This is mainly the accomplishment of Nietzsche, who brought the antitraditional offensive of the Enlightenment as well as its self-criticism to completion. In a note to one of the lectures, Strauss explains:

The end of this struggle is the *wholesale rejection* of the tradition: not only of its answers, also not only of its questions, but of its possibilities: the pillars on which our tradition was based: prophets and Socrates-Plato, have been demolished since Nietzsche . . . Nietzsche the *last* Enlightenment thinker."[65]

With his probing and incisive critique, Nietzsche completely dismantled the two basic principles of European culture. Against the contemplative ideal of classical philosophy and the moral ideal of the Judeo-Christian tradition, he advocated the will to power, which replaces the contemplation of reality by its production and which operates beyond good and evil. In Nietzsche's celebration of the will to power, modern philosophy achieved the ultimate negation of tradition, claiming to have attained total freedom.[66] When, however, one asks in what this freedom consists, the Enlightenment proves to be unable to go beyond the negation of tradition. Its own answers, but also its own questions, have no other foundation than the negation of the traditional answers and questions, and hence it is incapable of asking truly original questions. In Strauss's own words, the freedom it attains is "the freedom to *answer*, but not the freedom to question; only the freedom to a No instead of the traditional Yes."[67] The Enlightenment remains entangled in a negative dependency on the tradition, as Strauss will later observe in the introduction to *Philosophy and Law*.

This incapacity to develop original questions comes to the surface when we observe how late modern philosophy tackles the issue of how to deal with the ultimate freedom, Strauss argues. The contemporary philosophical landscape is characterized by confusion and pandemonium. Different systems coexist alongside and against each other, each as convinced of its own truth and value as of the historical relativity of all truths and values.[68] Some, like Max Weber, are resigned to this "polytheism" by accepting and affirming plurality and relativity as the inexorable fate of all philosophy.[69] They contend, moreover, that it is impossible ever to gain a free outlook on the reigning turmoil, since every appraisal is based on one interpretation among many. Others regard the present situation as a phase within a process of decline and decay. Still others, finally, try to find a way out by looking for a new synthesis.[70]

Regardless of their differences and similarities, however, what unites all these positions is a conviction that the past can provide no solution to contemporary problems. An answer to the question as to how to cope with the ultimate freedom can be found only in the present. For despite the confusion, they continue to view the present as a progress in comparison with the past. Thus, the relativists are persuaded that relativism signifies an improvement on the old and obsolete view that the truth exists. And even the most pessimistic thinkers of decadence still expect that, following dusk, the owl of Minerva will yet take wing.[71] However, Strauss asks, isn't this view based on a number of unchallenged presuppositions? Those who resign themselves to the prevailing disorder are guilty of making an unwarranted inference. That human thought is dependent on its situation does not exclude the possibility that it is able to oversee the situation adequately: "From the insight in the dependency of thought on the situation (*die Situations-Bedingtheit des Denkens*), it does not follow that one cannot catch sight of the situation in an original way, free of the prevailing opinions."[72] From the observation that so far man has failed to discover the truth, it does not follow that he has to acquiesce in this failure as in some fatality. Whoever does acquiesce, commits the fundamental mistake of trying "to determine the task from the fate" or to elevate the fate of philosophical inquiry into the principle of philosophical inquiry.[73]

What modern philosophy presents as an incontrovertible progress in fact hides a painful stagnation, Straus argues. The eradication of all prejudices has not led to knowledge, but to a radical ignorance: "Our freedom is the freedom of radical ignorance."[74] The absence of all prejudices is an empty freedom, a freedom unaccompanied by an instruction manual, and which will not tolerate any instruction manual. Instead of knowledge, contemporary thought rests on the unwarranted belief that it knows something, even many things. This belief is the main obstacle that keeps philosophy from seeking a way out of its ignorance: "*Fundamentally ignorant, we cannot attain knowledge, because we know too much*. Because we *believe* too much that we know."[75] When we abandon this belief and admit our ignorance, modern philosophy with all its learning is incapable of telling us what to do with our hard-won freedom.[76] Yet we cannot avoid any less than previous periods to raise the question what we must do, what the right or the good way is. In our attempts to do so, however, we face the same problem: "compelled to question like any previous age, the present is more incompetent to question than any age. We must question, without being able to question."[77] For not only our answers but our questions as well are based on the negation of traditional questions and answers.

How do we escape from this deadlock? Perhaps our ignorance nevertheless points to a way out, Strauss suggests. When we admit our ignorance, the question of what to do with our present freedom turns out not to be all that different from an old, traditional, even classical question: how should we live, or *pôs biôteon*? For, as Strauss indicates, its origin is Greek or, to be even more exact, *Socratic*: for Socrates, the question regarding the good or the right life was nothing less than the focal point of his thinking, and even of his life.[78] In defense of both, he asserts in the *Apology*: "the un-examined life is not worth living."[79] The importance of this discovery for Strauss's investigations can hardly be overestimated, as it profoundly changes his understanding of the theological-political problem. Underlying and preceding the two questions that occupied him as a political Zionist concerned with the claims of religion—the question of "politics" and the question of "God"—an older, more original, and more fundamental question has become visible—how should I live?—as well as the model of a life entirely dedicated to this question. By the same token, we understand the enigmatic and almost concealed remark he makes in *Philosophy and Law*: the "old love of truth" he distinguishes from the "intellectual probity" of Nietzsche, Weber, and Heidegger is nothing other than the philosophic *eros* that is at the heart of the "Socratic program."[80]

Of course, Strauss adds, Socrates was well aware that the quest for an answer to this question more often meets with failure than with success. In fact, the experience of failure is so recurrent and so powerful that his most famous student immortalized it in a well-known image. For what is Plato's famous simile of the cave, if not an evocation of the enormous difficulties that naturally beset the philosophic quest for the good and the true?[81] Before the cave dweller can even attempt to leave the cave and contemplate the sun, he must overcome a great number of obstacles. As Plato's image shows, every stage in the liberation and ascent is accompanied by much effort and pain, and an overwhelming likelihood of failure. And even if the cave dweller succeeds in reaching the exit of the cave, scorn and ridicule await him upon his return to the cave from those who have remained inside. If the intrinsic difficulties are of such magnitude, Strauss asks, need one wonder that the cave dwellers hold so many divergent and contradictory opinions concerning the good and the right way of life?

But even if the way out of the cave is strewn with obstacles, and even if so many different opinions exist, this does not justify the conclusion that it is impossible to leave the cave.[82] On the contrary, Strauss holds, these difficulties compel us to try again and try harder. That is why we as moderns should not acquiesce in the reigning pandemonium when we raise the question regarding the right way of life: "Mindful of the Platonic simile, we will not allow ourselves to be led astray by the anarchy of opinions, but rather strive as much as possible to get out of the cave."[83] Differently stated, instead of elevating the fate of philosophy into its guiding princi-

ple, we should philosophize like Socrates and Plato. Viewed from this perspective, Strauss argues, at least one prevailing view loses its self-evident
character, namely, the view that the question regarding the right way of life
can and should be directed exclusively to the present. Before the rise of
modernity, the present had little or no importance for the way in which
philosophy raised the question of how to live. It was only concerned with
what goes beyond the temporal, or with those aspects of the temporal that
had proven their durability.[84] That the present became the center of philosophical attention is in many respects a historical novelty. Perhaps the most
important philosophic characteristic of the present situation is that it in-
cessantly and exclusively asks after *itself*: "This situation is characterized by
the question regarding it (*die Frage nach ihr*)."[85] As we saw previously, however, this self-referentiality only leads to the confrontation with our radical
ignorance regarding the right way of life.

Why does modern philosophy raise the question of the good life
with exclusive regard for the present? This, according to Strauss, is due to
the deep-seated conviction that the present constitutes an indisputable
progress in comparison with the past or, in other words, to modern historical consciousness.[86] The latter tells us that every view of the good
life is historically determined and that therefore the right way of life does
not exist, while presenting this particular insight itself as a decisive progress compared to the unhistorical way of thinking of the past. As a result,
our question automatically focuses on the presently reigning ideal, while
simultaneously the meaning and the seriousness of this ideal are histori-
cized and relativized. This brings us to the cause of the present deadlock:
the historical consciousness compels modern thought to focus the question of the good life on the present and thus makes the question impossible. The only way out of this stalemate, therefore, is to call into question
the historical consciousness:

> [P]recisely the historical consciousness is the factor that makes the
> question regarding the right life come to grief. For if man is essentially
> historical, *the* right life does not exist; but every age, every historical
> situation has *its own* "right life," *its own* ideal of life (*Lebensideal*) . . .
> Under the assumption of the historical consciousness, the question re-
> garding the right way of life forces the question regarding the intel-
> lectual situation of the present. Because *this* question cannot be
> answered, the question regarding the right way of life appears to be no
> longer answerable. Should it be answerable, then this is only possible
> while the *historical consciousness is called into question*."[87]

A philosophical critique of the historical consciousness, however, is a hazardous undertaking, because it impinges on a number of deep-rooted modern convictions. To begin with, Strauss asserts, it has to point out that the historical consciousness, when carried to its ultimate consequences, must be applicable to itself. The view that all human thought is historically conditioned must be admitted to be itself historically conditioned and thus destined to be superseded—as it was preceded—by another, possibly non-historical view. This possible change may not be forthwith rejected as a regression or a relapse into a barbaric condition, for this would presuppose that the historical consciousness is an exception to its own rule, which would amount to a reaffirmation of its questionable premise. If the critique of the historical consciousness is taken seriously, one must admit one's radical ignorance and abandon this premise. Similarly, one must take into account the possibility that the present is a time of decay, without the unique opportunities attributed to it by the thinkers of decadence.[88]

A second and more important task of the critique consists in calling into question the universal claims of the key concept of prejudice. As we saw earlier on, this claim is closely connected with the genesis of the concept as a return to, an improvement on, and a rejection of the classical philosophical notion of *doxa*. Hence, it is necessary to inquire into the causes of this transformation. To this end, Strauss appeals to an author we already encountered in the second chapter. In the *Guide for the Perplexed*, Maimonides refers to the Greek philosopher Alexander of Aphrodisias, who distinguished three "causes of disagreement about things" in philosophy, analogous to the obstacles to philosophizing in Plato's simile of the cave. According to Maimonides, the Greek failed to mention a fourth cause because it was unknown to him:

> In our time there is a fourth reason which Alexander did not mention because it did not exist among them, viz. habit and training . . . So it goes with the opinions in which a man has grown up: he loves them and holds them fast and keeps himself away from diverging opinions. Thus for this reason, too, man is prevented from knowing the truth. This is the situation of the multitude with regard to the corporeality of God . . . because of their habituation to the texts in which they have a firm belief, to which they are habituated, and whose literal meaning appears to indicate the corporeality of God."[89]

As Strauss explains, the difference between the Middle Ages—"our time"—and Antiquity does not consist in the fact that the Greeks knew no texts expounding the corporality of God; on the contrary, many examples are to be found, and Maimonides was certainly aware of them. Rather, the decisive difference lies therein that these texts did not pose an obstacle to philosophy, because they were not authoritative and thus did not constitute a fertile breeding ground for customs and education. By contrast, the "texts" Maimonides refers to are of an entirely different nature: the Bible is regarded as divine revelation by a religious orthodoxy, and as such it is a document with an absolute and unconditional authority, the ultimate and definitive answer to all human questions, not least the question regarding the right way of life. The tradition based on this authority has brought into the world customs and opinions that have become incomparably more entrenched, and that form an additional and more formidable obstacle to philosophy. This fourth obstacle, Strauss emphasizes, is not natural but *historical*: it is not intrinsic to the situation of philosophy, but it has been introduced "from the outside" by the tradition of revelation. In his account, Strauss explains this new situation with a striking elaboration on the Platonic simile of the cave:

> The fact that a tradition based on revelation entered the world of philosophy has added the *historical* difficulty to the *natural* difficulties of philosophizing . . . The natural difficulties of philosophizing received their classical depiction in the Platonic simile of the cave. The historical difficulty can be illustrated when one says: at present there is another cave *below* the Platonic cave."[90]

Thus, the problem philosophy faces since the entry of revealed religion is the following: whoever wants to philosophize is henceforth compelled first to find his way out of the second cave in order to return to the first cave with its natural obstacles. In other words, he must return to the "world of philosophy" as it was before the entry of revealed religion.[91] This, Strauss argues, is precisely what the Enlightenment originally attempted to do:

> To a certain extent, Maimonides's observation [concerning the fourth obstacle to philosophizing] outlines, maps out the battle of the entire last three centuries, the battle of the Enlightenment: in order to make possible philosophizing in its natural difficulties, the artificial complication of philosophizing must be removed (*aus der Welt geschafft*); the struggle has to be against *prejudices*.[92]

As the words "to a certain extent" (*gewissermassen*) indicate, however, according to Strauss there is an important difference between the "outline" and its eventual realization. In fact, the Enlightenment's fight against prejudice has failed to bring us back from the second to the first cave. First, as Strauss discovered in his study of Spinoza, the fourth obstacle was relegated to the margins of modernity, where it nevertheless remained essentially intact. Second, Strauss finds, the Enlightenment quickly lost sight of its original goal. As a result of the claim to universal validity that accompanied it, the concept of prejudice was soon applied to premodern philosophy as well. In terms of Strauss's emendation of the Platonic simile, it may be said that not only the prospect of leaving the first cave, but perhaps even the notion of the first cave itself was consigned to the realm of prejudice.[93]

In the light of Maimonides's remark, however, this claim to universal validity turns out to be unfounded, and thus also the dismissal of premodern philosophy based on it. In its original sense, Strauss points out, the concept refers exclusively to the prejudices of revealed religion.[94] Since it was introduced to combat the new obstacle to philosophizing, it had to be attuned to the obstacle's characteristics: as opposed to the classic notion of *doxa*, it had to be a *historical* category. Moreover, while overcoming the natural obstacles was essentially an individual effort, eliminating the historical obstacle required a long-term collective effort, the ramifications of which were discussed in the previous chapter. In order to generate the dynamic necessary for this effort to succeed, a strong historical consciousness was indispensable. Because of its spectacular success in challenging all traditions, including the Enlightenment itself, this historical consciousness has acquired a seemingly universal authority in our times. This success, however, obscures but does not obliterate the fact that it originated in a very particular opposition, insofar as it continues to rely on the persuasive force of the historical category of prejudice.

In this way, we can see how Strauss's critique of the historical consciousness ties in with his critical analysis of modern atheism from probity. Instead of making a return to the first cave possible, modern philosophy has become entangled in its battle against the historical obstacle of revealed religion. Hence, its questions and answers can exist only as negations and denials of the traditional questions and answers. By the same token, it has failed to regain the original freedom to question, the freedom of the first cave. On the contrary, Strauss claims, in the course of three centuries, it has entrenched itself ever deeper in the second cave. In addition, it has all but closed off the exit with a proper "tradition" that discredits both the attempt to return to the first cave and the effort to leave it as a meaningless enterprise, a flight from the stark reality of the human condition. Hence, it is no accident that the late modern atheism from probity goes hand in hand with an intensification of the historical consciousness: in the perspective of Nietzsche and Heidegger, not only thought but man and eventually Being itself become time.[95]

The result of this process is the present quandary, Strauss concludes. The religious and philosophical traditions have been almost completely dissolved, and underneath the contemporary pandemonium is our radical ignorance. Unlike the natural ignorance of the first cave, our modern ignorance continually makes us collide with the walls of the second cave. It tells us that our question regarding the right way of life can be answered only by the present, while that same present dismisses our question as pointless. Nevertheless, Strauss does not judge the situation to be entirely hopeless. In his view, the present situation has one major advantage: as a result of the total alienation with regard to all traditions, the latter are no longer obvious or self-evident in any sense. This was not the case at the beginning of the Enlightenment: the latter turned against traditions it regarded as obviously outdated and indefensible. As a result, it did not feel compelled to seriously question their source, not even in moments of crisis, as the example of Mendelssohn shows. Strauss even goes so far as to suggest that this blindness was constitutive of the Enlightenment's struggle:

> However, what is "obvious" (*selbstverständlich*) is always fundamentally *not understood* (*unverstanden*). This not-being-understood (*Unverstandenheit*) is the ultimate reason why the battle against the tradition has become possible and necessary. The final outcome: the factual ignorance of the origins.[96]

Now that modern thought has undermined itself and the traditions have vanished as an object of conflict and contention, it becomes possible again to approach their foundations in a nontraditional and nonpolemical way.[97] This is the positive side of the philosophical iconoclasm of thinkers like Nietzsche and Heidegger. When Strauss introduces the image of the second cave in the 1930s, Heidegger is gathering renown with his project of *Destruktion*, the attempt to rethink more than two thousand years of philosophy, resulting in groundbreaking interpretations of Greek philosophers. In his autobiographical writings, Strauss acknowledges the profound influence of Heidegger's undertaking on the development of his own thinking.[98] Nonetheless, he also insists on important differences. In Heidegger's as in Nietzsche's thought, the dismantlement of the philosophical tradition ultimately aims at the final overcoming (*Überwindung*) of the tradition. Both thinkers lay bare the roots of Western metaphysics with the intention to eradicate them and replace them with a wholly new way of thinking. Underlying this intention, we already learned in the previous section, is the atheism from probity, the rebellious heir to biblical morality, which refuses to accept any illusion masking the groundlessness of human existence. In their conscientious determination, however, both Heidegger and Nietzsche neglect to consider an important possibility: "to see the roots of tradition as they are and thus perhaps to know, what so many merely believe, that those roots are the only natural and healthy roots."[99]

Before bidding a final farewell to the tradition of philosophy, Strauss argues, we have to inquire whether its foundations are indeed as deficient and faulty as Nietzsche and Heidegger claim. More particularly, we have to ask whether the Socratic question regarding the right way of life is indeed an absurd, unanswerable question. In the present condition, however, we cannot raise the Socratic question directly and without further ado, Strauss warns. After all, our present ignorance is anything but Socratic: our inquiries regarding the right way of life are conditioned by the historical consciousness. The latter's spell, however, cannot be broken at one fell swoop—it must be demolished gradually, bit by bit. The privileged means to do so is a certain form of historical research, to wit the renewed study of the founding documents of the philosophical tradition. This study is the appropriate response to the specific difficulties of the present age. In our radical ignorance, the question regarding the right way of life compels us to reconsider whether the premodern traditions really have nothing to say to us, as the historical consciousness would have us believe.[100]

In order to raise this latter question, we have to detach ourselves in the very first place from what Strauss calls the modern prejudice par excellence: "namely, the prejudice that *the* truth has not already been found in the past."[101] Of course, Strauss does not mean to say that we should therefore rashly and uncritically embrace the contrary prejudice that the truth has indeed already been found in the past. All we should do is learn to reckon with the *possibility* that it may have been found.[102] Only with this disposition will we be sufficiently motivated to take ancient thinkers seriously and try to understand them without preconceptions. This does not mean a blanket submission to their authority, but merely a readiness to be "taught" by the old philosophers, to be guided by them in studying their works.[103] In this way, the historical research is put at the service of what Strauss calls "learning through reading" (*lesendes Lernen*). The latter, he cautions, is not yet philosophizing; at most, it is a preparation to it: "we need history first of all in order to *ascend* to the cave from which Socrates can lead us to the light; we need a propaedeutic, which the Greeks did not need, namely, learning through reading."[104]

The propaedeutic of learning through reading is thus peculiar to the second cave. It is a prosthesis that helps us rehabilitate our natural consciousness, but which nevertheless remains an artificial, unnatural medium, characteristic of the reigning incapacity to raise the question regarding the right way of life in an original, natural way.[105] To confuse its use with actual philosophizing would be a grave error, Strauss emphasizes: historical research is only an inevitable detour, a means and not an end in itself.[106] Our interest in the past can no longer be merely antiquarian, since this past has lost its self-evidence. Precisely for this reason, however, our interest can be put at the service of the return to the first cave and the retrieval of the Socratic question.[107] According to Strauss, we owe this possibility to the same thinker who radicalized the consequences of the Enlightenment to the extreme. In a telling passage, he spells out the ramifications:

> In any case, Nietzsche has enabled us to understand again the Socratic question, to recognize it again as *our* question. The Platonic dialogues are for us no longer self-evident (*selbstverständlich*)—no longer obviously all right, no longer obviously wrong, outdated, irrelevant, but we read them in this way, that we would conduct them ourselves, if we were able to. However, we are unable to do so, because all the concepts we have on our part (*von uns aus*) stem from the modern tradition.[108]

This passage reveals that, for Strauss, "learning through reading" is a double task: it consists in studying both premodern *and* modern philosophy. Habituated for a long time to viewing and judging the former through the lens of the latter, in order to remove the lens we must get to know its construction by studying the concepts of the modern tradition. Since the validity of these concepts is based on the conviction that modern philosophy has decisively defeated premodern thought, it is necessary to reopen *la querelle des anciens et des modernes*, the quarrel between the ancients and the moderns.[109]

The passage just cited also shows how this task hinges on the other task Strauss sets himself: in order to recover the Socratic question as *our own* question, we must first learn to understand the Platonic dialogues again. The latter have lost their self-evidence, since both the traditional reading and the modern critique of that reading have become problematic. As we try to remove the modern lens, we are compelled to start reading all over again, without prejudice and prepared to learn. In his later work, Strauss formulates this task as follows: we must cease to try to understand the old thinkers better than they understood themselves, convinced as we are that we dispose of much more advanced equipment than they did. Before passing such judgment, we must first try to understand them as they understood themselves. These two related undertakings more or less delineate the entire program Strauss begins to carry out from the second half of the 1930s. In the following four decades, his primary occupation as a scholar will be to study major philosophical, theological, and literary texts, prompted by the attempt to recover the Socratic question, breaking the spell of the historical consciousness by reopening the quarrel between the ancients and the moderns. The results of this program will be discussed more extensively in the following chapter. By way of transition, two questions must be addressed that have remained largely unanswered in this chapter. To begin with, how is a return to the first cave, to the world of philosophy before the entry of revealed religion, possible if the additional obstacle has a foundation that cannot be refuted theoretically, as Strauss argued in *Spinoza's Critique of Religion*? And second, how does Strauss's new orientation affect his understanding of the theological-political problem? Although these questions may seem to point into completely different directions, both reappear in the next stage of his investigation, when he takes his first steps back toward the first cave. Not entirely by accident, he initially focuses on the author who inspired him to introduce the image of the second cave: Maimonides.

# CHAPTER 4

# The Order of Human Things

*. . . what do we, adherents of the true religion,
have to do with the son of Sophroniscus?*

—Moses Mendelssohn, Letter to H. Wessely (1768)

## Medieval Enlightenment: *Nomos* and Platonic Politics

In *Spinoza's Critique of Religion*, Strauss presented Maimonides as a classic Aristotelian, the Jewish equivalent of Thomas Aquinas. When, two years later, he takes his leave of modern philosophy and turns to the recovery of the Socratic question, his view of Maimonides has altered dramatically. Once again, the occasion is a controversial statement by Hermann Cohen. In an article written in 1908, Cohen praised Maimonides as "a classic of rationalism," and defended the striking thesis that the medieval thinker was "in deeper harmony with Plato than with Aristotle."[1] Like Cohen's contentious appraisal of Spinoza, this divergent opinion galvanizes Strauss's research. Moreover, as in his study of Spinoza, Strauss develops his own perspective in a critical discussion with Cohen, on which he reports in a lecture written in 1931 and tellingly entitled "Cohen and Maimonides."[2]

In his article, Cohen commemorates Maimonides as the greatest representative of what he calls "the medieval Jewish Enlightenment." By introducing Greek philosophy, he argues, Maimonides enabled the Jewish tradition to enlighten itself by purging its mythical elements and developing its rational elements.[3] Among the instruments he developed to this end was the allegorical exegesis of the Bible already discussed in chapter 2. Precisely because of these accomplishments, however, Maimonides *cannot* have been an Aristotelian, Cohen contends. To begin with, there is a fundamental theological difference: "All honor to the God of Aristotle, but truly he is not the God of Israel."[4] The biblical God is a personal, inscrutable, and provident God: whoever wishes to know him must obey him and comply with his commandments and prohibitions. The God of Aristotle, on the other hand, is an impersonal and intelligible God: whoever wishes to know him must engage in contemplation. As a son of Israel, Maimonides was compelled to give precedence to obedience over contemplation. As a result, he could not follow the metaphysics of his Greek example on this crucial point.[5]

Second, Cohen asserts, the central characteristic of both medieval and modern Enlightenment is the practical—moral and political—concern for the improvement of the human condition. Insofar as Maimonides was both a devout Jew and an Enlightenment thinker, ethics and politics must be regarded as the center of gravity of his thinking, and not metaphysics and logic, as is generally assumed.[6] For Aristotle, however, the practical sciences—ethics, politics, and economics—are subordinated to the theoretical sciences, such as logic and metaphysics. In this respect as well, then, Maimonides cannot have been an Aristotelian, Cohen infers. On the contrary, the two arguments mentioned above can only lead to the conclusion that Maimonides was a *Platonist*. What distinguishes Plato from Aristotle is precisely the fact that the former gives priority to the ethical and political over the theoretical. Among other things, this is borne out by the fact that in the famous Platonic doctrine of the Ideas, the Idea of the Good transcends the Idea of Being, which for Aristotle is the highest object of contemplation.

The point on which Maimonides is "in deeper harmony with Plato than with Aristotle," Cohen explains, is the priority he accords to morality (*Sittlichkeit*). If one wants to understand Maimonides as a proponent of medieval Enlightenment within Judaism, one must view his Enlightenment against a Platonic rather than an Aristotelian background. As Strauss puts it: "When Cohen is concerned with *enlightened Judaism*, he means thereby: *a Judaism understood within Plato's horizon*. And when he discovers Maimonides as an enlightened Jew, this means: he discovers Maimonides as a Jew who understands his Judaism within Plato's horizon."[7] In his critique, Strauss aims to show that while Cohen's conclusion is basically correct, the argument that leads up to it is not.[8] Thus, contrary to Cohen's assertion, there is no opposition between Maimonides and Aristotle as regards the primacy of *theoria*: for both thinkers the contemplative life is the highest human goal. As a result, Cohen's attempt to detach him from Aristotle on this issue is unjustified.[9] Moreover, Strauss points out, there is no opposition between Aristotle and *Plato* as to the primacy of contemplation either. The difference between them is that while Aristotle views contemplation as an entirely free activity, for Plato contemplation is under an obligation to justify itself to society. This requirement is expressed in the *Republic*: the philosopher, who after much toil and effort has succeeded in leaving the cave, is subsequently compelled to return to it, in order to care for his fellow citizens.[10]

This, however, leaves intact Cohen's more fundamental objection that the Aristotelian God is not the God of Israel. Strauss admits that this fact cannot remain without consequences for the interpretation of Maimonides: how, to begin with, can it be reconciled with his Aristotelianism? In response to Cohen, Strauss develops an interpretation of his own, which confirms Cohen's basic intuition with regard to Maimonides's Platonism, albeit in an unexpected and remarkable way. This interpretation constitutes the basis of *Philosophy and Law*, to which reference was already made in the previous chapter.[11] Although this book will only appear four years later in 1935, in fact nearly all of the main insights of this book are already developed in the lecture on "Cohen and Maimonides." For this reason, our discussion will include both texts.

As we saw, Cohen's argument founders on the fact that there is no difference of opinion between Maimonides and Aristotle as regards the priority of theory over ethics and politics. Strauss's own point of departure is that there is indeed a disagreement between the two, albeit on an entirely different and, as we will see, more fundamental point. In his lecture, Strauss revisits an observation he had already made in *Spinoza's Critique of Religion*: although Maimonides follows Aristotle in viewing theory as the highest human goal, he departs from Aristotle in asserting that the highest human perfection cannot be attained by the philosopher, but only by the *prophet*. Hence, Strauss points out, the fundamental point of divergence with Aristotle must be sought in Maimonides's teaching on prophecy or prophetology, which was already mentioned in the second chapter.[12]

According to this teaching, the prophet receives divine revelation in a direct encounter with God and subsequently mediates it to the community of the faithful. Although revelation itself has a supernatural character, Maimonides asserts that the prophet is able to receive and communicate it only due to certain natural human capabilities that are developed to perfection to such an extent as to surpass the perfection of the philosopher.[13] To begin with, the prophet possesses perfect knowledge and understanding: not only does he have direct knowledge of those natural truths the philosopher can only discover through reasoning, he also has direct access to supernatural and superhuman truths that remain inaccessible to the philosopher. Second, the prophet has a perfect imaginative faculty, which is at the service of his perfect cognitive faculties. Due to the unique cooperation between both, the prophet is able to use corporeal images to transmit divine revelation to a multitude incapable of understanding its purely intelligible content without assistance.[14] According to Maimonides, this combination of a perfect imaginative faculty and the skill to educate and guide the multitude by means of images is characteristic of statesmen, lawgivers, soothsayers, magicians, and seers. For Maimonides, prophecy is thus an exceptional cooperation of philosophy, politics, lawgiving, soothsaying, and magic; in short, a combination of theoretical and practical perfection that exceeds the perfection of both the philosopher and the statesman.[15]

Hence, the prophet is not only a perfect philosopher but also a perfect lawgiver who enacts a perfect law and thus founds a perfect society.[16] In the *Guide of the Perplexed*, Maimonides substantiates this claim in Aristotelian fashion. Man, he argues, is a political being who by nature needs to live in community. The natural heterogeneity among human beings, however, continually threatens the community with disintegration. For this reason, human society requires political rule capable of forging unity and harmony. Political rule can be effectuated in two distinct ways: either by government or kingship, or by law. Since a government or a king generally rules by applying the law, the latter is the original and higher form of political rule.

Maimonides further distinguishes two types of legislation by looking at their respective goals. The first type of legislation constitutes a society that is solely aimed at securing the well-being and perfection of the human body. Such a law, he explains, can only be of human origin. The second type constitutes a society that aims at both the perfection of the body and the perfection of the soul, which is the specifically human perfection. Only a divine law promulgated by a prophet can attain this higher goal, since he alone has the theoretical and practical capacities required to receive and transmit it. Since the prophet surpasses the philosopher on this point, the latter is obliged to obey the divine law: as a political being, he is subject to the authority of the prophet. Even if he were to equal the prophet on the theoretical level, he still would lack the practical perfection required for legislation.[17]

According to Strauss, Maimonides is neither the only one nor the first to propose this view. On closer inspection, his prophetology emulates a model introduced and developed by medieval Islamic philosophers such as Alfarabi, Avicenna, and Averroës. These *falasifa*, as they were called in Arabic, attempted to reconcile Greek philosophy and Islam by presenting the prophet Mohammed as a philosopher, seer, statesman, lawgiver, and founder of the perfect state.[18] Maimonides, who was familiar with the work of Alfarabi and who similarly attempted to harmonize philosophy and Judaism, adapted this approach by presenting Moses as the perfect legislator.

As Strauss goes on to show, however, the prophetology of the *falasifa* itself points to an even older source. In the introduction to a treatise entitled *On the Parts of the Sciences*, Avicenna states that the science dealing with prophecy is a part of the practical sciences, more specifically of *political* science.[19] The goal of prophecy, he explains, is primarily political, since the prophet's principal task is to provide political guidance to the community. In the same treatise, he points to the source of this particular view:

> Of this, what has to do with kingship is contained in the book [*sic*] of Plato and of Aristotle on the state, and what has to do with prophecy and the religious law is contained in both of their books on the laws . . . this part of practical philosophy [viz. politics] has as its subject matter the existence of prophecy and the dependence of the human race, for its existence, stability, and propagation, on the religious law.[20]

When Avicenna refers the treatment of prophecy to political science, he invokes the authority of *Plato* and *Aristotle*. In this approach, he is no exception. As Strauss shows, all of the *falasifa* as well as Maimonides understand revelation and the revealed law in the light of classical political philosophy or, more exactly, of *Platonic* political philosophy.[21] For they did not have access to Aristotle's *Politics*, nor was any Aristotelian work on the laws extant.[22] On the other hand, they did possess Plato's principal political works, the *Republic* and the *Laws*, at the core of which is the ideal state or, to be more exact, the best regime (*aristè politeia*) led by a philosopher acting as lawgiver and statesman. Hence, the *falasifa* and Maimonides regarded revelation as the realization of Plato's model: they identified the prophet with the philosopher-king-legislator and the revealed law with the divine law that constitutes the best regime.[23]

Moreover, Plato's work provides justification for the subordinate position of philosophy under the revealed law, which proved to be an important point of divergence between Maimonides and Aristotle. In the *Republic*, Socrates forbids the philosophers "what is now permitted," namely, to remain outside the cave and devote themselves to contemplation in splendid isolation, "and not be willing to go down again among those prisoners or share their labors and honors, whether they be slighter or more serious."[24] Hence, Socrates proposes legislation that compels the philosophers to be concerned for and participate in the life of the political community. Only when they obey these laws and dedicate themselves to the common good can a truly harmonious state come into being, as opposed to the existing states that are governed "in a dream."[25] According to Strauss, Plato's Socrates thus subjects philosophy to "the state by means of the harsh commandment of the lawgiver, which considers the order of the whole and not the happiness of the parts. The philosopher is *subordinate to* the state, *subordinate to* the law. Philosophy must justify itself *before* the state, *before* the law: it is not simply sovereign."[26]

Nevertheless, Socrates formulates a specific requirement the law has to meet. It can claim the philosopher's obedience only if it is truly divine, that is, if its ultimate goal is the perfection of the soul, which is tantamount to philosophizing. Thus, in the *Laws*, the Athenian Stranger names prudence and intelligence as the most important among "the divine goods" ordained by the divine law.[27] According to the *falasifa*, the revealed law fulfills this requirement more than any other law. On the one hand, it surpasses the understanding of the philosopher and thus legitimately commands his obedience.[28] On the other hand, it aims above all at the perfection of the soul: both the Torah and the Koran command man to acquire knowledge, the highest form of which is knowledge of God and creation. For the *falasifa*, this means that the law not only allows but also obliges them to philosophize, since this is the way toward knowledge of God.[29]

Thus, it is no coincidence that the prophetology of Maimonides and the *falasifa* appeals to Plato, Strauss argues. Living, in fact, under the authority of a religious law, they had no other choice: "The Platonism of these philosophers is given with their situation, with their standing in fact under the law."[30] Platonic political philosophy provides them with the means to justify their philosophic activity, something the Aristotelian framework fails to do: as we saw, Aristotle frees contemplation from political or legal tutelage. Thus, Strauss suggests, even if the *Politics* had been accessible to the *falasifa*, the work would not have lent itself for medieval prophetology, since it does not furnish analogies that would allow a prophetically revealed law to be explained philosophically.[31] Platonic political philosophy is therefore nothing less than the *conditio sine qua non* of medieval Islamic and Jewish Aristotelianism, he asserts. The *falasifa* can "Aristotelianize" *because* they are authorized to do so by a revealed law understood in Platonic terms.

In this way, Cohen's intuition about Maimonides is confirmed, albeit on different grounds. While Maimonides is indeed "in deeper harmony with Plato than with Aristotle," this is not because both are committed to "morality," Strauss argues. The actual reason is that as a Jew, Maimonides could justify his Aristotelianism over against the absolute authority of the Torah only by using Plato's political philosophy. The latter enabled him to "enlighten" the Jewish tradition by understanding Mosaic revelation as a politically constitutive moment in which philosophy and the social order were perfectly attuned to each other.[32] For this reason, Cohen's second thesis is also in need of correction. The fundamental difference between the God of Aristotle and the God of Israel is indeed undeniable, Strauss concedes, but it cannot be properly understood in terms of an opposition between theory and morality. Rather, the difference must be investigated starting from what the Jewish tradition and the Greek philosophical tradition have in common, namely, the concept of a divine law, understood as a comprehensive moral, legal, and political order:

> Cohen's outset—"all honor to the God of Aristotle, but truly he is not the God of Israel"—leads no further if one interprets the God of Israel as the God of morality (*Sittlichkeit*). Instead of morality, one should say: law. It is the concept of law, of *nomos*, which unites Jews and Greeks: the concept of the concrete binding order of life.[33]

As Strauss explains, the original concept of *nomos* has been obscured and suppressed by two later traditions that continue to dominate modern thought. First, there is the Christian tradition, based to a large extent on Paul's critique of the Jewish law. Paul rejected the detailed and comprehensive system of rules regulating human life the Torah imposes on the faithful. The true law, he argued, is a law "written in the heart," the core of which is the commandment to love one's neighbor.[34] Second, there is the natural law tradition, founded among others by Spinoza and Hobbes. In their work, the concept of law as a comprehensive binding and obligating order has been replaced by the concept of law as a system of abstract norms, based on inalienable rights. Both of these traditions, moreover, are interrelated, since Paul's critique played an important role in preparing the modern concept of natural law.[35] Since Cohen's notion of *Sittlichkeit* is one of the products of this confluence, it is part of the obscuring veil that has been thrown over the ancient concept of *nomos*.[36]

Whoever wishes to unearth the common background of Maimonides and Plato, of Judaism and Greek philosophy, is therefore compelled to follow two trajectories, Strauss holds. To begin with, the Platonism of medieval Jewish and Islamic philosophy must be examined further in its own terms, without reverting to ulterior—either Christian or modern—concepts. The rediscovery of this Platonism casts an entirely new light on the thought of Maimonides and the *falasifa*, the interpretation of which up to now was determined by the reception of their work by medieval Christian Aristotelianism.[37] Maimonides and the *falasifa*, Strauss claims, "are 'more primitive' than the modern philosophers, because unlike the latter they are not guided by the derivative idea of natural law, but by the *original, ancient* idea of *law* as a uniform, total order of human life; in other words, because they are pupils of *Plato* and not pupils of Christians."[38]

Furthermore, the spell of the Christian and the natural law traditions must be broken by means of a thorough examination of the basic concepts with which they shrouded the ancient concept of law.[39] Among other things, this requires that the oppositions characteristic of modern thought and politics be transcended:

> We will not be able to understand Plato and thus also Maimonides completely before we have gained a horizon beyond the antagonism Progress—Conservatism, Left—Right, Enlightenment—Romanticism or however one wishes to characterize this antagonism; not before we understand again the concept of the *eternal* good, the *eternal* order, free from all consideration of progress or decline.[40]

In the light of this intention, it does not come as a total surprise that Strauss's first step on this second trajectory will be to commence an in-depth study of Hobbes, one of the founders of modern natural law doctrine and of modern political thought. This study will be discussed further on. At this point, we must continue to follow the first trajectory. For Strauss, the discovery of the *falasifa*'s Platonism by way of Avicenna's utterance constitutes nothing less than a turning point. By focusing on the divine law as a common ground, it opens a wholly new perspective on the relationship between philosophy and revealed religion. In this way, it launches a new chapter in Strauss's struggle with "*the* theme" of his thought: the Platonism of the *falasifa* shows that they view the relationship between philosophy and revelation within a *theological-political* framework.[41] The transcendent, divine order they appeal to is a political order, in this sense that it concerns human living together rather than the life of the individual. To appreciate the importance of this discovery, and to show that it remained central for Strauss, it suffices to refer to a letter he wrote in 1951 to his colleague Eric Voegelin, in which he writes: "With regard to *Philosophy and Law*, I believe that I basically still stand on the same ground. . . . I still believe today that the *theioi nomoi* is the common ground of the Bible and philosophy—humanly speaking."[42]

The presence of a common ground does not, however, entail the absence of differences or even disagreement. Even if the God of Aristotle is not the God of Israel, this does not yet mean that Plato and Israel—let alone Islam—worship one and the same God. When the *falasifa* rely on the analogies supplied by Platonic political philosophy, they do so in order to justify their activity as philosophers before the authority of the divine law. For why would one philosophize if all the essential questions of human life have been answered by God's revealed law? Strauss asks. "For at first the revealed law makes philosophizing questionable from the ground up. A God-given and therefore perfect law necessarily suffices to guide life to its true goal. What then is the sense of philosophizing?"[43]

Unlike classical philosophy, its medieval counterpart faces a new situation, which was concisely summed up in Maimonides's reference to the fourth historical obstacle. Although the *falasifa* revert to Platonic political philosophy in order to find an adequate response to this situation, their response differs from the Platonic model in certain decisive respects, not least by its reliance on the figure of the prophet, whose theoretical and practical capacities exceed those of the philosopher. Thus, in the *falasifa*'s view, the revealed law not only fulfills all of the requirements set by Plato, it even seems to surpass these requirements. If this is the case, Strauss asks, to what extent is it still legitimate to regard them as "pupils of Plato"? Differently stated, doesn't medieval Enlightenment make the fourth obstacle into its very foundation, instead of trying to overcome it?

In *Philosophy and Law*, Strauss seems to conclude that this is indeed the case. From the perspective of their own perfect revealed law, the *falasifa* can only regard the Platonic concept of the divine law as a propaedeutic, a deficient prefiguration: "if they were not to lose confidence in the revelation because of Plato, then it had to be the case that Platonic philosophy had suffered from an *aporia* in principle that had been remedied only by the revelation."[44] For the *falasifa*, the political thought of the pagan Plato is necessarily limited and incomplete: it can only propose as a desideratum that which revelation has perfectly fulfilled. In this sense, Strauss points out, medieval prophetology contains a critique of the Platonic point of view: "From the *factual* answering of the Platonic inquiry into the true state there follows a modification of the Platonic blueprint (*Entwurf*), that is, a critique of the Platonic answer."[45]

As Strauss further indicates, however, this critique can be reversed. What may seem to be a decisive improvement on Plato's thought is actually a degradation: "Since, therefore, for them [the *falasifa*] the law was not truly open to question (*fraglich, fragwürdig*), their philosophy of law does not have the sharpness, originality, depth and—ambiguity of Platonic politics. Since Plato's requirement is now *satisfied*, Plato's questioning inquiry about this requirement is *blunted* (*nivelliert*)."[46] According to Strauss, while the *falasifa* critically appropriate the Platonic answer, they harbor fundamental reservations regarding the question that underlies it, the question regarding the best regime. This is the fundamental point of difference between the two, and in this sense, they indeed seem to make the fourth obstacle to philosophizing into the foundation of their thought.

While this conclusion clarifies Strauss's interpretation of the *falasifa*, it raises questions regarding his view of Plato. For what does he mean by "the sharpness, originality, depth and—ambiguity of Platonic politics," which apparently are lacking in the work of the *falasifa*? And why does he single out the final characteristic, ambiguity, by separating it with a dash? To say the least, these characteristics suggest that for Plato the law is more doubtful and problematic than it is for the *falasifa*. But how should we construe this suggestion? Nowhere in *Philosophy and Law* does Strauss explain his rather cryptic remark about Plato. Discussing the Platonic approach of the *falasifa* to the revealed law, he writes that "the philosophic foundation of the law . . . is the place in the system of the Islamic Aristotelians and their Jewish pupils where the presupposition of their philosophizing comes under discussion."[47] In this sense, the philosophic foundation of the law includes the philosophic foundation of philosophy itself. We have already seen why for the *falasifa* this self-foundation of philosophy occurs in the field of politics: their situation confronted them with the acute political problem of having to justify their activity before the authority of the law. As Strauss goes on to claim, however, the self-foundation of philosophy is a political problem for *Plato* as well: "the political problem, in which is concealed nothing less than the foundation of philosophy."[48]

Why this enigmatic addition? And how does this relate to the specific character of Platonic political philosophy, its ambiguity? To answer these questions, some bibliographic exploration is required. The fourth and final chapter of *Philosophy and Law*, devoted to the philosophical foundation of the law, is, in fact, the revised version of an article published separately in a Swedish journal.[49] In revising the original article for inclusion in the book, Strauss removed an instructive passage at the end:

> Platonic philosophy is the execution of the "Socratic program". . . The Socratic question regarding the right way of life asks after the right way of living together, after the true state; the Socratic question is political. Since Plato has always philosophized in the sense of the "Socratic program," one may say: philosophizing platonically means to ask after the good, after the idea of the good.[50]

In this way, Strauss establishes an intriguing connection between Plato's philosophy and the Socratic question regarding the right way of life, which was already discussed in the previous chapter. Not only does he identify Platonic philosophy as a whole with the "Socratic program," the question regarding the right way of life, but he also goes on to specify that this question is a *political* question. Why he omitted this instructive and in a sense crucial passage in *Philosophy and Law* is not clear; all we can do is try to assess its significance.

Once again, the explanation points to Hermann Cohen. The latter, we learned from "Cohen and Maimonides," put Strauss on the track of the "deeper harmony" between Maimonides and Plato. In the same lecture, Strauss indicates that Cohen adds another important element to this bold assertion. What distinguishes Plato from Aristotle, Cohen argues, is the former's "Socratic capacity": in giving priority to morality and politics over theory, Plato recognizes with Socrates that the primary and fundamental question of philosophy is the question regarding the right way of life. Moreover, Cohen adds, the right way of life is "a problem, which has to rejuvenate itself time and again, which occurs in ever new questions, which in every new solution only raises new questions."[51] In other words, the Socratic question remains an open question. Finally, Cohen argues, the question regarding the right way of life is meaningful only when it is systematically related to human society, when it is understood as a political question. "There is no self-consciousness that could be obtained without taking into account the state and without guidance by the concept of the state."[52]

Thus, Cohen proves to be a source of inspiration not only for Strauss's rapprochement of Plato and Socrates, but also for his interpretation of the Socratic question as a political question. In addition, Cohen supplies a third important insight: the Socratic question is necessarily an open question. In "Cohen and Maimonides," Strauss explicates and develops the connection between these three insights in a strikingly radical way. His point of departure is Plato's *Apology*, where Socrates defends his way of life against the accusations of his fellow Athenians. In this context, Socrates famously tells his audience that all he knows is that he knows nothing, an utterance traditionally understood by some as ironical or even as dishonest by others. This, however, is not necessary, Strauss rejoins, provided one heeds an important nuance. Granted, every reader of Plato's dialogues is aware that Socrates knows many things: he has an exceptional understanding of the characters of his fellow citizens, as well as of the affairs of the polis. His insistence on his ignorance is based on the recognition that he knows nothing about the most important and most pressing human issue, the right way of life. This recognition is precisely what impels him to raise the question regarding the right way of life. Measured by this fundamental ignorance, the many things he does know appear paltry and without significance.

When Socrates's utterance is understood in this radical way, it follows that there is no such thing as a Socratic teaching or doctrine. This is not because he did not leave any writings, as tradition has it, but because he was unable to develop any doctrine on the basis of his queries. All Socrates is able to do is ask questions in the awareness of his ignorance, and call himself and others to account for their life and their opinions about the good and the just. Since the answers he obtains always prove to be deficient, inconsistent, or contradictory, they compel him to continue his inquiries.

Because the evidence of the question always exceeds that of the answers, Socrates persists in his questioning, Strauss writes: "he *wants* to remain in the question, namely because questioning is what it comes down to, because a life that is not questioning is not a life worthy of man (*menschenwürdig*)."[53] According to Strauss, Socrates's assertion in the *Apology* nevertheless contains an—albeit paradoxical—answer to the question regarding the right way of life. As long as no answer stands firm, questioning itself is the only right and justifiable way of life: "Thus, Socrates does give an answer to the question regarding the right way of life: *asking after the right way of life—this alone is the right way of life*."[54] Of course, this does not do away with the fact that even this paradoxical answer is an *answer* that Socrates must critically challenge, insofar as he wishes "to remain in the question." Thus, it is essential to philosophy that it ceaselessly questions its own presuppositions. In the *Apology*, Socrates points to this self-questioning in his well-known story about the Delphic oracle's curt negative response to the question whether any man was wiser than he. For Socrates, this answer was the occasion to refute the oracle by searching for someone wiser than he.[55]

This, however, is not the only characteristic of Socrates that is generally overlooked. As Strauss stresses with Cohen, for Socrates human life is essentially living *together*: the life of the individual is essentially oriented toward the community, toward the polis, and it cannot be dissociated from the latter without losing its meaning. This means that both the questioning life and its object must at all times be considered in relation to the political community. On the one hand, Socrates always raises his question regarding the right way of life in a dialogue with others. In doing so, his primary goal is not to teach nor to convince, for he has no teaching, but only to reach agreement and accord regarding the good and the just. Such agreement, after all, is indispensable if the community is to be truly a community. This shows, according to Strauss, that the question regarding the right way of life is always and inevitably a question regarding the right way of living *together*, regarding the best regime. Because of this double orientation on the polis, Strauss summarizes, the Socratic question is in essence *political*:

> Thus, the knowledge sought by Socrates is agreement, resulting from discussion, on the good, which as a human good is a common good. *Socratic questioning regarding the right way of life is an asking-together (Zusammenfragen) after the right way of living together (Zusammenleben) for the sake of the right way of living together,* for the sake of the true state. The questioning of Socrates is essentially *political*.[56]

As Strauss goes on to point out, the term "political," as it is used in this context, is ambiguous. It refers both to actual "day-to-day" politics and to that which is of the utmost importance to the community, that which is most controversial among its members, the good and the just. While this controversy is what impels Socrates to seek the good and the just in conversation with others, it is also that which makes his own activity political in the practical sense. This ambiguity is inevitable, Strauss affirms, insofar as human life itself is essentially political.[57] In general, this characteristic only becomes explicit when man turns expressly toward the community, as in the case of the politician. The latter, however, is concerned with the affairs of the polis in the opinion that he knows what the right way of living together is, and propagates this opinion in order to convince the public. When one turns toward the community as Socrates does, guided by the question regarding the right way of living together, the political action is rather implicit. Socrates only knows that he does not know the right way of life, let alone the right way of living together. Unlike the politician, therefore, he is unable to proclaim a specific opinion, either orally or in writing. Nor is he able to address a multitude of citizens, since the latter can only be swayed by means of a doctrine, and this would mean the end of questioning. With his questions, Socrates can only address individual human beings in oral conversation:

> Because Socrates knows that he knows nothing, that all understanding (*Verständnis*) can only be agreement (*Einverständnis*), he does not address the multitude but only individuals; his conversation with others is a dialogue. That is why he speaks and does not write. For what is written is necessarily misunderstood; it cannot protect itself against misunderstanding; it always says one and the same thing only—whereas it is necessary to always say the one true thing (*das Eine Wahre*) ever differently.[58]

Hence, Strauss asserts, Socrates's political action is paradoxical, both literally and figuratively. His persistent query regarding the right way of life leads beyond the *doxai*, the multifarious and conflicting opinions regarding the good and the just. As a result, his insights cannot straightforwardly be expressed in the nonparadoxical language of opinion. But the concrete political implications of his query are equally paradoxical: sustained asking-together, philosophizing in dialogue constitutes a form of living together that oddly enough seems to meet the demands put forward by the Socratic question as a political question. For, as Strauss argues, on this level as well, the question paradoxically points to an answer. If, in the absence of a conclusive answer to the question regarding the right way of life, questioning itself proves to be the right way of life, then under the same conditions asking-together after the right way of living together itself proves to be the right way of living together.[59] Still, we should not forget that even this paradoxical answer is subject to philosophical questioning.

Taking leave of "Cohen and Maimonides," we return to the two questions raised concerning *Philosophy and Law*: why is the self-foundation of philosophy a political problem for Plato as well, and in what does the ambiguous character of Platonic politics consist? On closer inspection, both questions prove to be intimately related. In order to clarify this relationship, however, we must first address another question that imposes itself when we compare the passage omitted from *Philosophy and Law* with the account of the Socratic question in "Cohen and Maimonides." Platonic philosophy, according to Strauss, is the execution of the Socratic program, the question regarding the true state, the best regime. In this respect, there is no difference between master and pupil. However, if Plato always philosophized "in the sense of the 'Socratic program,'" how are we to cope with the seemingly very un-Socratic fact that he *wrote* dialogues that strongly appear to convey some kind of teaching? Don't the Platonic dialogues provide exemplary proof of the observation that what is written is necessarily misunderstood? In this case, is it at all possible to maintain that Plato, like his teacher, "wants to remain in the question"?

The only way in which the rapprochement of Plato and Socrates can be upheld would seem to be by suggesting that the dialogues do not convey a teaching either, but only serve to bring to light the Socratic ignorance. This, however, would presuppose that Plato somehow solved the problem of the written word, and that his written dialogues somehow preserve the peculiar qualities of Socrates's spoken dialogue. Looking at the research Strauss conducts after *Philosophy and Law*, this hypothesis cannot be dismissed. In fact, he finds it confirmed by none other than the medieval Islamic philosophers, the *falasifa*, and his Jewish pupil Maimonides.

## Between the Lines: The Art of Writing

*Speech was given to man to hide his thoughts.*

—Gabriel Malagrida[60]

The *falasifa* justified their philosophic activity by presenting it as a legal commandment. As Strauss shows, however, this commandment was accompanied by specific conditions. In *Philosophy and Law*, he discusses these conditions by referring to Averroës's *Decisive Treatise Determining the Nature of the Connection between Religion and Philosophy* (*Kitâb Fasl-al-Maqâl*), a classic example of the *falasifa*'s viewpoint. In this treatise, Averroës raises the question whether philosophy is prohibited, permitted, or commanded by the revealed law.[61] Appealing to various verses of the Koran, he argues that the law enjoins the investigation of the beings in relation to their Maker, and thus commands the practice of philosophy after the manner of the Greeks. Philosophy distinguishes itself from other human activities commanded by the law by the fact that its goal coincides with the highest purpose of the law, which is to attain happiness in the knowledge of God. As a result, Averroës concludes, philosophy can never contradict the law. Both ways lead to the truth, and the truth cannot contradict the truth.

If the law differs from philosophy on certain issues, the philosopher is obliged to interpret the law figuratively or allegorically. This procedure is justified, Averroës affirms, since the law originally has two meanings. The prophet, who had direct access to the intelligible divine truth, could reveal it in human language only by means of similes and enigmatic expressions.[62] For the multitude of nonphilosophers, this outer meaning suffices to guide them toward the right way of life.[63] The philosopher, however, is capable of grasping the inner, intelligible meaning of the revealed law, even though his understanding never equals that of the prophet. For this reason, the philosopher is not merely allowed but in fact obliged to interpret the literal sense of the revealed law figuratively or allegorically.[64]

At the same time, it is forbidden for the philosopher to communicate this figurative interpretation to the multitude, since it would easily cause misunderstanding and confusion.[65] For this reason, he must use a way of communicating that Strauss calls "esoteric": by means of a complex, reticent, and lapidary style, he must make his views and insights inaccessible to unqualified and unauthorized eyes and ears. In fact, the medieval Islamic and Jewish philosophers indicate that they themselves employ this technique in their own writings. Thus, in the introduction to the *Guide of the Perplexed*, Maimonides announces that he will not treat the parts of metaphysics systematically, but

"scattered, and . . . interspersed with other topics." The reason for this procedure, he explains is the following:

> No intelligent man will require and expect that on introducing any
> subject I shall completely exhaust it; or that on commencing the expo-
> sition of a figure I shall fully explain all its parts. Such a course could
> not be followed by a teacher in a viva voce exposition, much less by an
> author in writing a book, without becoming a target for every foolish
> conceited person to discharge the arrows of folly at him.[66]

An "intelligent man," Maimonides implies, is aware that certain philosophical subjects cannot be discussed openly in public, either in a conversation or in written form, without arousing suspicion and unrest. At the same
time, when these subjects are addressed in a book in an incomplete and al-
lusive way, scattered and mixed with other topics, an intelligent man is able
to supply what is missing and to reconstruct the argument independently. In
any case, the formal qualities of the book in question are such that an "ignorant" reader would fail to notice the omissions and to reconstruct the
inner coherence of the work. Moreover, Maimonides's remark indicates
that esoteric communication serves the *mutual* protection of philosophers
and nonphilosophers: while the former are saved from public suspicion and
persecution, the latter are protected against confusion and discord.

In addition, the *falasifa* indicate that they are not the only thinkers,
nor the first to make use of esoteric communication. In the same treatise in
which he refers the treatment of prophecy to Platonic political philosophy,
Avicenna writes, "Thus in their writings the most renowned philosophers of
the Greeks, and their prophets, employed images and figures in which they
concealed their secrets, e.g., Pythagoras, Socrates, and Plato."[67] Similarly, in
the *Guide of the Perplexed*, Avicenna's Jewish follower Maimonides points
out, "This principle was not peculiar to our Sages: ancient philosophers and
scholars of other nations were likewise wont to treat of the *principia rerum*
obscurely, and to use figurative language in discussing such subjects."[68] Subsequently, the only ancient philosopher mentioned by name is Plato.

Esoteric communication, Avicenna and Maimonides assert, is a
legacy of the classical Greek philosophers. According to the latter, not
every human being is capable of leading a life of questioning and contemplation: there is an ineradicable qualitative difference between the small
group of philosophers and the multitude of nonphilosophers. What is intelligible to the former creates confusion and distrust among the latter. For
this reason, the philosophers are compelled to hide their views from the
multitude by means of a variety of literary devices such as the images and

figures mentioned by Avicenna, but also the literary artifices discussed by
Maimonides. This "exoteric" procedure obscures controversial views from
the public eye, covering them with a conventional and publicly acceptable
facade. Only the diligent and perceptive reader is able to read beyond this
facade and discover the original insights.

Although the medieval Islamic and Jewish philosophers are instrumental in revealing to Strauss the intrinsic connection between the contemplative ideal of classical philosophy, the division of humanity into
philosophers and nonphilosophers, and the art of esoteric/exoteric writing,
they are not the only, perhaps not even the primary, source. In his introductory commentaries on Moses Mendelssohn's works, he already suggested that Leibniz's defense of religious orthodoxy with regard to
providence, the immortality of the soul and eternal damnation in *Causa Dei*
and in the *Théodicée* is rather a form of exoteric lip service. What Strauss
omits, however, is that he merely repeats a suggestion by Lessing. The latter wrote the following about Leibniz:

> He did no more and no less than what all of the ancient philosophers
> used to do in their exoteric speech. He observed a sort of prudence
> for which, it is true, our most recent philosophers have become much
> too wise. . . . I admit that Leibniz treated the doctrine of eternal
> damnation very *exoterically*, and that *esoterically* he would have ex-
> pressed himself altogether differently on the subject.[69]

At the end of the same text, Lessing indicates that one ancient philosopher who observed this sort of prudence was Socrates, who "believed in eternal punishment in all seriousness, or at least believed in it to the extent that
he considered it expedient (*zuträglich*) to teach it in words that are least susceptible of arousing suspicion and most explicit."[70] With these words as well
as in other writings, Lessing indicates that, unlike most of his contemporaries, he had not become too wise for the wisdom of the old philosophers.
Similarly, he made the distinction between the esoteric and the exoteric into
the guiding principle of his writing. This is borne out by the flexible, playful, and scintillating style as well as by the great erudition he displays in his
philosophical, theological, and aesthetical works. This guise was so effective
that even his close friend Mendelssohn admitted to being exasperated at
times by what he called Lessing's "theatre logic," his love of paradoxical positions in both conversation and writing. As opposed to Mendelssohn, the
staunch adherent of the Enlightenment, Lessing espoused the ancient view
that a "radical, i.e. non-dogmatic way of thinking" is inevitably at odds with
prevailing opinions and must therefore conceal its views.[71] As Strauss will

later argue, "Lessing was the last writer who revealed, while hiding, the reasons compelling wise men to hide the truth: he wrote between the lines about writing between the lines."[72]

By the same token, Lessing may well have been the first writer from whom Strauss began to learn how to read between the lines. Moreover, as an assiduous student of his undogmatic way of thinking and of his art of writing, Strauss knew that Lessing was familiar with medieval Jewish and Islamic theology and philosophy. It is not unlikely that this had some bearing on his investigations.[73] Thus, in 1946 he sketches the plan of a book tentatively titled *Philosophy and the Law*, the final chapter of which was to be devoted to Lessing's *Nathan der Weise*. Although this well-known play is generally regarded as a tribute to Mendelssohn, the symbol of enlightened tolerance, Strauss hints at a strikingly different interpretation: "The recollection of the man Maimonides was probably one of the motives underlying Lessing's *Nathan the Wise*, the outstanding poetic monument erected in honor of Jewish medieval philosophy."[74] Whether Lessing actually guided Strauss to Maimonides's art of writing, however, cannot be determined with certainty.[75]

At any rate, Strauss's investigations reveal that the original esoteric-exoteric character of classical and medieval Islamic and Jewish philosophy is closely related to the problematic relationship between philosophers and nonphilosophers. As the example of the *falasifa* shows, this problem is primarily a *political* problem: philosophy is suspect from the perspective of the community and thus requires a political justification, a demonstration that it does not threaten or undermine the community. The painstaking care with which the *falasifa* rely on Platonic politics to supply such a justification suggests that this challenge also posed itself for Plato. Obviously, the latter was all too familiar with public and political distrust and opprobrium against philosophy, as it ultimately led to the execution of his teacher. In the *Apology*, Socrates points to the dangers attendant on the persistent questioning regarding the right way of living together: "Now from this investigation, men of Athens, many enmities have arisen against me, and such as are most harsh and grievous, so that many prejudices have resulted from them and I am called a wise man."[76] The spoken word need not even be written down in order to be misunderstood. As soon as it starts to lead a life of its own, it gives rise to misapprehensions, such as the view that Socrates's ignorance is feigned and that he is truly wise. A more striking illustration of the political character of Socratic questioning can hardly be found.

For whoever subscribes to the Socratic program, then, the conviction and execution of Socrates are a problem of primary importance. How can one "remain in the question," asking after the right way of life and the true state, in the dark shadow of suspicion and persecution? How can one preserve "the sharpness, originality, and depth" of the Socratic question? How else, if not by means of—ambiguity? As the allusions of Avicenna and Maimonides, as well as their approach to the revealed law suggest, Plato adopted and developed the veiled and veiling mode of communication in response to the political problem, the tension between philosophy and the political, legal and moral order of the polis.

In this way, we have found answers to the questions that remained suspended in *Philosophy and Law*. If the foundation of philosophy, understood as self-foundation, is a political problem, this means that the primary question of philosophy, the question regarding the right way of life, is a political question regarding the true state. At the same time, it means that philosophy is continually obliged to give the highest priority to reflecting on its problematic relationship to the law and the polis. The main reason is not only that its incessant questioning of reigning opinions undermines the foundations of the polis, but also that it permanently questions itself as a way of life. In both senses, philosophy must first and foremost be *political* philosophy: philosophy concerned with political matters, which always point to the question regarding the right way of life, but also philosophy that has to become political in order to justify itself vis-à-vis the law and the polis.[77] This means, among other things, that philosophy in its dealings with the polis may have to don the public attire of a teaching or doctrine. The latter, however, cannot but be ambiguous, since underneath it the persistent questioning regarding the true state continues.

How this ambiguity pervades Plato's dialogues will be discussed shortly. At this point, it is necessary to return once more to Strauss's interpretation of the *falasifa*. As we saw, in *Philosophy and Law* he concludes that the latter correct and thereby blunt Platonic political philosophy in a decisive respect, since they assume that the question regarding the right way of life and the true state has been decisively answered by revelation. For this reason, they subject the philosopher to the authority of the prophet and the revealed law, both politically and intellectually. For Strauss, however, this finding is unsatisfactory, for how can one claim that the *falasifa* are Platonists if they dismiss an essential characteristic of Plato's thought as an aporia? Either one must assume that prophetology's use of Plato's philosophy is inappropriate since its intrinsic and vital ambiguity is flatly overlooked and even denied. Or one must consider whether prophetology may not in some way have preserved the ambiguity. This, however, would require a fundamental revision of the interpretation.

In a series of articles published shortly after *Philosophy and Law*, Strauss is seen to have taken the second path. As he pursues his research in medieval Jewish and Islamic prophetology, he comes to entertain the view that the *falasifa* do not blunt or mutilate Platonic political philosophy, but rather *emulate* and *continue* it. To this view he is led in particular by closer study of the founder of medieval Islamic philosophy, Alfarabi. The latter, Strauss had already noted in *Philosophy and Law*, "denies the possibility of super-philosophical knowledge of the upper world through prophecy: through the influence of the active intellect on his intellect the prophet becomes a philosopher—nothing other and nothing higher than a philosopher."[78] In other words, for Alfarabi the superiority of the prophet over the philosopher is restricted to the political, and does not include the theoretical. In his subsequent research, Strauss gathers increasing evidence suggesting that Alfarabi regards revelation chiefly and even exclusively as a political matter. Thus, he flatly subordinates theology and jurisprudence, the religious sciences par excellence in Islam, to political science. In doing so, he does not hesitate to regard religious knowledge as the lowest form of knowledge, below even grammar. Just like language, this ranking implies, religion is characteristic of a particular—that is, *not* a universal—society. Finally, Alfarabi completely assimilates ethics, the doctrine of virtue, to politics. Virtues, he indicates, are not ends in themselves, but merely means by which man can attain happiness, human happiness being a purely political—that is, worldly—matter.[79]

According to Strauss, this politicization of revealed religion bears a Platonic stamp, as becomes apparent from the part of Alfarabi's prophetology devoted to divine providence. This teaching chiefly consists in a demonstration supporting the law's assertion that God's knowledge and caring concern extend to even the smallest things, and thus also to human affairs such as happiness. Divine providence, the law states, is a particular providence, which punishes or rewards the individual in accordance with the moral quality of his actions. In his demonstration, however, Alfarabi indicates that this view belongs to the outer or exoteric meaning of the law. According to its inner or esoteric meaning, providence has no bearing whatsoever on human action, but only on human thought. True human happiness, this distinction implies, cannot be attained through action but only through seeking knowledge or philosophizing.

As Strauss shows, Alfarabi's demonstration, including its distinction between the inner and the outer meaning of the law, is derived from Plato's *Laws*. In the tenth book of the *Laws*—a discussion of criminal law—the Athenian Stranger argues in favor of the coordination of just actions and happiness, on the one hand, and unjust deeds and unhappiness on the other, by referring to divine providence. In order to buttress his claim, he develops a theology that displays remarkable formal and substantial resemblances to the Old Testament: the God, who is called "Father," is a benevolent though strict God, creator of heaven and earth, and concerned with the minutest details of his creation.[80] The Athenian Stranger's dazzling rhetoric, however, makes the reader forget that earlier on, in the second book, he had already discussed the divine coordination of virtue and happiness and vice and unhappiness. In this context, the Stranger had added the following considerations, formulated in a deceptively conditional mode:

> Even if what the argument established were not the case, could a lawgiver of any worth ever tell a lie more profitable than this (if, that is, he ever has the daring to lie to the young for the sake of a good cause), or more effective in making everybody do all the just things willingly, and not out of compulsion?[81]

Having named one such lie by way of example, the Stranger continues:

> Indeed, this myth is a great example for the lawgiver of how it is possible to persuade the souls of the young of just about anything, if one tries. It follows from this that the lawgiver should seek only the convictions which would do the greatest good for the city, and he should discover every device of any sort that will tend to make the whole community speak about these things with one and the same voice, as much as possible, at every moment throughout the whole of life, in songs and myths and arguments.[82]

Divine providence, Plato's Athenian Stranger suggests, is a story that is politically salutary and necessary for stability and concord in the state. By distinguishing between esoteric and exoteric providence, and by characterizing the teaching on providence as a part of political science, Alfarabi intimates that he has understood Plato's hint. In his prophetology, he closely follows the Athenian Stranger's advice to the lawgiver: for what conviction is more beneficial for the *umma*, the Islamic community of the faithful, than the teachings of the Koran, interpreted in terms of Platonic politics? The transformation of the prophet into a legislator, statesman, and philosopher, and of the law into a truly divine law with a double meaning, is a necessary artifice that exoterically shores up Islamic orthodoxy, while esoterically it creates latitude for philosophy.[83]

In this way, Platonic politics enables Alfarabi to restore philosophy in its original, radical sense without exposing it to the hazards of religious persecution. As Strauss points out, however, the aim is the *mutual* protection of philosophy and the community. In Alfarabi's lifetime in the tenth century, Islam is threatened with disruption and disintegration, by febrile chiliastic expectations on the one hand, and by a radical critique of Epicurean stamp on the other. Because these turbulences endanger both the community of the faithful and philosophy, Alfarabi is compelled to defend religious orthodoxy against both overzealous fanatics and radical skeptics, as well as philosophy against religious orthodoxy, Strauss explains:

> In a century that was not considerably less "enlightened" than that of the sophists and Socrates, when the foundations of human life, i.e., of political life, were shaken by chiliastic convulsions on the one hand, and by a critique of religion the radicalism of which is reminiscent of the freethinkers of the 17th century on the other, Alfarabi had rediscovered in Plato's politics the right mean (*le juste milieu*) equally removed from a naturalism that only aims to hallow the savage and destructive instincts of "natural" man, the instincts of the master and conqueror, and from a supernaturalism that tends to become the basis of a slave morality— a right mean that is neither a compromise nor a synthesis, that is not based on the two opposite positions, but which annuls both and uproots them by a preliminary question, more profound, raising a more fundamental problem, the work of a truly critical philosophy.[84]

What this "more fundamental problem" is becomes clear when Strauss goes on to define the core of Platonic philosophy as "the quest for the perfect state."[85] In other words, the more fundamental problem Alfarabi raises is nothing other than the Socratic question that at once examines the reigning *doxai* and itself as a way of life, and which thus brings to light the problematic relationship between philosophy and politics. From Socrates and Plato, he learns that the self-foundation of philosophy is a political problem, in the double sense discussed above: a problem that makes the political things into the object par excellence of philosophy, and a problem that compels philosophy to justify itself politically. In Plato's work, the self-foundation of philosophy takes the form of the foundation of a divine law: in the *Laws*, Strauss claims, Alfarabi finds "the unbelieving, philosophic foundation of the belief in the revelation."[86] The ambiguous character of this foundation points the attentive reader back to the problem of the self-foundation of philosophy, and thus to the Socratic question. As Alfarabi writes, Plato's works give us "an account of philosophy, but not without giving us also an account of the ways to it and of the ways to re-establish it when it becomes confused or extinct."[87] By presenting the constitution of the best state as the ultimate goal of Islamic revelation, he succeeds both in upholding orthodoxy and in reviving the Socratic-Platonic query where it has been jeopardized or even oppressed by revelation's absolute claim to authority.[88] By presenting the revealed law equivocally as the answer to the requirements of Platonic politics, he draws the philosophic reader's attention to the questions and the problems underlying these requirements.

After Alfarabi, the other medieval Jewish and Islamic philosophers are driven by identical concerns, Strauss argues. At the end of the twelfth century, Maimonides is faced with a similar problem: rising messianic fever, on the one hand, and the controversy surrounding the rediscovery of Aristotelian philosophy, on the other, jeopardize obedience to the revealed law as well as the freedom of philosophical inquiry. As a result, the need arises for a new and adequate defense and foundation of the law, as well as of philosophy.[89] Responding to this need, Maimonides turns to Platonic politics, adapting its means and methods to his religious community. Thus, he identifies Moses with the legislator-philosopher, and the Messiah with the philosopher-king who will restore the perfect order of the law to the people of Israel and bring eternal peace, enabling all to attain knowledge of God according to their capacities.[90] For in the messianic era the distinction between philosophers and nonphilosophers will continue to exist, Maimonides asserts. Like Alfarabi, he emulates Platonic politics by attributing a double meaning to the law: one consisting of politically necessary beliefs, and a philosophical meaning.[91] As Strauss explains, Maimonides "could make this essential distinction only in a disguised way, partly by allusions, partly by the composition of his whole work, but mainly by the rhetorical character, recognizable only to philosophers, of the arguments by which he defends the necessary beliefs."[92]

Once prophetology is recognized as the core of their thinking, one sees that Maimonides and the *falasifa* are political philosophers in the original, Socratic-Platonic sense of the word: their thought is entirely in the service of the question regarding the right way of life, a question that must be raised and discussed with due regard for the difference between philosophers and nonphilosophers.[93] Already in *Philosophy and Law*, Strauss availed himself of this distinction in order to point to an essential difference between medieval and modern Enlightenment:

> The esoteric character of the "medieval religious Enlightenment" is based on the prevailing ideal of the *theoretical* life, just as the exoteric character of the modern Enlightenment is based on the conviction— prevalent long before its formulation, foundation and radicalization by Kant—of the primacy of *practical* reason.[94]

Modern Enlightenment rejects the theoretical ideal of life, and thus dismisses the distinction between the philosophers and the multitude as irrelevant, as well as the distinction between esoteric and exoteric meaning. In its view, the complete enlightenment of the multitude is not only possible but even desirable: the new scientific method is capable of fully developing practical reason in all men. Animated by this prospect, it strives to make public all the truths of philosophy, which thereby becomes completely exoteric. A telling example is the famous exhortation of Denis Diderot, one of the compilers of the *Encyclopédie*: "Let us hasten to make philosophy popular!"[95] More importantly, the exoteric character of modern Enlightenment and the primacy it accords to practical reason rest on the presupposition that there is no fundamental tension between philosophy and society, which philosophy must address and attempt to mitigate. On the contrary, modernity sets the stage for an unprecedented alliance between philosophy and politics that profoundly changes the face of the world within a few centuries.

However, as we saw in the previous chapter, Strauss finds that this alliance has exacerbated philosophy's entanglement in the impasse of the second cave. The way out of this predicament, we learned, runs along two parallel and interrelated paths: the rediscovery of premodern philosophy in its original form, and the critical reassessment of modern philosophical tradition. As regards the first path, Strauss's research into the medieval Enlightenment shows the potential of "learning through reading." A meticulous study of medieval Jewish and Islamic prophetology reveals that the *falasifa* may have found a way of overcoming the fourth historical obstacle to philosophizing in Plato's philosophy, showing them how "to re-establish it when it becomes confused or extinct." For a young scholar caught between Jewish religious orthodoxy and atheism from probity, neither of which he was willing or able to adhere to, the prospect of resuscitating the Socratic-Platonic inquiry must have been appealing, to say the least.[96] As he notes in the autobiographical preface to *Spinoza's Critique of Religion*, it offered a way out of the dilemma in which he found himself:

> Other observations and experiences confirmed the suspicion that it would be unwise to say farewell to reason. I began therefore to wonder whether the self-destruction of reason was not the inevitable outcome of modern rationalism as distinguished from pre-modern rationalism, especially Jewish-medieval rationalism and its classical (Aristotelian and Platonic) foundation.[97]

But what about the second path? Obviously, Strauss's remarkable rediscovery of Platonism is not barren of consequences for his investigation into the foundations of modern thought, an investigation that is similarly guided by the restitution of the Socratic question. An important and conspicuous sign is that Strauss comes to focus this research on the meeting ground of Plato and the *falasifa*: political philosophy. What this means is borne out by a seemingly odd remark in a letter of 1935 to the renowned Jewish thinker Gerschom Scholem, in which Strauss reports enthusiastically on his breakthrough understanding Maimonides: "If I have the time and the strength, I want to write a book on the *Guide [of the Perplexed]* in the course of about ten years. For the time being, I'm publishing an introduction to the *Guide* under the title: Hobbes's political science in its development."[98] In the work of Thomas Hobbes, the process is brought to completion that Strauss, in his introductions to Mendelssohn, had circumscribed as "the suppression of law understood as obligation in favor of right understood as claim." For this reason, Hobbes is not only one of the fathers of political liberalism, but also one of the founders of modern political thought in general. The Hobbesian revolution in political philosophy decisively contributed to suppressing the ancient concept of *nomos* and supplanting it by the concept of natural law, clearing the path for the rise of practical reason. For this reason, Strauss regards a long and detailed study of Hobbes's work a *conditio sine qua non* to break the spell of modern concepts.

## "A Horizon Beyond Liberalism": The Debate with Carl Schmitt

In the previous chapters, we saw that the most important turns and breakthroughs in Strauss's research are accompanied by a debate with a contemporary thinker. His research on Hobbes is no exception, although this time his interlocutor is not Hermann Cohen but a passionate advocate of Hobbes in interbellum Germany: the notorious legal scholar and political thinker Carl Schmitt. The latter, in a controversial book of 1932 entitled *The Concept of the Political*, undertakes a spirited defense of the political against what he considers to be its neutralization by modern liberalism. According to Schmitt, the political is ultimately predicated on the distinction between friend and foe, and thus on the possibility of armed conflict. In this context, he hails Hobbes, the philosopher of the war of all against all, as an ally and a kindred spirit. In the same year, Strauss publishes a lengthy review of the book, in which he critically assesses Schmitt's position and brings to light its presuppositions, contradictions, and aporias.[99] Moreover, he offers the reader an intriguing glimpse of his own premises.[100]

Strauss's review consists of three sections, the first of which presents the chief argument of Schmitt's book, as well as its philosophical background, and offers some criticisms. Thus, he begins by observing that according to

Schmitt all human concepts are polemical: they do not express timeless truths, but are always directed against some opponent and thus determined by the specific context in which they are formulated. As a result, Schmitt's concept of the political must likewise be understood not as a timeless truth, but as a polemical assertion. In particular, his defense of the political is directed against modern liberalism's attempt to negate it by eradicating enmity and to establish a state on the basis of this negation. According to Schmitt, liberalism has only succeeded in obscuring the political, not in eliminating it. With his defense, he wants to rescue the political from liberal oblivion by recalling the problem of the foundation of the state. In doing so, however, he acknowledges one major obstacle to his endeavor: despite its shortcomings, liberalism possesses a remarkable systematic consistency that can be refuted and replaced only with great difficulty. As Strauss will show, Schmitt's endeavor proves to remain entangled in the system of liberal thinking, precisely because it is polemical and aimed against it.[101]

This may explain why Strauss only discusses Schmitt's understanding of the political in the second section. If the thesis of the political is itself necessarily polemical or political, this implies that its content is defined, at least in part, by the polemic and thus by the enemy. Hence, Strauss opens the second section by noting that Schmitt purposely declines to provide an exhaustive definition of the political. The main reason is that it is characteristic of liberal thought to define the political as an autonomous field of culture, whereby the latter is understood as a sovereign human creation. For Schmitt, this is an inadmissible and even dangerous reduction: as a result, Strauss observes, a renewed understanding of the political presupposes a fundamental critique of the liberal concept of culture. Nevertheless, this implication is obscured by the fact that Schmitt frequently refers to the political as if it were indeed an autonomous "province of culture" (*Kulturprovinz*) like morality or aesthetics, each of which is characterized by its own basic distinction, such as good and evil or beautiful and ugly. When he goes on to flesh out this distinction, however, it becomes apparent that this is not the case. In comparison with the other "provinces," the political is fundamental, encompassing and normative because the distinction between friend and foe has an existential dimension: it is oriented toward the *Ernstfall*, the case of emergency, the real possibility of war and physical annihilation. Hence, the reaffirmation of the political necessarily requires a critique of the leveling concept of culture underlying liberalism. In order to highlight this implication, which is merely "adumbrated" by Schmitt, Strauss reverts to a tactic he will repeatedly employ throughout the review.[102] He makes Schmitt's position stronger and more coherent than it

really is, by rendering explicit certain ambiguities and hesitations, and trying to "resolve" them in accordance with Schmitt's guiding intention.[103]
This means that he elaborates the critique of the modern liberal concept of
culture that is implied in Schmitt's defense of the political. As we will see,
this exposition reveals a number of crucial flaws.

At the heart of the modern concept of culture, Strauss argues, is the
view that culture as a whole is the autonomous and sovereign creation of
the human mind, of which the political is just one particular instance.[104]
This view, however, fails to appreciate that in its original meaning culture
is never simply autonomous and sovereign, since it always presupposes
something that is cultivated: *nature*.[105] In order to recall this relationship,
Strauss makes a distinction crucial to his critique. He reminds the reader
that "to cultivate" can have two distinct meanings. Either it can be understood in the original classical sense, as "the careful cultivation of nature—
whether of the soil or of the human mind; in this it obeys the indications
that nature itself gives."[106] Or it can be understood in the modern sense as
"overcoming nature by obedience to nature. . . . In that case, culture is not
so much faithful cultivation of nature as a harsh and cunning fight *against*
nature. Which understanding of culture is accepted depends on how nature
is understood: whether as an order seen as a model or whether as disorder
which is to be removed. In either view culture is cultivation of nature."[107]

Recalling this original dependency does not suffice, however. One
also has to raise the question of what is exactly understood by "nature." As
Strauss specifies, "culture" refers primarily to *human* nature as its basis.
Human nature, moreover, has specific characteristics:

> since man is by nature an *animal sociale*, the human nature underly-
> ing culture is the natural living together of men, i.e. the mode in
> which man—prior to culture—behaves towards other men. The term
> for the natural living together thus understood is *status naturalis*. One
> may therefore say: the foundation of culture is the *status naturalis*.[108]

On the basis of this definition of nature, Strauss further determines
the modern concept of culture. In the modern sense, "culture" denotes the
struggle against the *status naturalis*, against the natural form of living together. The most original formulation of this view, he notes, can be found
in the work of Hobbes, who defines the *status civilis* as the *negation* of the *status naturalis*. For Hobbes, the state of nature is the greatest conceivable disorder, a *status belli* or condition of war. As Strauss goes on to remark, there
is a noticeable parallel between Hobbes's state of nature and the political as

Schmitt understands it, which explains why the latter acts as a modern defender of the Hobbesian state of nature against the neutralizing oblivion of modern liberalism.

Closer scrutiny of this parallel, however, reveals profound differences between Schmitt and Hobbes. As Strauss points out, if the parallel is sound, the Hobbesian negation of the *status naturalis* actually means the negation of the political in the sense of Schmitt. He notes, ironically enough in an unassuming footnote, "In fact [Hobbes] is *the* anti-political thinker, if we understand 'political' in Schmitt's sense."[109] Hobbes's definition of the state of nature is polemical, Strauss points out: it is intended to justify the negation of the *status naturalis* and the transition to the *status civilis*. That is why the state of nature is for him an untenable condition of war of all against all, a war with only enemies and no friends.[110] In comparison, and contrary to his own claim, Schmitt's defense of the state of nature as a struggle between hostile groups no longer appears as polemical and negative, but rather as positive or affirmative.[111]

Moreover, Hobbes's definition of the state of nature shows that his concept of the state is, in fact, opposed to that of Schmitt. For Hobbes, the natural right to self-preservation is the ultimate limit of state power, to the extent that the state must guarantee full security to the individual and can never demand the latter's total self-sacrifice. By providing security, the state guarantees freedom to the citizens in order to freely acquire wealth, not by waging war, but by trade, labor, and frugality, assisted by science and technology. For this reason, Strauss argues, Hobbes cannot be the ally Schmitt takes him to be. On the contrary, Hobbes is no less than the founder of the modern ideal of civilization and thus of the liberalism Schmitt opposes so vehemently: "Hobbes is to a much higher degree than, say, Bacon, the originator of the ideal of civilization. By this very fact he is the founder of liberalism."[112]

By providing man with an inalienable right to self-preservation limiting the power of the state, Hobbes laid the basis for the rise of other human rights. Nevertheless, there is a fundamental difference between the founder and those who continued to build on his foundation, Strauss holds: Hobbes was still aware that he had to defend the liberal ideal of civilization against the "illiberal" state of nature, against what he considered to be the "natural evil" of man. In his view, this natural evil set limits to the abolition of the state of nature, so that it was necessary to expand the authority of the state as far as possible as was consistent with the individual right to self-preservation. Once the ideal of civilization had been constituted, however, this original opposition was forgotten. Awareness of the limits of the civilizational project yielded to the belief in the unlimited creative powers of the human mind, expressed in the concept of culture. According to Strauss, Schmitt also seems to partake of this oblivion in making Hobbes a champion of the political. It strengthens Strauss's impression that Schmitt's critique of liberalism remains dependent on liberal presuppositions: "Whereas Hobbes, living in an illiberal world, lays the foundation of liberalism, Schmitt, living in a liberal world, undertakes the critique of liberalism."[113]

In the third section of his review, Strauss will argue that this is indeed the case and assess the implications for Schmitt's endorsement of the political. Before considering this section, however, it is necessary to return to Strauss's discussion of the relationship between culture and nature. The reader cannot but be struck by the fact that Strauss only broaches the contrast between the ancient and the modern concept of culture in order to argue that in both cases culture always relates to nature: in the classical view, this relationship is complementary, while the modern view sees it as an opposition. However, when he goes on to specify nature as human nature, he focuses exclusively on Hobbes as the founder of the modern concept of the culture, who viewed the *status civilis* as the negation of the *status naturalis*. The classical view and its ramifications, it seems, are passed over in near silence.

Or are they? As Strauss specifies, man is by nature an *animal sociale*, a social animal: human nature is equivalent to the natural living together of human beings, the *status naturalis* that lies at the basis of culture. Within the context of Strauss's discussion, this specification is noteworthy: Strauss cannot but have been aware that Hobbes's understanding of the state of nature implies that man is not a social animal, but rather an "arrant Wolfe" engaged in a struggle for life with others.[114] By remaining silent on this implication, he draws our attention to the connection between the classical concept of culture and the classical understanding of the state of nature. This connection can be elaborated as follows: if culture is the careful cultivation of nature in accordance with the indications of nature, if nature is primarily human nature, and if man is by nature a social animal, it follows that cultivating human nature consists in developing the natural living together of man in accordance with the indications of nature. It is important to note that, according to the classical view, the state of nature is a social or *political* condition, *animal sociale* being the Latin translation of the Aristotelian definition of man as a *zôion politikon*.[115] "Culture" in the classical sense thus means the careful development of political life in accordance with the indications of nature.[116] Similarly, the reference to culture as the cultivation of the human mind in obedience to the indications of nature echoes the Ciceronian definition of philosophy as *cultura animi* or cultivation of the soul.[117] Thus, in referring to the ancient concept of culture and the social animal, Strauss appropriates the classical understanding of the political. As we will see, this understanding differs both from the Hobbesian and from the Schmittian view.

At the beginning of the third section, Strauss recapitulates the results of the comparison between Schmitt and Hobbes: while Hobbes polemically negates the political, Schmitt unpolemically posits it. According to Schmitt, the political, the possibility of physical death is a reality impervious to normative and evaluative judgment, an inescapable destiny that manifests itself most strongly where man tries to escape or suppress it. The political is a fundamental trait of human life, so much so that it determines man's humanity: for Schmitt, abandoning the political signifies abandoning humanity. Nevertheless, this firmness is relative, Strauss observes, for even if the political is real and incontrovertible in the present, Schmitt confesses to being uncertain whether the future will not be entirely neutralized and depoliticized.

According to Strauss, the ultimate premise of the political in Schmitt's view proves to be an anthropological position: man is by nature evil, not in a moral sense, but in the sense of "dangerousness," and thus in need of being kept in check. Once again, however, Schmitt undermines his own position by asserting that human dangerousness is ultimately an "anthropological profession of faith."[118] If that is the case, Strauss rejoins, the thesis of the political is based on a belief that is no more plausible than the belief underlying the opposite view, according to which man is by nature good. Moreover, in that case the political is not an inexorable fate, but something that is threatened by the exertions of the opposite camp. As a result, Schmitt is forced to do more than simply posit: he is compelled to affirm the political and thus to affirm human dangerousness.

The affirmation of the political, however, cannot belong to the political itself, in the sense that it can be described as an inescapable destiny: groups of human beings engaged in a life-and-death battle do not wish or affirm the dangerousness of their enemies. Nor do they wish or affirm their own dangerousness for its own sake, but only to ward off the enemy.[119] Hence, Schmitt's affirmation of the political must have extrapolitical grounds, Strauss suggests: more particularly, it conceals a *moral* stance that is not based on the glorification of war and warrior virtues, but on the conviction that man needs authority and guidance because of his dangerousness. Nevertheless, Schmitt denies that his authoritarian premise has a moral character. Following seventeenth-century philosophers of the state such as Hobbes, Spinoza, and Samuel von Pufendorff, he characterizes human dangerousness and evil as a natural, animal force (*naturae potentia*). Here again, however, Schmitt chooses the wrong allies, Strauss contends: the seventeenth-century thinkers embraced this definition of human dangerousness because they denied that man is a sinful creature and because they rejected the primacy of duty and the state over individual natural right. In addition, they held the view that man is an animal capable of acquiring wisdom through negative experiences, and thus educable. While Hobbes still held this possibility to be so limited as to warrant a defense of state absolutism, his views did not prevent his successors from expanding human educability exponentially. In this respect, seventeenth-century anthropology lies at the basis of both liberalism and anarchism, and as such it is unsuited for Schmitt's purposes. His authoritarian affirmation of the political and his critique of liberalism require that a meaningful distinction can be made between good and evil, and that human evil can be regarded in moral terms:

> In order to launch the radical critique of liberalism that he has in mind, Schmitt must first eliminate the conception of human evil as animal evil, and therefore as "innocent evil," and find his way back to the conception of human evil as moral depravity. Only by so doing can Schmitt remain in agreement with himself, if indeed "the core of the political idea is the *morally* exacting decision" (*Political Theology*, 56).[120]

That Strauss quotes from Schmitt's *Political Theology* (1922), something he only does twice in the whole review, is anything but coincidental. It tacitly suggests that Schmitt's moral concern has theological roots. In this respect, it is noteworthy that Strauss points out the difference between Schmitt and the seventeenth-century thinkers on the issue of sin and human evil. Moreover, we should not forget Schmitt's own characterization of the thesis of human dangerousness as "an anthropological confession of faith." Contrary to Schmitt's denial, his defense of the political has an unmistakable moral core. Nevertheless, the question remains as to how he can affirm the political, understood as human moral wickedness. According to Strauss's explanation, the affirmation of the political is, in fact, an "objectifying" and "value-free" guise underneath which Schmitt hides his deep moral aversion at the prospect of a completely neutralized and depoliticized world. Behind the thesis of the political is a defense of the moral seriousness of life, threatened with complete extinction by the onslaught of a society focused on amusement and consumerism. This seriousness is dependent on fundamental moral disagreements that confront human beings with existential and moral decisions, and which remind man of—as Strauss calls it—"the things that really count" (*worauf es eigentlich ankommt*).[121] Hence, Strauss concludes, Schmitt in reality wishes to affirm the moral: "The affirmation of the political is in the last analysis nothing other than the affirmation of the moral."[122]

Further corroboration of this thesis, Strauss adds, is found in Schmitt's perception of the modern process of depoliticization. According to Schmitt, this process did not so much cause changes in the "fatal" character of the political—conflicts continue to occur in modernity—as in the object of political disagreement, "the things that count." The latter always depend on a dominant background theme, such as theology, metaphysics, morality or economics. In its pursuit of agreement, security and peace at any price, modernity has tried to introduce a dominant background theme that no longer would give rise to conflict, an ultimate neutral ground: technology, which would allow man to concentrate exclusively on the means without having to refer to the contentious and explosive issue of the ends. For Schmitt, however, turning away from this issue would mean turning away from the moral seriousness that determines man's humanity. Strauss encapsulates this view in a passage that at the same time allows us to catch a glimpse of his own position:

> Yet agreement can always be reached in principle about the means to an already established end, whereas the ends are always controversial: we disagree with one another and with ourselves always only about the just and the good (Plato, *Euthyphro* 7b–d and *Phaedrus* 263a). If therefore one wishes agreement at any price, there is no other way than to abandon altogether the question of what is right and to limit one's concern exclusively to the means.[123]

As the passage shows, once again Strauss interprets and assesses Schmitt's problem against a classical background. While he agrees that behind the political struggle there is a moral concern, his understanding differs from that of Schmitt, insofar as it is guided not by political theology, but by Platonic political philosophy. In the passage of the *Euthyphro* he cites, Socrates asks his interlocutor what things cause disagreement between human beings to develop into enmity. A dispute about numbers, size, or weight, he observes, can easily be resolved by counting, measuring, or weighing. This resort is lacking, however, when the object of disagreement is the good, the noble, and the just or their opposites. These are "the questions about which you and I and other people become enemies, when we do become enemies, because we differ about them and cannot reach any satisfactory agreement."[124] In the passage of the *Phaedrus* cited by Strauss, Socrates makes a similar distinction. Everyone agrees to the meaning of words like "iron" or "silver," he says. But what happens in the case of terms such as "justice" or "goodness"? "Do we not part company, and disagree with each other and with ourselves?"[125] "The things that count," the things that are really contentious, Strauss holds with Socrates and Plato, are the good, the noble, and the just. These matters divide human beings in opposed groups and thus determine the content of the political.

It is no accident that, in the passage just quoted, Strauss tacitly replaces the "moral" by "the question of what is right." Although he nowhere mentions Socrates by name in the review, he indicates that both the framework and the criterion of his critique of Schmitt are defined by the Socratic question. The latter not only addresses the most serious moral issues, but also the most serious political matter: "the things that count," the right and good way of life, is essentially the right and good way of living together. Moreover, the Socratic question recognizes the primacy of duty—the laws—over the rights of the individual, even if it understands this duty in a very specific way, as something to be scrutinized by the philosopher.[126]

Against this background, Strauss develops his own perspective on the process of neutralization and depoliticization. The modern pursuit of peace and agreement at any price and the search for a neutral ground, he argues, are ultimately based on a rejection of the Socratic question regarding the right way of life. However, insofar as the capacity to raise this question is the highest and most urgent human task, neutralization and depoliticization also entail the loss of man's humanity:

> Agreement at any price is possible only as agreement at the price of the meaning of human life, for such agreement is possible only when man abandons the task of raising the question regarding what is right, and when man abandons this question, he abandons his humanity. But when he asks the question of what is right in earnest, there arises (given the "inextricably problematic character" of what this question is about) conflict, life-and-death conflict: by the seriousness of the question of what is right, the political—the division of the human race into foes and friends—is justified (*hat das Politische . . . seinen Rechtsgrund*).[127]

The fundamental and often volatile disagreement about the good and the just that divides humanity is justified by the seriousness of the philosophic question regarding the right way of life, which is a political question. The same problem that underlies the political also propels the Socratic question, and finds its ultimate justification in it. Without disagreement regarding the right way of life, the question would come to a halt. It should be noted that, once again, Strauss selects his words carefully: while the term *"Rechtsgrund"* doubtless has particular resonance for an eminent legal scholar like Schmitt, it is also an important pointer to his own position. As it was argued in the previous chapters, one of the keys to Strauss's early works is the *Rechtsfrage*, the question of the legitimacy of modernity in its pervasive critique of the premodern religious and philosophical traditions. In the wake of his investigation of Spinoza's critique, and guided by his study of Lessing and medieval Jewish and Islamic philosophy, he learned to see this question as an instance of an older and more fundamental question: the Socratic question of the right life.

In contrast to Schmitt, Strauss starts from the classical concept of the political: the civil or political condition of man is the natural state of man, and the question regarding nature, regarding the most natural way of living together, is therefore a political question.[128] The philosophical affirmation of the political thus entails a critical positioning with regard to both Hobbes and Schmitt. To begin with, it is aimed as much against the Hobbesian negation of the political as against its historical effects. To some extent, Strauss shares Schmitt's aversion of the prospect of a depoliticized global community of consumers, of the pursuit of peace and security at any price, and of the blind faith in the stabilizing power of technology.[129] Nevertheless, he is less interested in the consequences of Hobbes's negation of the political than in the philosophical motivation that informs it. As we will see later on, his principal objection against Hobbes is not so much that he has made the Socratic question impossible, but rather that he gave rise to the ideals of culture and civilization without having properly raised or even understood the question in the first place.[130] Second, the Socratic understanding of the political indicates a decisive step in bringing to light the hidden premises and difficulties of Schmitt's position. Strauss's general tactic consists in approaching and reinforcing Schmitt's thesis as a political-philosophical thesis, in order to show subsequently that it can only lead to a radical critique of liberal thought when it is based on classical political philosophy and thus on the Socratic question.

In the remainder of his review, Strauss returns to his earlier observation that underlying Schmitt's affirmation of the political is, in fact, an affirmation of morality. More specifically, he wonders how this concern can be brought into line with Schmitt's vituperations against those who uphold the primacy of morality over politics. Once again, the explanation can be found in Schmitt's polemics: his critical stabs are chiefly aimed against humanitarian and pacifist morality, which attempts to usher in the end of politics. As Strauss remarks, however, this means that Schmitt implicitly recognizes and acknowledges the object of his critique as a genuine morality, instead of dismissing it as a fraud or a nonentity. Moreover, Schmitt rejects this morality on the basis of his own contrary moral position, which he claims has become necessary in response to the process of neutralization. In Schmitt's Weberian view, however, all moral convictions and ideals are based on a private decision without any publicly binding character. Since this necessarily also applies to his moral defense of the political, he is only able to posit the publicly binding character of the political by reverting to the subterfuge of presenting it as an ineluctable destiny. The success of this stratagem, however, does not do away with the fact that Schmitt's understanding of morality as essentially private is, as Strauss remarks, a typically liberal view. This shows that Schmitt's polemic remains essentially tied to the conceptual framework of its opponent.

However, there is another, albeit related, difficulty. Insofar as Schmitt's affirmation of the Hobbesian state of war concerns the state of war *as such*, it is entirely indifferent and neutral regarding what is actually at stake in the conflict, the specific content of the distinction between friend and foe, and thus also regarding the particular decision that underlies it. In this neutrality and indifference, it is nothing less than the mirror image of liberal neutrality and tolerance regarding every moral conviction. In this sense, Strauss argues, Schmitt's position is in fact "liberalism preceded by a minus-sign (*mit umgekehrtem Vorzeichen*)."[131] In this way, Strauss finds confirmation for his initial suggestion: Schmitt remains caught within the system of liberal thought. By dint of both its polemical and its essentially private character, his critique exhibits the strength and coherence of this system.

On the basis of this result, Strauss suggests that even the affirmation of the moral is not Schmitt's ultimate target. Rather, his "last word" lies beyond the affirmation of both the political and the moral: it is to restore "the order of human things" (*die Ordnung der menschlichen Dinge*) by means of "pure, unpolluted knowledge" (*integres Wissen*) that must be gained from a return to "undefiled, uncorrupted nature" (*unversehrte, nicht korrupte Natur*).[132] As Strauss goes on to point out, however, this goal contradicts Schmitt's own premises: the notion of "pure, unpolluted knowledge" is incompatible with his basic proposition that all concepts are polemical and dependent on their political and existential condition. Here again, Strauss's criticism is at once revealing of his own orientation:

> For pure, unpolluted knowledge is never, except accidentally, polemical; and pure unpolluted knowledge cannot be gained from "the concrete political existence," from the situation of the age, but only through a return to the origin, to undefiled, not corrupt nature."[133]

The return Schmitt envisages is possible only through a recovery of Socratic-Platonic political philosophy, Strauss argues. Although this orientation is not made explicit, it is, in fact, the key by which he understands Schmitt's guiding intention from the outset. Already at the beginning of his review, he notes that "Schmitt sets out to do no more than to ascertain *what is*," as if *The Concept of the Political* were a typical Socratic inquiry.[134] This rapprochement, however, is only intended to bring to light the profound differences between Schmitt's position and the Socratic position. From the perspective of the latter, only the classical philosophic question regarding the best state can lead to "unpolluted knowledge" and thus to an understanding of the political that is neither purely private nor liberal "preceded by a minus-sign," and that avoids the pitfalls of historicism and decisionism.

From the Socratic point of view, moreover, it is possible to develop a moral-political outlook on human evil without reverting to a hidden religious framework as in the case of Schmitt. According to Socrates's well-known dictum, "virtue is knowledge" and thus vice is based on ignorance. However, when one recalls that true, unpolluted knowledge is Socratic knowledge of one's ignorance regarding the fundamental issues, it follows that only the philosopher is truly concerned with knowledge and thus is truly virtuous. The qualitative difference between philosophers and non-philosophers implies that political disagreement regarding the good and the just will continue to arise. Genuine agreement is possible only on the basis of philosophic knowledge of ignorance regarding these issues. Strauss's philosophical affirmation of the political, unlike that of Schmitt, thus leaves room for a form of friendship that is not completely determined by the distinction between friend and foe: the friendship between philosophers who agree on the fundamental problems.[135]

For Strauss, restoring "the order of human things" is nothing less than the retrieval of the Socratic question from liberal oblivion. Schmitt's unpolemical version of the Hobbesian state of nature, however, is unsuited as a source of pure, unpolluted knowledge. Moreover, Strauss suggests, Schmitt's polemical entanglement in liberal thought is not the only thing that prevents him from pursuing a philosophical affirmation of the political. Ultimately, Schmitt's affirmation of the political and the moral has a *theological* foundation: his polemic against liberalism is based on a political theology of Christian origin, which contains a specific conception of the order of human things and thus also a specific answer to the question of the right way of life. The supra-individual obligation Schmitt advocates is that of a faith in revelation and incarnation, which views human moral evil in the light of the doctrine of the Fall and of original sin. In his review, Strauss alludes to this background when he argues that Schmitt's affirmation of the political can only *prepare* the radical critique of liberalism, since the latter is not the opponent he really envisages:

> The polemic against liberalism can therefore have no meaning other than that of a subsidiary or preparatory action. It is undertaken only to clear the field for the decisive battle between the "spirit of technology," the "mass faith of an anti-religious, this-worldly activism" and . . . the opposite spirit and faith, which, it seems, does not yet have a name. In the end, two completely opposed answers to the question of what is right permit no mediation and no neutrality. . . . Schmitt's ultimate concern is then not the fight against liberalism. For this very reason the affirmation of the political as such is not his last word. His last word is "the order of human things."[136]

With measured irony, Strauss intimates that the name of "the opposite spirit and faith" is all too well-known to him. The final battle Schmitt wishes to initiate is the fight between his Christian faith and modern activist atheism. It is hardly surprising that Strauss characterizes *both* opponents as *answers* to "the question of what is right." As we saw in the previous chapter, he criticizes modern atheism from probity as a form of belief tributary to biblical morality. In this respect, both opponents are distinguished from classical, Socratic-Platonic philosophy, which does not attempt to mediate let alone synthesize, but rather harks back to and persists in what precedes both answers: the question of what is right. For we should not forget that, according to Strauss, "by the seriousness of the *question* of what is right, the political is justified."[137]

With his remark about Schmitt's "last word," Strauss reveals the chasm between political theology and political philosophy, precisely by indicating how Schmitt conceals his political-theological position behind an ostensible return to nature and the thesis of the ineluctability of the political. His critical reading of *The Concept of the Political* shows that Schmitt's stratagem is inspired by the power of liberal thought, which continues to exhibit an "astoundingly consistent system" despite the failure of the process of neutralization.[138] From Schmitt's attempt, Strauss learns that, in order to escape from the hold of the liberal system, one must face its originator:

> The critique of liberalism that Schmitt has initiated can therefore be completed only when we succeed in gaining a horizon beyond liberalism. Within such a horizon Hobbes achieved the foundation of liberalism. A radical critique of liberalism is therefore possible only on the basis of an adequate understanding of Hobbes.[139]

While this is indeed the "urgent task" Strauss sets himself, its formulation is somewhat deceptive. It seems to suggest that adequately understanding Hobbes is both the necessary and the sufficient condition for gaining a horizon beyond liberalism. In fact, as Strauss's scattered allusions in the review show, he has *already* begun to recover the horizon beyond liberalism within and against which Hobbes founded liberalism and the modern concept of culture: the horizon of *nomos* or law as a "concrete binding order of life," common to revealed religion and Socratic-Platonic philosophy. This is corroborated by a remark in *Philosophy and Law*, where he argues with explicit reference to his review of Schmitt that "'religion' and 'politics' are *the* facts that transcend 'culture' or, to be more precise, the *original* facts."[140] According to its own self-understanding, religion cannot be reduced to one cultural product among many because it is based on a claim to truth and obedience that is not of human but of divine origin. Similarly, politics in the classical view is not a cultural product but a natural condition of man. If religion and politics are *cruces* or stumbling blocks for liberalism and the modern concept of culture, by the same token they are the necessary point of departure for a radical critique:

> [T]he radical critique of the concept of "culture" is possible only in the form of a "theologico-political treatise,"—which of course, if it is not to lead back again to the foundation of "culture," must take exactly the opposite direction from the theologico-political treatises of the seventeenth century, especially those of Hobbes and Spinoza. The first condition for this would be, of course, that these seventeenth-century works no longer be understood, as they almost always have been up to now, within the horizon of philosophy of culture."[141]

Here again, Strauss is reticent about the fact that *Philosophy and Law* itself is *already* an attempt to meet these requirements. It is a "theologico-political treatise" that aims to recover the ancient "illiberal" horizon of *nomos* against which Hobbes and Spinoza established liberalism, modern culture, and civilization. In this process, Strauss is guided by the medieval Islamic and Jewish philosophers, whose own theologico-political treatises indeed run counter to those of Hobbes and Spinoza, insofar as they point back to Socrates and Plato.[142] In this sense, *Philosophy and Law* shows how Strauss is learning to look at modernity from the perspective of premodern thought, an effort that also informs his review of Schmitt. This may clarify a particularly enigmatic statement in his autobiographical preface to *Spinoza's Critique of Religion*, in which he alludes to his breakthrough. Taking a stern and critical look at his first book, he writes:

The present study was based on the premise, sanctioned by powerful prejudice, that a return to pre-modern philosophy is impossible. The change of orientation which found its expression, not entirely by accident, in the article published at the end of this volume, compelled me to engage in a number of studies in the course of which I became ever more attentive to the manner in which heterodox thinkers of earlier ages wrote their books.[143]

The "article published at the end of this volume" to which Strauss refers is none other than the review of Schmitt's *The Concept of the Political*, which was reprinted at the end of the first edition of *Spinoza's Critique of Religion*. The "change of orientation" that found its first expression in this writing is his overcoming of the historicist prejudice and the rediscovery of original Platonic philosophy, its Socratic program, and its particular art of writing. Nevertheless, why does Strauss add that this change found its first expression "not entirely by accident" in the review of Schmitt? With the benefit of hindsight, it is possible to suggest an answer. As we have seen, the moment of his philosophical breakthrough coincides with his departure from political Zionism, political activism, and modern politics as such. With the recovery of the Socratic question and the Platonic horizon, Strauss encounters a way of life that proves to be more fulfilling than the political life. As he notes in one of the early lectures mentioned earlier, "Socrates gives an answer to the question regarding the right way of life: *raising the question regarding the right way of life—this alone is the right way of life*."[144]

This may help explain why Strauss chooses to divulge his "change of orientation" in a commentary on *The Concept of the Political*. In Schmitt, he finds not only an acute critic of liberalism, but also a powerful defender of the two authoritative alternatives to the philosophic life he is trying to recover.[145] For within the illiberal horizon, politics and religion are the two "original facts" the philosophic life has to face in order to justify itself and thus be truly philosophic. Schmitt's political theology offered an appropriate opportunity for Strauss to test this new understanding of the theological-political problem. Subsequently, he is able to turn to a thinker who, like Spinoza, wrote theological-political treatises in order to establish the liberal horizon that would eclipse the original facts.

# CHAPTER 5

# Socrates and the Leviathan

*We may as bootless spend our vain command*
*Upon the enraged soldiers in their spoil*
*As send precepts to the leviathan*
*To come ashore.*

—Shakespeare, *Henry V*, III.3

## Hobbes's Motive

Strauss's review of Schmitt already provides some brief indications as to how he intends to approach his new object of research. As he notes in the conclusion, Hobbes, "living in an illiberal world, lays the foundation of liberalism" against the "illiberal" state of nature. The Hobbesian state of nature is thus a "counterconcept" (*Gegenbegriff*), directed as much against the Biblical notion of original sin as against the classical understanding of nature. This observation, however, gives rise to the same question that animated *Spinoza's Critique of Religion*: what is the mainspring, the motive underlying this opposition? As Strauss argued, Hobbes's negation of the state of nature is diametrically opposed to Schmitt's affirmation of the political. If the latter proves to be based on an ulterior concern (morality, in Schmitt's case), might not this apply to the former as well?

That this question indeed forms the Leitmotiv of Strauss's subsequent research on Hobbes is borne out by an article of 1933 entitled "Some Remarks on Hobbes's Political Science."[1] In this article, Strauss discusses the conditions and prerequisites of what he considers to be "an adequate understanding of Hobbes." First, he asserts, we must assume that we can learn from Hobbes certain things we cannot learn from the present. By admitting that Hobbes can actually teach us something, moreover, we admit that we know too little or perhaps even nothing at all about important present matters. It also implies that we have to read his work with the utmost seriousness:

> This imposes on the interpreter the duty of seeing to it with the utmost care that the opinions reigning or tending to reign today are not carried over into Hobbes's thought. For every such modification of the "facts" would from the outset deprive the study of Hobbes's politics of the possible benefit it might have for the elucidation of current political opinions.[2]

Subsequently, Strauss goes on to explain what this approach consists of: one must pay attention to the internal coherence of Hobbes's work, and look for its most original and most authentic "tendency" (*Tendenz*). The latter, he claims, comes to light most clearly where Hobbes turns against the tradition. On this point, Strauss takes issue with contemporary interpretations, which locate Hobbes's antitraditional thrust in his naturalistic and scientific approach to ethics and politics. Against this view, he submits a crucial historical observation with important philosophical consequences: Hobbes only discovered natural science and its method at an advanced age, *after* his basic ethical and political views had already taken shape.[3] Of course, the older Hobbes subsequently attempted to deduce these views from the new scientific premises. Nevertheless, Strauss wonders, doesn't this mean that his original antitraditional tendency can already be found in his earlier views and thus be understood independently of its later scientific elaboration?

> [I]sn't it possible to fully understand his political science without taking into account the ulterior naturalistic foundation? . . . This possibility becomes a necessity, if it should turn out to be the case that Hobbes's most profound anthropological and political thoughts are obscured rather than clarified by the ulterior naturalistic foundation (not to say anything about the fact that, in the end, naturalism as such is not so "natural" that one would not also and precisely have to query *its* human and not already scientific roots.[4]

As Strauss argues, there are indications that this original, antitraditional and nonnaturalistic basis is *moral*. Thus, he points out that Hobbes distinguishes between justice and injustice already on the most fundamental level of his naturalistic theory, when he establishes the "right of nature," and not, as is generally assumed, when he goes on to establish the "law of nature."[5] More particularly, Hobbes asserts that, in the state of nature, man moves between two poles. On the one hand, there is the unlimited natural desire to please oneself and to be recognized as superior by others. This drive, Strauss observes, has a negative moral connotation: Hobbes characterizes it as *vanity*, because it makes man live as if in a dream and thus prevents him from recognizing his real situation. In this way, it leads to an increasing striving after power and thus to ever more violent conflict.

Vanity, however, is limited and held in check by the other pole: the human fear of violent death at the hands of others. This fear originates when man is in mortal danger and is compelled to recognize death as *summum malum*, the greatest evil. For Hobbes, this pole has a positive connotation: fear of violent death awakens man from his dreams of power, confronts him with reality, and makes him realize that he must squelch his desire in order to survive. In this way, the unlimited and *unjustified* natural desire is reduced to a limited and *justified* and reasonable demand, which subsequently comes to determine the content of the right of nature. Fear thus has an essentially rationalizing and enlightening effect: it is the source of human self-consciousness, reason, and conscience. With this view, Hobbes reveals himself to be an early Enlightenment thinker, Strauss holds: "In the opposition between vanity and fear the Enlightenment character of Hobbes's philosophy reveals itself."[6]

What is more, this fundamental opposition makes Hobbes the founder of liberalism. It points toward the modern opposition between politics and economics, more particularly to the battle of the latter against the former, which for Strauss, as for Schmitt, is characteristic of liberalism:

> For every fight against the political in the name of the economical presupposes the preliminary depreciation of the political. However, this depreciation occurs in this way, that the political, understood as the domain of vanity, prestige and the will to dominate (*Geltungswille*), is opposed—either covertly or openly—to the economical, understood as the world of rational, pragmatic and modest labor.[7]

The bourgeois ideal of civilization and enlightenment founded by Hobbes aims at general stability for the sake of peaceful production and trade. Since politics is perceived as the realm of vanity and strife, this goal can only be attained through economics, the realm of rationality and sobriety. At the same time, Strauss holds, the Hobbesian opposition of vanity and fear also points back to the past. At first view, it may seem to be the secularized equivalent of the old Christian opposition between *superbia* (pride) and *humilitas* (humility). According to Strauss, however, this opposition, while influential, was not decisive, since Hobbes denies sin, and his natural law doctrine aims precisely to distinguish meaningfully between good and evil on the basis of man's natural state. Rather, the opposition between vanity and fear is a modern modification of an antagonism introduced by Socrates and Plato, between the illusory good pursued in politics and the true good pursued by philosophy, or between opinion and knowledge. As Hobbes characteristically claims, his modern version of this old antagonism exhibits a more profound understanding of human nature. In order to assess this claim, Strauss suggests, it must be compared and confronted with the Socratic-Platonic claim:

> The path from vanity to fear is the way from unreflectiveness (*Besinnungslosigkeit*) to circumspection (*Besonnenheit*), from the shining delusion of "the political life" to the truly Good that is only accessible to rational understanding. This means: the opposition vanity-fear is the modern modification, determined by Christianity, of the opposition classically expounded by Socrates-Plato. For this reason, a radical understanding and a well-founded judgment of Hobbesian politics is in fact only possible if one confronts it directly with Platonic politics. Only in this way can it be ascertained whether the modification, intended by Hobbes and in fact determined by Christianity, of ancient ideas is actually based on a more profound understanding of human nature, and what this concern for "profundity" actually entails.[8]

As in the case of Spinoza, Hobbes's claim to greater originality and profundity—to modernity—can only be assessed correctly "in its act or exercise," in direct confrontation with the two dominant forces of the premodern illiberal horizon: Christian revealed religion and Platonic political philosophy.[9] This approach indeed determines Strauss's subsequent investigations, as becomes apparent from two separate book manuscripts he prepares between 1933 and 1936: *The Political Philosophy of Hobbes: Its Basis and Its Genesis* and *Hobbes's Critique of Religion: A Contribution to the Understanding of the Enlightenment*.[10] While the first manuscript is mainly devoted to Hobbes's critical reception of Greek historians and philosophers, the title of the second clearly indicates that it is intended as a continuation of *Spinoza's Critique of Religion*, focusing on Hobbes's polemic against Christianity and revealed religion in general.

In spite of the difference in focus, however, the texts are intended as two complementary parts of one and the same endeavor. As Strauss already suggests in the preliminary article, Hobbes's critical reception of Platonic politics was determined by his critical reception of Christianity. Read in conjunction, the two texts make the remarkable case that Hobbes's critique of classical political philosophy misses its mark because he remains entangled in his polemic with Christianity. As Strauss contends at the beginning of *Hobbes's Critique of Religion*: "it is revelation, respectively the polemic against revelation, which makes it impossible for Hobbes to recognize and appreciate ancient politics."[11] In good Aristotelian fashion, then, *The Political Philosophy of Hobbes* identifies the error, while *Hobbes's Critique of Religion* goes on to locate the source of the error. However, just as with Maimonides and the *falasifa*, Strauss's path ultimately leads to Socrates and Plato, and just as with the medieval Enlightenment, Strauss not only looks *at* Plato's perspective from a different vantage point, but he also looks back at the vantage point *from* Plato's perspective.[12]

## "The Right Order of Society"

Strauss's Platonic orientation is reflected mainly in the composition of *The Political Philosophy of Hobbes: Its Basis and Its Genesis*. After a brief introduction, the second chapter deals with "The Moral Basis," while the eighth and final chapter, "The New Political Science," is entirely devoted to a confrontation between Hobbes and Plato. In the preceding chapters of the book, however, the relationship between Hobbes and classical thought is constantly present. In the introduction, Strauss makes three decisive points that clearly elaborate on the preliminary article previously discussed. Already in the opening sentence, he indicates that Hobbes will be investigated within a framework and with a focus that cannot be identified otherwise than as Socratic-Platonic:

> Hobbes's political philosophy is the first peculiarly modern attempt to give a coherent and exhaustive answer to the question of man's right life, which is at the same time the question of the right order of society. . . . Hobbes's political philosophy is of supreme importance not only for political philosophy as such, i.e. for one branch of knowledge among others, but for modern philosophy altogether, if the discussion and elucidation of the ideal of life is indeed the primary and decisive task of philosophy.[13]

The second point takes up Strauss's earlier position on the question of interpretation: Hobbes's political philosophy has a moral basis that precedes and is independent of the naturalistic, scientific approach he adopted later. Nevertheless, this basis is entirely new when compared with the tradition: "The moral attitude which underlies Hobbes's political philosophy is independent of the foundation of modern science, and at least in that sense 'pre-scientific'. It is at the same time specifically modern. One is inclined to say that it is the deepest stratum of the modern mind."[14] Third, Strauss connects the situation in which Hobbes thought and wrote with the present situation. Hobbes, he argues, raised the question of the right way of life at a moment when the traditional answers to this question had lost their authority, and with his own answer he laid the foundation of modern thought. This foundation, however, has been hidden from view by the further development of modern thought. "The structure which Hobbes, led by the inspiration of the moment, began to raise, hid the foundation as long as the structure stood, i.e. as long as its stability was believed in."[15] Now that the belief in its stability has ceased to be self-evident, it is necessary to return to the foundation of the structure. The necessity of this return, however, points back to the question of the right life, which remains the focus of Strauss's investigations throughout.

Thus, the tone is set for the second chapter, devoted to the moral basis and basically an elaboration of the argument proposed in the preliminary article: at the core of Hobbes's political philosophy is a moral position that is independent of his ulterior naturalistic and scientific approach. Underlying Hobbes's theory of human nature, Strauss now explains, is a tension between an anthropological orientation on the one hand and a naturalistic orientation on the other. This tension can be made visible by focusing on two postulates of Hobbes's theory, namely, "natural appetite" and "natural reason." As Strauss observes, Hobbes offers both a purely mechanistic and a vitalistic definition of the first postulate. Despite the fact that these definitions point in markedly different directions, both refer to an irrational and unlimited striving for superiority and recognition, which Hobbes defines as "vain-glory," "pride," or "vanity." This, Strauss argues, reveals the true origin of the postulate.[16] In either of its definitions, the determination of natural appetite as vanity presupposes a *moral* judgment. Thus, on the fundamental level, Hobbes distinguishes between admissible and inadmissible striving for power, while defining the natural striving for power of man as inadmissible, vain, evil.

For this reason, Strauss firmly rejects the interpretation that Hobbes somehow attempts to construct an "amoral morality": "Hobbes's political philosophy rests not on the illusion of an amoral morality, but on a new morality, or, to speak according to Hobbes's intention, on a new grounding of the one eternal morality."[17] At first view, this seems to be a departure from the line of argument he had developed against Schmitt's moral understanding of human dangerousness, arguing that for Hobbes and Spinoza human dangerousness is mere natural force. If this is the case, however, it does not yet mean a vindication of Schmitt's position. Rather, Strauss tries to show that for Hobbes the normative moment is indispensable in order to establish the core of his "new morality," the primacy of individual right over transindividual obligation. This becomes apparent when we look at the second postulate, that of natural reason. Here again, Strauss points to an ambiguity: Hobbes defines this postulate both as "avoiding violent death as the greatest natural evil" and as "preserving life as the primary good." As Strauss explains, the solution lies in the difference between "the primary good" and the "greatest evil": for Hobbes, there is no *summum bonum*, or highest good, only a *summum malum* or greatest evil. Hence, only the fear of violent death can be a reliable foundation for a theory of human nature.[18] Although this fear, like vanity, is irrational, it has a rationalizing effect. The threat of violent death is an unexpected resistance that awakens man from his delusions of power and confronts him with reality. The power of this experience is such that Hobbes goes so far as to identify human self-consciousness and human conscience with the fear of violent death. Fear causes man to understand that only the minimal demand of self-preservation is legitimate and reasonable: in this respect, it constitutes the basis for morality, law, and the state.

Like vanity, fear has a moral significance. This, Strauss holds, is borne out by the fact that, in the state of nature, Hobbes holds every action to be admissible, but not every intention. While every action can be considered necessary for self-preservation, only those intentions that spring from the fear are justified. As a result, the right of nature also has a moral content: contrary to what is generally assumed, Hobbes makes a meaningful distinction between just and unjust that *precedes* the conclusion of the social contract and the subsequent obligation to honor it. According to Strauss, this distinction, the basis of Hobbes's political philosophy, is "not the naturalistic antithesis of morally indifferent animal appetite (or of morally indifferent human striving after power) on the one hand, and morally indifferent striving after self-preservation on the other, but the moral and humanist antithesis of fundamentally unjust vanity and fundamentally just fear of violent death."[19] Moreover, Strauss again cautions against reducing this antithesis to a secularized version of the biblical antithesis between *superbia* and *humilitas*. Regardless of whether there is actually a connection, this would fail to do justice to the specific, positive significance of Hobbes's endeavor: to find a meaningful distinction between just and unjust that is in accordance with human nature as such. Without such a distinction, his political theory would end up in a complete naturalism incapable of differentiating between power and legitimacy, between force and law. Only by giving the fundamental antithesis a moral content was Hobbes able to present his natural right doctrine as an answer to "the specifically human problem of right."[20]

In the fourth chapter of his book, Strauss further elaborates the connection between the moral character of fear as the basis of legitimate intentions and the primacy of natural right. This he does by focusing on the historical shifts in Hobbes's attitude with regard to aristocratic virtue. As he shows, Hobbes initially had great admiration for the moral views of the aristocratic Cavendish family, for whom he worked as a teacher and a secretary. He integrated this admiration in an Aristotelian framework by means of the concept of *megalopsuchia* (*magnanimitas* or "great-souledness"), by which he understood ambition, heroism, and courage. As he developed his new political philosophy, however, he moved away from both the aristocratic ideal and Aristotelianism. At first, Hobbes no longer regarded magnanimity as a state (*hexis*) in which man exists, but rather as an intention. Subsequently, he discarded magnanimity altogether and only retained intention as a moral principle.[21] The turn toward intention was thus accompanied by a departure from the Aristotelian framework in which virtue was measured by a binding natural order:

> The intention becomes for Hobbes the one and only moral principle, because he no longer believes in the existence of an "objective" principle according to which man must order his actions—in the existence of a natural law which precedes all human volition . . . The denial of a natural law, of an obligation which precedes all human contracts, is the final reason why the intention . . . is considered as sufficient reason for all virtue."[22]

The denial of a natural law preceding all human volition is accompanied by the recognition of a natural right that precedes all obligations. Behind this natural right, we saw earlier, is ultimately the antithesis between vanity and fear of violent death. Only the latter can give rise to a legitimate intention, which shows that for Hobbes fear is indeed the foundation of morality.[23] By regarding the fear of violent death and the right to self-preservation as the basis for all virtues, Hobbes breaks decisively with aristocratic virtue. Every motive other than fear that could impel man to risk his life is suspect in his eyes: courage, ambition, self-sacrifice, heroism, but also patriotism. As a matter of consistency, he therefore holds desertion in wartime to be justified, though dishonorable.[24] In this way, Strauss argues, he became the founder of bourgeois morality, which puts politics at the service of the development and cultivation of justice, charity, thrift, and industry—the necessary conditions for comfortable self-preservation.[25]

Fear of violent death as the source of human self-consciousness is Hobbes's "last word," Strauss asserts. It comes as no surprise, then, that he goes on to discuss Hobbes's relationship to classical political philosophy. Thus, he points out that for Hobbes fear is not only the basis of morality, law, and the state, but also of science or philosophy. Vanity gives rise to presumption, ignorance, prejudice, and superstition, all of which can only be eradicated by the sudden threat of violent death and the fear that accompanies it. As Strauss indicates, this implies that "the world is originally revealed to man not by detachedly and spontaneously seeing its form, but by involuntary experience of its resistance."[26] In other words, Hobbes's view is directly opposed to classical *theoria*: the origin of science is not contemplation of the natural order, but the compulsive involvement of fear, which forcibly imposes reality on man and thus has a liberating, enlightening effect. It also implies that Hobbes in fact puts science at the service of the human interest in self-preservation and acquisition of power, an eminently practical function.[27] As man in his naked, precarious existence comes to occupy the center of Hobbes's reflections, the primacy shifts from theory to praxis. Thus, in the third chapter, where he discusses the changes in Hobbes's perception of Aristotle, Strauss notes: "He [Hobbes] certainly knew and valued the joys of knowledge no less than any other philosopher; but these joys are for him not the justification of philosophy; he finds its justification only in benefit to man, i.e. the safeguarding of man's life and the increase of human power."[28]

Although Hobbes abandoned scholasticism at an early stage, he held on to Aristotelian ethics and politics for some time. According to Strauss, however, this was a "decapitated" Aristotelianism, since Hobbes replaced theoretical philosophy and metaphysics with practical philosophy as the highest science. This difference is closely related to a difference in their respective views on man's place in the cosmos: "Aristotle justified his placing of the theoretical sciences above moral and political philosophy by the argument that man is not the highest being of the universe. This ultimate assumption of the primacy of theory is rejected by Hobbes; in his contention man is 'the most excellent work of nature.'"[29] According to Strauss, the essentially practical and anthropocentric orientation underlying Hobbes's new political science becomes most visible in the fact that his departure from Aristotelianism is accompanied by a turn toward history and historiography. This turn, as well as in the philosophical motives that animate it, contains Hobbes's greatest achievement, but also his greatest shortcoming.

The reason Hobbes focuses on history is his increasing doubt regarding the applicability and the effectiveness of traditional Aristotelianism's ethical precepts. Initially, he turns to history in search of examples of success and failure in their application, with a view to better understanding its conditions and rendering it more efficient. In this study, he pays particular attention to the passions, because in his view they provide the most reliable knowledge about the real motives of man.[30] Subsequently, however, he radically calls into question the effectiveness and applicability of the traditional precepts, and replaces them with the study of history now understood as *magistra vitae*, a teacher of life. According to Hobbes, only the study of man as he really is allows the creation of applicable and effective norms, whereas the traditional approach fruitlessly focuses on how man ought to be. As Strauss remarks, with this latter view Hobbes joins the critique of tradition formulated by Machiavelli and elaborated by Francis Bacon and Spinoza.[31] Finally, Hobbes comes to doubt the utility of historiography altogether. For, as Strauss observes, the practical need for applicability is ultimately determined by the fundamental question of the right order of society. To this question, historiography seems unable to offer any effective answer.

As a result, Hobbes is led to construct a hypothetical "typical" history from which the right order may be deduced: the abolishment of an untenably defective state of nature into a stable and secure civil state.[32] The defectiveness of the state of nature must be magnified as far as possible, so that the necessity of the transition to the civil state can be seen to spontaneously follow from it. In this construction, the study of the passions no longer fulfills a merely subordinate role, but it becomes the cornerstone. The norms of a new morality, the morality of the right order, are defined with a view to the most extreme situation and to the passions that attend it in order to guarantee a maximum of applicability.[33] In this way, we are led back to the fundamental antithesis of vanity and fear of violent death.

In this way, the development that began with the turn to history comes to an end. Hobbes integrates history in his new political philosophy by founding the principles of a new applicable morality on a typical account. In this way, the appeal to existing historiography becomes superfluous. The right social order realizes itself out of and against the chaos of the state of nature, driven by a perfectly human principle: the will, driven by fear of violent death, to abolish the state of nature.[34] According to Strauss, the movement encapsulated in this anthropocentric premise is the basis of the modern concept of progress. Henceforth, the historical course that led up to the present is regarded as a process of irreversible improvement that guarantees the possibility of further improvement.[35] Since all order is immanent and of human origin, there are no limits to man's ordering activity: this, Strauss holds, is the historical core of Hobbes's political thought as well as the basis of the modern concept of culture.

Hobbes's doubts regarding the effectiveness and applicability of the traditional precepts, which deepen as he turns toward history, are a clear sign that he is fundamentally convinced of the impotence of human reason to apply and live according to the precepts, Strauss argues.[36] The study of man as he really is reveals that disobedience is the rule and obedience the exception. Hence, in turning to history, Hobbes aims to replace the old morality of obedience to a transcendent order with a morality that makes obedience realizable, by enabling man to comply with its norms despite the impotence of reason. Hobbes's political philosophy, which makes the political order completely immanent, is thus the most coherent and profound response to this requirement. The way in which he first turns to history, only to incorporate it into his new philosophy, shows that he raises the question of the right political order exclusively and from the very beginning with a view to practical applicability. Only on the basis of his fundamental anthropocentric orientation does his attempt to raise the Socratic question require the turn to history.[37] The Hobbesian answer to the question—bourgeois morality *in ovo*—no longer points towards a higher order and man's place within it, but only to intersubjectivity: "the right life of man is understood exclusively as an emanation of his right self-consciousness. . . . [I]t is, in other words, not knowledge of the place which is essentially due to man in the cosmos, but is a right consciousness in the human individual of himself in relation to other human individuals."[38]

Once again, Strauss contrasts Hobbes's position with the classical view he opposes and rejects. Still, he goes on to ask, what exactly does Hobbes oppose when he puts man at the center, doubts the power of human reason, and turns to history? After all, he could raise the issue of the applicability of the traditional moral precepts only because he assumed that the preliminary issue—the philosophical foundation of the precepts themselves—had been settled in an authoritative and thus self-evident manner by tradition, more precisely by Aristotle:

> Because the formulation and the explanation of these precepts had been fully and adequately completed by Aristotle, because the primary philosophic problem had been solved, because its solution had become a matter of course, because of all this a philosopher like Hobbes had the leisure and the opportunity to give thought to the secondary problem of the application of the precepts.[39]

In this passage, Strauss implicitly passes a critical judgment: instead of relying on the traditional view and taking the Aristotelian solution for granted, "a philosopher like Hobbes" should have concentrated first on "the primary philosophic problem." What this problem entails is made clear in the final chapter of *The Political Philosophy of Hobbes*, where Strauss develops his initial remark into a full-fledged and incisive critique, the core of which can be summarized as follows. In conceiving his new, antitraditional political philosophy, Hobbes starts from the traditional assumption that political philosophy is possible and even necessary. In this assumption, however, the founder of modern political philosophy differs from the founders of classical political philosophy: for Socrates and Plato, the possibility and necessity of political philosophy are and remain a permanent problem, insofar as the question "How should we live?" is always coeval with the question "Why philosophy?" and thus insofar as the question of the right life is always a political question.[40]

Blinded on this decisive point by the Christian-Aristotelian tradition, Hobbes launches his antitraditional philosophy from a position that is insufficiently radical and thus insufficiently philosophical. This, Strauss argues, is the reason why he came to regard the conception of a new political philosophy as a question of method only after he had discovered Euclidean geometry and Galilean natural science. This discovery consolidated, as it were, the initial oblivion at the heart of his political philosophy:

> [T]he introduction of this method into political philosophy presupposes the previous narrowing-down of the political question, i.e. the elimination of the fundamental question as to the aim of the State. The introduction of Galileo's method into political science is thus bought at the price that the new political science from the outset renounces all discussion of the fundamental, the most urgent question. This neglect of the truly primary question is the result of Hobbes's conviction that the idea of political philosophy is a matter of course. Hobbes does not question the possibility and necessity of political philosophy; in other words, he does not ask first "what is virtue?" and "can it be taught?" and "what is the aim of the State?", because these questions have been answered for him by tradition, or by common opinion.[41]

Hobbes's blindness to the nontraditional origins of the tradition of classical political philosophy becomes apparent when we focus on the connection between his discovery of geometry and of the modern scientific method and his attitude with regard to Plato, Strauss argues. From the moment Hobbes becomes acquainted with the work of Euclid and Galileo, he begins to develop the idea of an exact and scientific approach to morality and politics. On the one hand, this *desideratum* leads to a departure from Aristotle, who contends that the scientific understanding of moral and political things can only be approximate and imprecise. On the other hand, Hobbes's quest for an exact science of politics is accompanied by a growing admiration for Plato. Unlike Aristotle, Hobbes holds, Plato succeeded in liberating himself from the spell cast over human understanding by the senses, the passions, words, and opinions. Plato's distrust of ordinary language and *doxa* led him to embrace a paradoxical political science critical of sense perception and guided by the Ideas and mathematics instead of by words.

According to Strauss, this view is nothing less than a caricature, based on a misunderstanding of the actual relationship between Aristotle and Plato.[42] For in reality Plato chooses to be guided by words, and by words alone. Of course, Strauss does not deny that Plato was critical with regard to ordinary language and its confusing, conflict-inducing imprecision. However, he rejects the inference that, as a result, Plato abandoned ordinary language altogether in his philosophy. On the contrary, he writes, "Plato's theory that the causes of things, the ideas, have a transcendent independent existence, rests on the fact that the ideas show this independence in speech. . . . Plato 'takes refuge' from things in human speech about things as the only entrance into the true reasons of things which is open to man."[43] Access to the ideas as the true causes is found in Socratic dialectic, which confronts contradictory opinions in search of the truth behind the contradiction. This truth is thus truly paradoxical and warrants the partial truth of the contradictory opinions:

> The most obvious contradictions which underlie every contention and every enmity, concern the just, the beautiful, and the good. And yet men are in greater concord as regards the good than as regards any other subject, and in such a fashion that this real concord is the ultimate ground of all possible concord.[44]

Precisely this "ultimate ground"—the object of Socratic inquiry—is absent in Hobbes's reading of Plato.[45] Inspired by the Cartesian pursuit of a *mathesis universalis*, a universal language, Hobbes starts from the erroneous—though immensely influential—assumption that Plato developed an ontology or "physiology" in order to transcend the contradictoriness of ordinary language. As a result, Strauss argues, he fails to see that Plato's paradoxical political philosophy is not based on any ontology or "physiology," but solely on dialectic.[46] The truth it uncovers are the fundamental and perennial problems that beget contradictory opinions about the good, the just, and the virtuous. To live in accordance with this truth, to lead a truly virtuous, philosophical life, is to be guided by these problems as an unchangeable normative order.[47]

Hence, Plato's political philosophy differs from that of Hobbes in its ambiguous, paradoxical attitude toward opinion. By way of illustration, Strauss discusses a theme crucial to political philosophy: courage. In Hobbesian politics, courage is not regarded as a virtue; rather, it is criticized as an illusion jeopardizing human self-preservation. In this way, Hobbes squarely opposed the prevailing opinion of his turbulent time, which valued courage highly. In fact, his new morality was aimed precisely at removing the grounds of this esteem, in order to secure the stability of bourgeois existence. Plato, on his part, also develops an incisive critique of courage, but in his case this does not lead to a wholesale rejection. Rather, Plato observes the reigning opinion—which views courage or *andreia* as the capacity to hold one's ground—but he remarks that glorification of courage in this definition ultimately leads to idealizing the life of the tyrant, who has the power to be fully autonomous.[48] From this, he infers that underlying courage is actually the natural self-love of man. For this same reason, however, courage cannot be the highest virtue for the philosopher, whose love primarily regards the truth. Rather, from the philosophical point of view, the highest virtue is wisdom. In that case, however, the problem arises that wisdom becomes more important than justice, which is the political virtue par excellence. As Strauss argues, Plato solves this difficulty by making a distinction that may sound more or less familiar: "It is not courage which is the highest virtue—self-mastery stands higher, and higher still than self-mastery stand wisdom and justice. In itself wisdom stands supreme, but justice stands supreme from an exoteric point of view."[49]

Although Strauss does not enlarge on this remark, he continues with a disquisition reminiscent of *Philosophy and Law*: although the philosopher as such transcends the political realm, as a human being he owes obedience to the laws of the polis and respect to its opinions. For this reason, Plato subjects the philosopher to the divine law of the best regime, which compels him to devote his wisdom to justice and the care of his fellow men. In this way, he exoterically preserves the primacy of justice and courage, while exoterically crowning wisdom as the highest virtue. We should not forget, however, that wisdom is understood here in the Socratic sense, as the awareness of ignorance regarding the good and the just.[50] The distinction between an esoteric and an exoteric dimension allows Plato to mediate between the political power of opinion and the philosophic pursuit of the truth, without detracting from either. In contrast, Hobbes's radical critique of courage starts from a passion that is equally developed in all human beings, and ultimately aims at eradicating the difference between esotericism and exotericism.

The only parallel between Hobbes and Plato, Strauss asserts, is that the antithesis between appearance and truth is of fundamental importance for both. "What Hobbes's political philosophy owes to Platonism is, therefore, its antithetic character, the constituent conception of the antithesis between truth and appearance, the fitting and the great, in the most extreme formulation, between reason and passion."[51] In this way, Strauss rejoins his earlier article, where he identified this antithesis as the touchstone of a genuine confrontation of Hobbes and Plato, allowing a correct assessment of Hobbes's claim to a more profound understanding of human nature. Hobbes's understanding of this antithesis, Strauss now finds, proves to be based on a complete break with Plato. The opposition between vanity and fear of violent death is the basis of an exact political science claiming universal applicability. In order to substantiate this claim, the place of reason in the original Platonic antithesis is now occupied by a passion. Hence, Strauss concludes, the basis of Hobbes's political philosophy is not the activity of reason, but a dynamic of opposed passions that is the sole guarantee of universal applicability. Hobbes's understanding of exactitude is diametrically opposed to that of Plato: while for the latter "exactness means the undistorted reliability of the standards," for Hobbes "exactness means the unconditional applicability, applicability under all circumstances, applicability in the extreme case."[52]

Unlike the Platonic standards, the Hobbesian criteria can easily be integrated in a scientific method, since they are designed from the outset with a view to practical application. In this context, Strauss refers to Hobbes's use of Galileo's "resoluto-compositive" method, the technique of resolving the studied object—this case the state—into its constituent parts and recomposing it with a view to improving it. The result of Hobbes's analysis is the antithesis between vanity and fear of violent death, out of which he subsequently proceeds to construct the improved state, the right state. As Strauss points out, however, this implies that there is no longer any need to ask for the "rightness" of the right state: the latter follows spontaneously and obviously from the results of the analysis. Precisely this assumption reveals Hobbes's fundamental obliviousness:

> The "resoluto-compositive" method thus presupposes nothing less than a systematic renunciation of the question of what is good and fitting. Convinced of the absolutely typical character of mathematical method, according to which one proceeds from self-evident axioms to evident conclusions, "to the end," Hobbes fails to realize that in the "beginning," in the "evident" presuppositions whether of mathematics or of politics, the real problem, the task of "dialectic" is hidden.[53]

Hobbes's faith in the resoluto-compositive method is the complement of his nominalist distrust of ordinary language and human reason. According to Strauss, this distrust is premature and unjustified: "For to give up orientation by speech means giving up the only possible orientation, which is originally at the disposal of men, and therewith giving up the discovery of the standard which is presupposed in any orientation, and even giving up the search for the standard."[54] Hobbes attempts to find a standard beyond ordinary language, opinion, and reason, by deducing it from the analysis of the existing state. However, Strauss argues, the principles that result from his analysis—vanity and fear—must already *imply* a specific answer to the question regarding the right state in order to be effective. For the analysis of the existing state only reveals its basic principles: it does not say anything about the goodness or badness of these principles. This means that Hobbes must tacitly *insert* an answer to the question of the right state between his analysis and his synthesis. As Strauss points out, Hobbes neither simply presupposes nor even posits the fear of violent death as a principle of natural reason and as the basis of the right of nature, but he actually *justifies* it, something that would be superfluous if it would follow spontaneously from the resoluto-compositive analysis. His failure to clarify the reasons for this justification shows that, from the outset, he has relinquished the Socratic question and the philosophic search for the standard.[55]

The absolute individual right posited and justified by Hobbes precedes both reason and society. According to Strauss, this signifies a decisive break with the traditional view, which gave primacy to a law that derived its authority from its ancestral or divine origin, or, from the point of the philosophers, from its superior rationality. Reason's claim to authority and the classical concept of rationality, however, are firmly rejected by Hobbes. In his view, reason is a product of fear, and since all human beings are driven by fear in equal measure, they are in principle equally rational. Moreover, the development of man's rational capacities can never eradicate disagreement regarding fundamental matters.[56] As a result, Hobbes is the first political thinker faced with the problem of sovereignty, Strauss points out: if all men are by nature equal, who shall exercise power, under what conditions and within what limits? Hobbes's solution to this problem has become familiar, not only to every reader of his great work *Leviathan*, but in fact to every modern individual: to secure the pursuit of comfortable self-preservation, every individual transfers his power to the sovereign in exchange for the latter's protection.[57] The unrivaled success of Hobbes's proposal, however, should not make us forget that it is based on a break with classical rationalism: it is "the decisive presupposition for the concept of sovereignty as well as for the supplanting of 'law' by 'right,' that is, the supplanting of the primacy of obligation by the primacy of claim."[58]

As Strauss explains, the break with classical rationalism is based on the rejection of ordinary language as a suitable philosophical point of departure, and this marks the decisive difference between Hobbes and Plato. The latter develops a paradoxical philosophy that acknowledges and preserves the importance of morality, while critically investigating its origins.[59] Hobbes, on the other hand, denies the intrinsic value of man's natural moral judgments and constructs a new morality that clears the path for the conquest of nature: "while Plato goes back to the truth hidden in the natural valuations and therefore seeks to teach nothing new and unheard-of, but to recall what is known to all but not understood, Hobbes, rejecting the natural valuations in principle, goes beyond them, goes forward to a new *a priori* political philosophy, which is of the future and freely projected."[60]

Thus, Strauss's final verdict can be summarized as follows: despite his undeniable originality and power of thought, Hobbes's claim to "a more profound understanding of human nature" proves to be based on a superficial and prejudiced appreciation of the foundations of classical political philosophy. His break with classical rationalism was only possible because of a failure to understand the complexity of its origins. A strong prejudice, partly determined by the Christian-Aristotelian heritage, prevented him from carrying his inquiry to a more fundamental level, where the question of the right order of society or of the true state and the question "Why philosophy?" find a common root in the Socratic question.[61] Moreover, on the basis of this omission Hobbes constructed a political philosophy that obscured the original Socratic question and hid it from view for a long time. Its success reinforced the prejudice that classical political philosophy was—and is—definitely a thing of the past. With his critical analysis, Strauss seeks to break the spell of this prejudice, by confronting Hobbes's political philosophy with its classical, Socratic-Platonic counterpart, and by showing that the Socratic question has not in the least been rendered superfluous by Hobbes and his philosophic descendants.[62]

## Fighting the Kingdom of Darkness

Having identified what he views as the errors in the Hobbesian reception of Platonic politics, Strauss goes on to investigate their roots and causes in *Hobbes's Critique of Religion*. As the reader of the manuscript will not fail to notice, in many respects his approach is reminiscent of that of *Spinoza's Critique of Religion*. Thus, Strauss begins by firmly rejecting the prevalent notion that Hobbes's critique of religion is a by-product or spin-off of either his philosophy of nature or his political philosophy. On the contrary, it is the basis of both: "the critique of revelation is not simply an ulterior if necessary *supplement* (*Ergänzung*) of Hobbesian politics, but rather its *presupposition* (*Voraussetzung*), indeed the presupposition of Hobbes's philosophy as such."[63] By the same token, "Hobbes's idea of natural science can be understood radically only from his critique of miracles. In this sense, at any rate, the critique of religion is the presupposition of his science."[64] In Hobbes's view, theological politics, the alliance of ancient political thought and revealed religion, was responsible for violent religious wars. Restoring order and peace required a new scientific politics that would radically overcome both ancient political science *and* revelation and thus solve the theological-political problem. Not surprisingly, Hobbes's major works, *De Cive* and *Leviathan*, in which this new politics is developed, deal extensively with both philosophical and theological issues.

On the same grounds, Strauss questions the view that Hobbes was a believing Christian. Guided by Lessing and the medieval Jewish and Islamic philosophers, he has become more attentive to Hobbes's own art of writing and concealing his subversive views.[65] As he explains, Hobbes makes use of the same twofold strategy as Spinoza: behind the facade of a purist critique of theological tradition on the basis of Scripture, he deploys a covert but fundamental critique of Scripture itself.[66] Similarly, in his critique on the basis of Scripture, although he ostensibly submits to the literal meaning of the biblical text, he interprets it as a human literary document in order to prove that it does not intend to teach anything regarding the objects of philosophy or science. According to Hobbes, the traditional distinction between the spiritual and the material realm has no foundation whatsoever in the biblical teaching, and neither does the dualism of power that threatens the unity and stability of the political regime.

Rather, the distinction between spirit and matter is one of many fraudulent heresies disseminated by what Hobbes calls "the kingdome of darknesse," a "confederacy of deceivers" that comprises the priesthood, but also Greek poets and philosophers, primarily Aristotle.[67] Their metaphysical dualism merely justifies the natural human tendency to take figments of the imagination as real entities. By the same token, their ethics and politics validate the human passions and thereby vindicate man's natural disobedience with regard to the law, as well as his vanity and pride.[68] These pernicious and anarchistic doctrines rooted in vanity were subsequently adopted and incorporated into the Christian church by the Roman priesthood, leading to Christianity's decadence. This does not mean, however, that Hobbes envisages any kind of renascence, Strauss argues:

In truth, Hobbes's critique of tradition on the basis of Scripture is not guided by the earnest will to find in Scripture the tree of life, the divine order of human life, but by the calculated intention to safeguard a view of the human order of human life established independently of Scripture, against objections on the part of the church and theology, by a subsequent appeal to Scripture.[69]

Thus, the professed purity of Hobbes's biblical investigations is merely a fiction, Strauss observes. In fact, his exegesis proves to be based on nonreligious, philosophical presuppositions that, as in the case of Spinoza, are of Epicurean origin. His critique on the basis of Scripture, most notably his rejection of the dualism of spirit and matter, is fundamentally animated by the effort to liberate man from the fear of divine powers and from the fear of death. However, like Spinoza's liberal interpretation of the Bible, Hobbes's new politics is called into question by the reality and the possibility of miracles, much more so than by the dualism of spirit and matter. For as long as this possibility has not been refuted, prophecy and revelation remain essentially possible. For this reason, his critique must go further and attack the fundamental claim to miraculous inspiration underlying the Bible itself: "Shaking the authority of Scripture, indeed, the possibility of revelation as such, is thus the *conditio sine qua non* for the definitive safeguarding, if not for the original possibility of Hobbesian politics."[70]

Here again, Hobbes proceeds in a manner that prefigures Spinoza's approach in the *Theological-Political Treatise*. More to the point, the failure of his critique foreshadows the failure of Spinoza's critique of religion. To begin with, Hobbes develops a historical critique of prophecy aimed at undermining the credibility of Scripture. In doing so, however, he treats the Bible like any other literary document, thus begging the question with regard to the interpretation of a believer. The mere fact of envisaging a historical critique, Strauss argues, shows that "his unbelief is not the consequence, but the precondition of the historical critique."[71] Thus, Hobbes must turn from the miracle of prophecy to miracles as such. On this point, he not only argues that miracles cannot be known by natural reason, but he sets out to prove that they are, in fact, impossible. In order to do so, however, he must have recourse to the philosophical distinction between miraculous or supernatural events and natural events. As Strauss already argued in *Spinoza's Critique of Religion*, however, this distinction is unacceptable to the true believer. Like Spinoza after him, Hobbes cannot refute the possibility of miracles directly, but only indirectly, by focusing on its consequences.[72] While his argument may have

some effect against Scholasticism, it utterly fails *vis-à-vis* a radical orthodox position like that of Calvin's.

To avert this threatening result, Strauss argues, Hobbes takes an almost desperate measure. Bent on refuting the knowability and possibility of
miracles, he carries the belief in miracles to its most radical consequence: if,
as revealed religion claims, creation is dependent on the workings of an inscrutable and omnipotent creator, it cannot but be altogether unintelligi-
ble. In one fell swoop, he rejects both revealed religion *and* the ancient idea
of nature as an intelligible order, both faith *and* natural reason. In order to
escape from this untenable position, he espouses the view that only what is
made freely and arbitrarily by the human consciousness is intelligible, since
human consciousness can withdraw from the reach of both nature and
God. Because only the principles and the content of human knowledge are
in the power of consciousness, natural science becomes the entirely hypothetical pursuit of the causes of things. This science is as "capable" of explaining nature as it is of explaining miracles, because it holds the things in
themselves to be beyond the power of consciousness. At the same time,
however, natural science remains constitutionally incapable of refuting the
possibility of miracles. In order to uphold itself, it must have recourse to
the same Cartesian-Napoleonic stratagem Strauss already brought to light
in *Spinoza's Critique of Religion* and *Philosophy and Law*:

> Modern science, which so little excludes the possibility of miracles that
> rather the admission of their possibility is its basis, protects itself *post
> festum* (*nachträglich*) against this possibility by asserting the relativity of
> belief in miracles to the pre-scientific stage of humanity, on the basis of
> its characteristic consciousness of being advanced (*Fortgeschrittenheits-
> Bewusstsein*), hence on the basis of historical reflection."[73]

This, Strauss argues, shows that the basis of Hobbes's critique of religion is not modern science: on the contrary, the latter merely serves to
shore up the indemonstrable assertions of the former regarding the impossibility of miracles. These assertions themselves are ultimately based on
what Strauss calls a "primary skepticism" regarding miracles, which merely
argues that knowledge of miracles is very difficult. This primary skepticism, he further observes, historically *precedes* the new science: it can already be found in the ancient and medieval critics of religion who had an
entirely different, premodern concept of science. In Hobbes's work, as in
Spinoza's *Theological-Political Treatise*, however, it is grafted on Cartesian
radical doubt and its "nihilist" retreat to the individual human consciousness in the face of the possibility of a deceitful God (*deus deceptor*).

Nevertheless, although Hobbes considers knowledge of things in themselves to be impossible, he does not deny their existence. This existence, however, he can only conceive of as *corporality*: being is for him identical to being-corporal, and being-corporal ultimately means being tangible or, more precisely, to offer resistance to human force. The tactile experience of resistance, Strauss explains, thus becomes the new universal paradigm for human knowledge: instead of seeing and understanding, sensing and feeling now become the source of human certainty about being. The epoch-making success of this shift, however, does not do away with the fact that the fundamental identification of being with being-corporal is an unwarranted *prejudice*, Strauss argues: "The prejudice that being is being-corporal thus originally signifies: being is resistance (*Widerständigkeit*) and palpability. Thus, for Hobbes, the existence of a resistant world is from the outset and always self-evident."[74] According to Hobbes, man is in the grips of an incomprehensible world that exists independently and resists his power, a view that remains essentially beholden to the unrefuted possibility of miracles. The only way in which man can hold his own in such a world, the only way in which the lingering threat of an intervention by the God of revelation can be averted, is by withdrawing to the inner world of consciousness with its figments and constructs.[75] For lack of an intelligible natural order in which guidance can be found, man can only orient himself by his own artfulness, "the capacity to produce useful effects on the basis of deliberation."[76]

This, Strauss argues, leads us to the core of Hobbes's critique of religion, and thus to the basis of his philosophical project: "The fact of art (*das Faktum der Kunst*) is authoritative (*massgebend*) for Hobbes's philosophy. For this philosophy is a philosophy of civilization: by means of the knowledge of the conditions of civilization, it wants to contribute to the safeguarding and furtherance of civilization."[77] Within the confines of the progressive work of civilization, man can finally confront and avert the claims of revelation regarding miracles as deceptions that distract and prevent him from seeking his own advantage. However, human art in the service of the pursuit of comfort, security, and happiness is no longer the imitation of nature understood as an intelligible and exemplary order. Instead, art becomes the sovereign creation of man in opposition to nature understood as an incomprehensible chaos. By dint of this momentous change in the relationship between art and nature, Hobbes can rightly be called one of the founders of modernity.

The main conditions and implications of Hobbes's historical project of civilization are discussed in more detail in *The Political Philosophy of Hobbes*. In the present inquiry, however, Strauss makes clear that this change

itself is rooted in an immense prejudice that originates in Hobbes's strenu-
ous but purely defensive effort to keep the persistent threat of miraculous
divine intervention at bay. Just as his extreme aversion to theological politics
leads him to a radical critique of the virtue of courage, it causes him to dismiss the idea of nature as an intelligible order. According to Strauss, however, Hobbes's wholesale rejection of ancient philosophy and politics is
precipitate, since his polemic against revealed religion prevents him from
seeing and understanding them in their original sense. Thus, his polemic
against the traditional dualism of power precludes him from addressing a
more fundamental question that Strauss calls the "primitive and principal
theme of politics": "for every discussion about dualism or monism of powers presupposes the clarification of the meaning of 'power,' the answer to
the question of the meaning and the purpose of the state."[78]

With this remark, Strauss rejoins his most fundamental criticism in
*The Political Philosophy of Hobbes*: even though he claims to repeat the Socratic foundation of classical political philosophy, Hobbes fails to properly
raise the Socratic question. As a result, and contrary to his own claim, his
new political philosophy is, in fact, less original and less radical than the
old.[79] In addition, Strauss returns to the questions he had raised in the preliminary article: "whether the modification, intended by Hobbes and in fact
determined by Christianity, of ancient ideas is actually based on a more
profound understanding of human nature, and what this concern for 'profundity' actually entails."[80] As his inquiry shows, Hobbes's claim to a more
profound understanding of human nature is at least questionable, since it is
based rather on his animosity toward revealed religion and theological politics than on a genuine understanding of ancient ideas. As for the concern
for profundity itself, it too proves to be problematic. As Strauss's formulation seems to suggest, it is somehow determined by Christianity. In the
draft of a letter to Gerhard Krüger, he elaborates this view as follows:

> Granted the greater *profundity* of Christian and post-Christian
> philosophy—is it a matter of depth, then? Is this perspective (of pro-
> fundity) not itself already a Christian perspective, which is in need of
> clarification (*Ausweisung*)? Is "profundity" identical with radicalism?
> Isn't it rather the case that "profundity" is not *really* radical? . . .
> Hobbes claims to be more profound than Aristotle (and Plato). What
> is hidden behind this claim? He fails to raise the question regarding
> the *eidos* [idea, shape] (either the question of the essence of *aretè*
> [virtue] or the question of the sociability of man), he assumes that the
> question has already been answered and that the answer is "trivial."[81]

As Strauss further explains, Christianity claimed to have brought to light certain facts about man that the ancients failed to recognize. In particular, their view of human nature and of the soul was judged to be superficial and incomplete, since it ignored or underrated crucial strata such as conscience and temporality. When the founders of modernity turned against revealed religion in order to reinstate philosophy, they did not raise the question whether this "deepening" was indeed justified.[82] Instead, it became the implicit framework of their revolutionary endeavor, as becomes apparent from Hobbes's turn to history, as well as from certain of his anthropological and ontological presuppositions. Spellbound by the premises of revealed religion and captivated by their polemic against the scholastic philosophic tradition, they failed to restore philosophy in its original sense, but instead launched a historical project.

In fact, Strauss argues, the "deepening" claimed by Christianity even continues to determine late modern philosophy. As we saw in chapter 3, he finds that the radical historicism and the intellectual probity professed by Nietzsche, Weber, and Heidegger remain decisively indebted to Christian morality. These three thinkers bring to completion the process that begins in the thought of Hobbes: modern philosophy's construction of a second cave underneath the Platonic cave. Designed as an artificial shelter from the threat of revealed religion, this second cave has become the place in which modern man has almost forgotten, if not denied, the existence of the first, original cave. In his various writings on Hobbes, Strauss attempts both to understand how the second cave came into being and to find a way back to the first, to the position from which Socrates raised the question of the right way of life. By the same token, he tries to detach himself from the modern concern for profundity and intellectual probity and to recover the Socratic love of truth.

Before concluding this chapter, a curious though important detail must be mentioned. Although numerous elements leave no doubt that *The Political Philosophy of Hobbes* is part of his attempt to recover the Socratic question, Strauss almost never mentions Socrates by name in the book.[83] Only in the final chapter, when explaining how Plato "takes refuge" in dialectics instead of ontology, he adds that this turn is an essential characteristic of "the tradition founded by Socrates-Plato, for the Socratic-Platonic reform of philosophy rests precisely on the perception of the unreliability and contradictoriness of ordinary speech."[84] It is not clear why the presence of Socrates, which is clearly crucial to the intention of the book, is limited to a discreet adjective. That it is indeed crucial is intimated in the autobiographical preface to the German edition of the book, where Strauss emphasizes that he "did not write about Hobbes as a Hobbesian."[85] By way of an explanation, he refers the reader to the words of his contemporary Gerhard Krüger, yet without quoting them explicitly: "That the decisive question remains *true*, even if it finds *no* answer, this he who questions thus can learn from the example of *Socrates*."[86] The bearing of this quote is clear: Strauss would only have been able to write about Hobbes as a Hobbesian if he had shared Hobbes's understanding of and answer to the decisive question. From this he was prevented by the example of Socrates, for whom the question of the right life always held more attraction than the answers that are given to it.

As became already apparent, the conspicuous absence of Socrates is not only characteristic of the Hobbes book: in the review of Schmitt's *The Concept of the Political*, as in *Philosophy and Law*, the teacher disappears behind the pupil, Plato, even though in the decisive respect there is no difference between them. For reasons that are not entirely clear, Strauss judged it necessary to conceal the focal point of his endeavor in his early work. Perhaps he estimated that a straightforward presentation would only be received with skepticism and even opprobrium in an academic world dominated by the philological-historical approach to philosophy. Perhaps he was guided by considerations similar to those of Plato and the *falasifa* with regard to the importance of caution and moderation in philosophy's relationship to the polis. However this may be, in his early works Strauss donned the garb of the historian of philosophy or the historian of ideas, who indulges in detailed and painstaking scholarly research. However, he left no doubt that this was in part a necessary camouflage, as may be inferred from a footnote in *Philosophy and Law*:

> To that end and only to that end is the "historicization" of philosophy justified and necessary: only the history of philosophy makes possible the ascent from the second, "unnatural" cave into which we have fallen less because of the tradition itself than because of the tradition of polemics against the tradition, into that first, "natural" cave which Plato's image depicts, to emerge from which into the light is the original meaning of philosophizing.[87]

# CHAPTER 6

# Epilogue

## The Surface and the Core

At the moment when Strauss uncovers what he regards as the rationality deficit in Hobbes's foundation of liberalism, that same liberalism is all but defunct in Germany. In 1936, when the Hobbes book is published, Hitler's National Socialist Party wins the Reichstag elections with a 99 percent landslide, the Nuremberg racial laws are coming into full effect, and everything that smacks of *Zivilisation* is denounced in the name of *Kultur*. The precarious and much-afflicted liberal democracy of the Weimar Republic is no more than a distant recollection. Strauss, living and working in England with his family, is unable to return, while his professional and financial situation is becoming increasingly difficult.[1] Fortunately, the fact that he failed to find a publisher for the German Hobbes manuscript and was forced to publish it in English now proves to be advantageous. The book is well received in the English-speaking academic world on both sides of the Atlantic, and turns out to be a bridgehead. Partly by its strengths, Strauss is able to obtain a position in the United States, where he will remain for the rest of his career.[2]

 With the passage to America, we enter the domain of the more "familiar" Strauss, who founded a school and aroused controversy. The change of continents, however, does not mean a change of intellectual pursuits. Strauss scrupulously continues his research on the two paths he has set out: the recovery of the Socratic question by studying premodern philosophy, and the critical investigation of modern philosophy by reopening the quarrel between the ancients and the moderns. At the same time, the theological-political problem remains the juncture of these two paths: religion and politics are the two fundamental challenges to which philosophy, both ancient and modern, must respond. On both paths, Strauss abides more than ever by his characteristic approach of "learning through reading." Clearly, the initial attempt to understand authors as they understood themselves and in their own terms has gathered additional momentum by the discovery of the art of veiled and veiling writing of Plato and his Jewish, Islamic (and German) students. It underscores the necessity of reading their works with the utmost care, impartiality, and hermeneutic openness, and with special attention to their formal—stylistic, rhetoric, and dramatic—characteristics. However, this requirement not only applies to the interpretation of Plato and the *falasifa*: in studying the works of other premodern authors, Strauss finds indications that they likewise concealed their intentions with the aid of literary techniques and devices.[3] In their case as well, this procedure is inspired by the tension between the philosophic pursuit of knowledge and the political community. In this respect, their writings can be regarded as political philosophy, in the double sense of the term.

As Strauss comes to attach more importance to this connection, the perspective of his research gradually changes, a process Heinrich Meier has aptly described as "the movement from the history of philosophy to the intention of the philosopher."[4] Instead of interpreting a text as a product of its historical context and its author as a child of his time, Strauss endeavors to detect to what extent the author detaches himself from his historical context and thus is a stepchild of his time. As Meier further points out, the discovery of the philosophers' art of writing arouses the suspicion that the history of philosophy as it was written since the nineteenth century is largely a *fable convenue*, a likely story: the most salient features of a premodern philosophic text, those privileged by the conventional historical approach, may in fact be part of its outer meaning, the exoteric casing with which the author adapted his mode of expression to the prevailing views of his time.[5] In order to grasp the author's guiding intention, one first has to decipher this casing, for the art of writing only becomes visible to those who have mastered the art of reading.

The result of Strauss's studies is a large number of commentaries of varying length on numerous classic philosophic texts, in which he investigates how their authors responded to the theological-political problem. To provide a summary or even an overview of these interpretations is impossible, if only because of the wide range they cover, but also for more intrinsic reasons. In each of his interpretations, Strauss emphasizes that he can only indicate the first steps on the way to an adequate interpretation. A classic text, which has been composed and polished with exceeding care over a long period of time, only yields its full meaning to a sustained and protracted study that may take years, perhaps a lifetime. A careful author, it must be assumed, knew exactly what he was doing and left nothing to chance in the process of writing: every formal and substantial element, every detail was selected with deliberation and presented with precision, and thus merits the interpreter's full attention. For the art of writing owes its effectiveness not only to the competence of the author, but also to the fact that not all readers are equally thoughtful, perspicacious, patient, and leisured.

Precisely for this reason, it is of crucial importance to make the right beginning in interpreting a philosophic text. As Strauss is well aware, at first view there is no essential difference between inner and outer meaning: both are part of one and the same text.[6] Whoever wishes to fathom the deeper meaning cannot avoid starting from the surface of the text as it presents itself. To speculate in advance as to an inner meaning is the surest path to failure, Strauss warns. Such assumptions may lead the reader to overlook certain aspects and details, so that from the outset he puts himself on the wrong track. "There is no surer protection against the understanding of anything than taking for granted or otherwise despising the obvious and the surface. The problem inherent in the surface of things, and only the surface of things, is the heart of things."[7] In other words, the only way to discover what is behind the mask is to study closely the mask, and nothing but the mask.

Obviously, this is no easy task. The art of writing has no standard instruments or fixed rules. It is a subtle and flexible means of communication that at once imitates and deflects the prevailing modes in order to convey a paradoxical insight.[8] How an author proceeded in writing a text depends on his assessment of the theological-political problem, and can only be gleaned from the indications he supplies in the text. On this point, the possibilities are well nigh infinite. Thus, the content of utterances, assertions, and propositions may be dependent on their function and place within the text as a whole. In support, Strauss concurs with Lessing's remark that "the same thought in a different place may have an entirely different value."[9] Thus, apparent repetitions may indicate that what has been repeated has acquired a different meaning. Moreover, the connection between larger wholes may also be important: the seemingly arbitrary composition of a text—its divisions into books, chapters, paragraphs, and sections—may conceal a well-ordered plan obliquely alluded to by the author.[10] Contradictions or grave errors in the text are not necessarily due to carelessness or neglect, but may have been inserted deliberately. A contradiction may even be hidden, for example, in the contradictory implications of two utterances that as such are not opposed.[11] In addition, we should not forget that a careful writer is *eo ipse* a careful reader. References to and quotations from the work of other authors may contain meaningful clues, particularly when they are incorrect or incomplete. Last but not least, the art of writing is the art of silence and omission: what an author does not say, especially when the reader is justified in expecting him to do so, may be as important as what he does say. In such cases, the reader must independently supplement what is unsaid or omitted. However, the reverse may also be possible. An author reputed for his ambiguous or obscure manner of expression may unexpectedly exhibit unusual frankness. Only a patient reader will resist the temptation not to take such utterances seriously.[12]

There is another reason why Strauss's commentaries resist review and summary. If, as he ventures to impress on his readers, a careful writer is by necessity a careful reader and vice versa, his own writings can be no exception. Alfarabi, who succeeded in decoding the clues in Plato's writings as well as their underlying rationale, thereby understood the necessity to communicate his discoveries in a similarly covert manner, albeit with the aid of different clues adapted to his surroundings. For this reason, he presented his insights in the guise of seemingly dry and tedious commentaries without a clear system and written in an erratic style, alternatingly concise and long-winded. In this way, he succeeded in only drawing the attention of diligent, philosophically minded readers, using his own covert clues to guide them to those of Plato.[13]

Strauss, who succeeded in decoding Alfarabi's pointers, follows suit. As his studies of other authors make him more familiar with their respective arts of writing, he begins to develop one of his own.[14] In doing so, he is guided by considerations similar to those of his medieval exemplars: the only way to draw the reader's attention to a specific author's art of writing is by means of an art of writing. Thus, initially he presents his interpretations in the garb of solid, scholarly, and detailed historical studies, as a result of which he is often mistaken for a historian of ideas. That this impression is indeed misleading is borne out by a telling remark of Strauss's about Alfarabi: "Fârâbî avails himself then of the specific immunity of the commentator or of the historian in order to speak his mind concerning grave matters in his 'historical' works, rather than in the works in which he speaks in his own name."[15] What one writer says about another may be an important clue to how he wishes to be read. Thus, it is no coincidence that Strauss rarely speaks in his own name in his "historical works."[16] In fact, he eventually discards the guise of the historian altogether. From the second half of the 1950s on, his interpretations increasingly come to resemble paraphrases of the texts under scrutiny, to the incomprehension and even disapproval of a host of contemporary critics.

Whoever opens Strauss's later works is thus compelled to proceed with caution. Like Alfarabi, he brings to light the problems inherent in the surface of the text under scrutiny only by covering it with the surface of his own commentaries. In other words, unveiling takes place by means of a new veiling. This does not mean, however, that his writings are entirely inaccessible or hopelessly idiosyncratic. In most cases, even a first superficial reading yields enlightening and intriguing insights that challenge the prevailing interpretations and raise disturbing questions. Since they defy summary or review, I will limit myself to discussing a few of the most salient and controversial aspects of Strauss's most important works. In doing so, I will attempt to situate these aspects as much as possible against the background of his philosophical project as a whole. It goes without saying that this procedure cannot in any way pretend to be a valid substitute for reading the commentaries themselves, let alone the original works commented.

## The Problem of Socrates

As said, Strauss's investigations remain focused throughout in the recovery of the Socratic question. Already at the beginning of the 1930s, he indicates that a thorough rereading of Plato is necessary to this end. In this respect, it is all the more remarkable that, in his publications, he commences his study of "the problem of Socrates" not with Plato, but with Xenophon, the only other pupil of Socrates whose writings are extant. Since the nineteenth century, the heyday of classical philology, Xenophon's reputation is mostly that of a historian, most notably as the author of the *Anabasis*, an account of a military expedition in which he took part. The philosophical works he wrote, most of which are dedicated to Socrates, are hardly, if at all, taken seriously. This reception has obscured the fact that up until the nineteenth century Xenophon was regarded as a philosophical author on a par with Plato.

The rehabilitation of Xenophon is perhaps one of Strauss's most important accomplishments. In his interpretations, this allegedly "feeble-minded" pupil of Socrates appears as a political philosopher and writer of the first rank who introduces his diligent readers to the Socratic program by means of superior irony. As Strauss shows, all of Xenophon's writings are parts of a tightly composed *Gesamtwerk* of which Socrates is the focal point: not only in the so-called Socratic writings, the *Memorabilia*, the *Apology*, the *Symposium*, and the *Oeconomicus*, but also in his so-called historical works such as the *Anabasis*, the *Hellenica*, and the *Cyropaedia*, and even in the *scripta minora*, the minor writings such as the *Agesilaus* and the *Hiero*. In its own way, Strauss argues, each of these works explores the theological-political problem,

the tension between the philosophic life and the theological-political authority of the city, as the fundamental problem of philosophy. At the beginning
of the 1950s, Strauss's interpretation of Xenophon's *Hiero* sparks a brilliant polemic with his colleague and friend Alexandre Kojève, an eccentric
Marxist-Hegelian whose lectures on Hegel were of momentous influence on
a whole generation of French thinkers. Against Strauss's classical understanding of the relationship between philosophy and politics, Kojève defends the
modern view, so that the debate becomes a contemporary installment of the
*querelle des anciens et des modernes*.[17]

Only when he has become acquainted with the deceptive sobriety of
Xenophon's art of writing does Strauss venture to address the more exuber-
ant and versatile ambiguity of Socrates's most beloved student. Here again,
his interpretations stray far from the beaten path. They resolutely dismiss
the deeply ingrained contemporary dogma that Plato betrayed his teacher's
critical and liberating inquiry by turning it into a conservative, even authoritarian, dogmatic system.[18] Rejecting this view, Strauss persists with his
original view that philosophically there is no difference between pupil and
teacher on the essential point: Plato carries out the Socratic program. The
dialogues, Strauss argues, do not transmit any doctrine or system. Rather,
they offer an intricate literary presentation of what Socrates stood for: a life
in the service of questioning.[19] Far from reflecting a certain stage in Plato's
development, each dialogue throws light on a specific aspect of the Socratic
question, in such a way that the various dialogues supplement each other. At
the same time, however, the dialogues are more than a representation of the
philosophic life: they incite the reader to ask questions in order to independently reconstruct and articulate the whole.[20] Their mutual connection re-
sembles that of shattered "hologram" (literally, a "writing of the whole").
Each dialogue is, as it were, a shard in which the whole is reflected, albeit indirectly and incompletely. Only by recomposing the shards does the image
become visible in its entirety.

Like all of his interpretations, Strauss's reading of the Platonic dialogues
begins with the surface. In this case, this means that their formal, literary characteristics are at least as important as their putative "doctrinal" content. As his
interpretations show, Plato is an extremely skillful writer who literally leaves
nothing to coincidence in his work: "Nothing is accidental in a Platonic dialogue; everything is necessary at the place where it occurs. Everything which
would be accidental outside of the dialogue becomes meaningful within the
dialogue."[21] In other words, the dialogues are governed by the author's intention down to their minutest details, just as the biblical universe is governed
by a divine providence without which not even a sparrow shall fall on the

ground.[22] In trying to understand them, we should keep in mind that, as a contemporary author has his protagonist assert, "a man of genius makes no mistakes; his errors are volitional and are the portals of discovery."[23]

For the reader, it is therefore necessary to study the choices and selections as well as the omissions that produced the surface of the dialogues, since they are the only guideposts to Plato's intention. Thus, it is necessary to begin by pondering various patent characteristics: the difference between the dialogues' titles, their formal setting—are they narrated or performed?—as well as the presence or absence of certain *dramatis personae*, not least of all Socrates.[24] By a careful study of these characteristics and details, Strauss argues, the reader discovers a complex network of connections between the dialogues that only gradually becomes apparent, as his attention turns from the most visible problems on the surface to less visible and eventually to implicit problems. Thus, a comparison of their titles already supplies certain clues, as does the difference between narrated and performed dialogues. Last but not least, the role of Socrates should be studied carefully: in some dialogues he clearly dominates the conversation, in others he merely participates, while in one dialogue, the *Laws*, he is completely absent. In Strauss's reading, all these details are the result of scrupulous selection, the rationale of which only becomes apparent in the course of repeated watchful reading.

The most salient aspect of Plato's dialogues is perhaps their dramatic character. Even the narrated dialogues are first and foremost a *drama*, a combination of *logoi kai erga*, speeches and deeds performed by certain persons with regard to each other, within a certain period of time and in one or more specific places. According to Strauss, it is no accident that Plato stages and dramatizes philosophy. For what medium is better suited to present the political dimension of Socratic questioning than the dramatic art? The dialogues are performances where what is said and done must always be considered in the light of who says or does it, to whom, about what, when, where, and in what circumstances. Whoever wishes to understand the meaning of a dialogue must therefore take into account each of these elements.

An important implication of this approach is that nothing of what is said in the dialogues may simply be regarded as a reflection of Plato's view. When discussing modern literature, no one will contend that the views of the character in a novel or a play are the straightforward expression of the author's opinion. Strangely enough, such caution is lacking in the case of Plato, a master playwright who remains conspicuously absent in his plays.[25] It seems to be a typically modern conceit that Plato shared the many views and arguments presented by his Socrates or by any other of his characters.

Moreover, as Strauss remarks, even if one were justified in taking Socrates to be Plato's spokesman, this would be to little avail: "it is one of Socrates's peculiarities that he was a master of irony. We are back where we started: to speak through the mouth of a man who is notorious for his irony seems to be tantamount to not asserting anything."[26] As in the case of all great writers, Plato's intentions must therefore be sought and found between the lines or in the interaction of speeches and deeds, in the vicissitudes of the characters, and in the composition of the dialogues, and also in what remains unspoken and unperformed.[27] For if nothing is accidental in a Platonic dialogue, neither is silence.

According to Strauss, this latter point becomes apparent in the overall composition of the dialogues. If each dialogue makes visible a part of the whole, it does so in a partial manner, since Plato deliberately left out something that is of vital importance for the theme. "Each dialogue, we venture to say, abstracts from something that is most important to the subject matter of the dialogue."[28] In this way, Plato engages in ironic play with his own design, indicating to the reader that an adequate understanding of the subject depends on whether he succeeds in discovering the fundamental abstraction and supplementing its implicit consequences, not least by studying the other dialogues. To provide some illustration of how an interpretation according to these "principles" proceeds, it is useful to turn to Strauss's reading of one of Plato's most political works, the *Republic*.

The theme of this dialogue is as famous as the way in which it is presented. With his young interlocutors, Socrates tries to answer the question: what is justice? Initially, they look for justice in the individual, but in the interest of the inquiry Socrates proposes to focus on the city, since justice "would be easier to observe closely" on this level.[29] In the ensuing discussion, the best city is conceived "in speech," a procedure that takes up almost the whole remainder of the dialogue.[30] In this best city governed by philosophers, a host of political distinctions generally deemed essential is obliterated: differences between the sexes, but also the boundary between the public and the private, as property goods, spouses, and children are held in common.

On closer inspection, the predominance of philosophy and the disappearance of social and political differences are connected in a way that is characteristic of the *Republic*, Strauss argues. This is already the case at the beginning of the dialogue, when Socrates enters the house of Polemarchus and meets the latter's father, Cephalus. The old man introduces the main theme of the dialogue by providing a definition of justice in passing. Justice, Cephalus suggests, is speaking the truth and giving back what one has borrowed. In reply, Socrates observes that in some cases it is not advisable to speak the truth or to render what has been borrowed, for example, when the owner of a weapon one has borrowed has in the meantime lost his mind.[31] Justice regarding the distribution and the possession of property, he implies, is a matter of knowledge of what is suitable for different people, of their needs and competences. As Strauss indicates, this reasoning, carried to its ultimate consequences, already points toward the abolition of private property and of the private sphere as such: an extreme communism ruled by "knowers," or a philosophic regime.

Of course, Strauss is well aware that this argument abstracts from a number of important elements.[32] However, he shows that in the continuation of the dialogue this abstraction gradually emerges as a Leitmotiv in the *Republic*. This is already the case in the debate between Socrates and the seemingly volatile rhetorician Thrasymachus who argues that justice is nothing but the interest of the stronger. As Socrates rejoins, even the strongest can make mistakes and thus unwittingly serve the interest of the weaker. In this way, Thrasymachus is forced to revise his thesis: the strongest are infallible since they possess knowledge, like the artisans and the wise. While justice is once again related to knowledge, Socrates avails himself of Thrasymachus's elucidation to tackle him, by pointing out that the good craftsman always looks to the interests of others. This shift in the definition of justice, from knowledge to art (*technè*) puts its mark on the whole discussion. Gradually, the image develops of a just city composed entirely of "technicians" who practice their own art with devotion and diligence: from the farmers and laborers to the guardians and the philosopher-kings. Since membership of this city consists exclusively in the practicing of an art, and since the capacity to do so is located in the soul, it is hardly surprising that the difference between the sexes disappears, Strauss observes. Thus, Socrates argues that women are by nature as capable as men of taking care of the surveillance and defense of the best city. For this reason, they must receive the same education, including physical training.[33]

According to Strauss, this argument tells us something more about the characteristic abstraction of the *Republic*: in various ways, the dialogue systematically abstracts from the *body*. Initially, the needs of the body are the prime reason for a city's existence: human beings are unable to fulfill them independently and are thus compelled to live together. At the same time, the needs of the body individuate: within society they distinguish people, and their recognition and fulfillment requires the creation of a private sphere distinguished and screened from the public sphere. In this way, the body determines the basic political distinctions, and these are systematically ignored in the construction in speech of the best city, which focuses on the soul. At the beginning of the *Republic*, when Socrates shifts the inquiry from the individual to the city, he does so at the urging of Glaucon, who demands that he demonstrate that justice is preferable for its own sake. In order to meet this demand, Socrates draws an implicit parallelism between the city and the individual, in particular between the city and the *soul*. In this parallelism, which becomes the basis for the construction of the best city, the body is left out of consideration. As Strauss observes, this particularity is reflected in the dramatic setting: Polemarchus entices Socrates to come to his house with the promise of a meal and a nightly spectacle. This promise is not kept: Socrates gets to spend the night in a long discussion where the only nourishment taken is "soul food." Thus, in the action of the dialogue as well, the body and its needs are suppressed.[34]

Behind the abstraction from the body, however, lies another abstraction. Within the city, the bodily needs also play an integrating role in the form of desire or *eros*: as the love of the other sex, as the love of one's kin or friends, as the love of one's property, and the love of one's country. Generally speaking, the fundamental significance of bodily *eros* consists in the love of *one's own*. Thus, the abstraction from the body that underlies the construction of the best city, modeled on the soul and guided by knowledge, is ultimately an abstraction from *eros*. In the *Republic* love in its various forms—from sexuality to familial ties to the pursuit of property—is subjected to the strictest political control. The underlying negative valuation becomes most explicit near the end of the dialogue, when Socrates connects *eros* to tyranny, presenting the tyrant as *eros* incarnate.[35] Completely dominated by his private bodily desires, the tyrant puts the public sphere at the service of his personal gratification.

The *Republic*, in fact, reverses this movement, insofar as it sacrifices all private ties to the public interest. Insofar as the abstraction from *eros* requires the disciplining of bodily needs and of the love of one's own, it demands the destruction of all existing social structures: the abolition of the private sphere and thus the collective care for wives, children, and property as well as the strict regulation of sexual relationships and the expulsion of the poets who praise *eros*. In other words, Strauss argues, the construction of the most just and most natural city is seen to require a number of most unjust and unnatural political measures.[36] The most notable of these is the so-called noble lie Socrates introduces with a view to maximizing cohesion in the best city: thus, the true city, in fact, proves to be based on a fundamental untruth.[37]

However, the fundamental abstraction regards *eros* not only as bodily desire, but also as psychological desire, the highest form of which is philosophy. Socrates's hypothetical parallelism between the city and the soul, which underlies the abstraction from the body and from *eros*, is also the basis for his well-known tripartite division of the city: the three parts of the soul—*eros* (desire), *thumos* (spiritedness), and *logos* (reason)—correspond to the class of farmers and craftsmen, the warrior class, and the class of philosopher-rulers, respectively. Remarkably enough, Socrates places *thumos* above *eros*, as an ally of *logos*. Philosophic *eros*, which surpasses *thumos* as a true ally of *logos*, is thus completely left out of consideration.[38] In the best city, both *eros* of the body and *eros* of the soul are curbed and demoted by the promotion of *thumos*, the quintessentially political part of the soul.[39]

As a result, Strauss submits, philosophy as a spontaneous and free activity disappears from the *Republic* as a whole. Its central thesis that justice can only be realized when philosophers become kings—when philosophy and political power coincide—implies that philosophy is introduced as a *means* to an end, instead of as an end in itself.[40] Thus, Socrates repeatedly suggests that philosophers must be forced to take charge of ruling the best city, since they cannot be persuaded to do so. Preoccupied by their erotic desire for knowledge, they regard political matters as a bothersome distraction.[41] Similarly, Strauss points to a feature of the *Republic* that is seldom noticed: the philosopher's ascent from the cave toward the light is characterized by compulsion throughout.[42] Finally, it should not be forgotten that the whole discussion of the *Republic* finds its origin in an act of compulsion: Socrates is forced to join Polemarchus under the threat of physical coercion.[43]

Does this mean that we must interpret the *Republic* as a plea for the political subjugation of *eros*? On the contrary, Strauss asserts: since nothing is accidental in a Platonic dialogue, the abstraction from *eros* and the body are a deliberate ploy on Plato's part. It aims to show that the best city ruled by philosophers is an impossible construct because it negates the specificity both of the city and of philosophy. In Strauss's reading, the *Republic* is thus the exact opposite of what many contemporary interpreters hold it to be. Instead of a totalitarian political blueprint, it is an ironic and incisive critique of every attempt to re-create politics in the image of philosophy: "the *Republic* conveys the broadest and deepest analysis of political idealism ever made."[44] The staged attempt to make the city just by reorganizing it in accordance with the correct order of the soul only serves to bring out the differences between the two as regards their fundamental needs, desires and ends. Moreover, at the end of the dialogue, Socrates bluntly remarks to his interlocutors that they have not yet investigated the true nature of the soul. In order to do this, he adds, it must first be "seen such as it is in truth, not maimed by community with body and other evils, as we now see it. But what it is like when it has become pure must be examined sufficiently by calculation."[45] In this way, Socrates calls into question the initial parallelism between the soul and the city and thus pulls the rug out from under his own construction. Moreover, he points the reader back to the initial question: what is justice? Instead of revealing the "true nature" or the "idea" of justice, the *Republic* seems only to present a fundamental problem.

In fact, Strauss argues, there is no difference: the dialogue is nothing other than an intricate literary articulation of the paradoxical character of the Socratic question of the good life.[46] True and perfect justice, as sought for in the best city, proves to be realized only in the philosopher for whom the pursuit of the well-ordered soul is his life's work.[47] However, the justice of the philosopher is at odds with that of the city. It is identical to his questioning in pursuit of knowledge, which not only queries itself but also the foundations of the city. The philosophic quest for truth and justice is permanently at odds with the city, which even in its best form is still dependent on unjust policies and noble lies. The *Republic*, Strauss concludes with Cicero, does not provide a model for political action; rather, it brings to light the limits of politics, the *ratio rerum civilium* or "the nature of political things."[48] Plato hides the insuperable tension between philosophy and politics by means of the abstraction from *eros*, in order to the make the attentive reader aware of it. Moreover, he intimates that philosophy can mitigate the risks that accompany this tension only through the use of noble lies. When, near the middle of the dialogue, Socrates announces that he and the rhetorician Thrasymachus have "just become friends, though we weren't even enemies before," he implies that philosophy needs rhetoric in its dealings with the city.[49] As Strauss does not fail to point out, Alfarabi already suggested that Plato's writings are the result of a combination of "the way of Socrates" and "the way of Thrasymachus."[50]

Plato chose a most political art in order to transmit the Socratic program to later generations. Moreover, he also offers the reader valuable clues as to its origins. In the *Phaedo*, which is set on the eve of his execution, Socrates points to an important turning point in his life as a philosopher. In his youth, he tells his companions, he conducted his investigations after the manner of the philosophers of nature: he studied the heavens and earth, trying to discover the first principles of nature. Eventually, he concluded that this direct approach to the beings led to a dead end. Abandoning the pre-Socratic method, he embarked on a "second sailing" in which he "took refuge in speeches in order to see the truth of the beings."[51] In this way, his inquiry shifted from what is *proton kata phusin*—first by nature—to what is *proton pros hèmas*—first for us. In other words, his quest became "political" in the sense outlined earlier: he focused on the opinions of his fellow citizens regarding the good, the just, the noble, and the beautiful.[52] Underlying the Socratic turn to speeches was the view that every opinion contains a partial and imperfect reflection of the truth, which can only be made visible by means of dialectic.[53]

This does not mean, however, that Socrates abandoned the fundamental distinction between *phusis* (nature) and *nomos* (convention) that is coeval with philosophy. Rather, he made the awareness of its political implications a primary philosophical concern. By dint of its quest for *phusis* as that which is reducible neither to human artifice nor to divine power, philosophy necessarily transgresses and corrodes the foundations of the religious and political community. For this reason, it is at once in need of justification and open to suspicion. As a quest for self-knowledge, philosophy must therefore take both of these issues seriously and become *political* philosophy for two reasons. First, the various opinions about the good, the just, and the noble are its necessary starting point, for "political philosophy is *the part* of philosophy in which *the whole* of philosophy is in question."[54] Second, it must defend and justify itself vis-à-vis the religious and political community by means of a rhetoric that emulates the latter's priorities.

According to Strauss, this is not the whole story of the second sailing. Regarding the "pre-Socratic" Socrates, none of his pupils who left writings offer much clarity. There is, however, another ancient source that may provide a clue, even if it is a comedy. In Aristophanes's *Clouds*, we find a portrait of Socrates that differs strikingly from its Platonic and Xenophontic counterparts. In the *Clouds*, Socrates displays a complete lack of interest in human matters: he does not care about religion and politics, is completely insensitive to bodily comforts or discomforts, and is only concerned with what happens above and below the earth. This indifference, moreover, is accompanied by a total lack of caution and prudence: Socrates is prepared to share his outrageous and blasphemous views with anyone. These shortcomings eventually lead to his demise: having persuaded one of his pupils that superiority of knowledge may justify beating one's father, at the end of the play his dwelling is burned down by the pupil's incensed father.

In the light of Socrates's execution, this criticism is sufficiently important for Strauss to pay attention to Aristophanes. In a detailed study of the latter's works, he shows that the paragon of Old Comedy mastered the art of writing like his philosophic contemporaries, and that his comedies constitute a hologram in their own right, based on a keen understanding of man's place in the cosmos.[55] In Aristophanean ridicule, all comic elements refer to serious equivalents in human reality, and so do Socrates's vicissitudes in the *Clouds*. According to Strauss, the comedy was intended as a friendly warning to Socrates who, it should not be forgotten, was a member of the audience when it was performed. Aristophanes wanted to make the philosopher aware of the danger he was courting: as a result of his complete lack of interest in human affairs such as politics, religion, love, and art, his incessant philosophic probing risked provoking the anger of the city. However, although the wise poet was sympathetic to the thick-skinned philosopher, he also failed to fully fathom the strange attraction exercised by Socrates. Thus, in the *Clouds*, no conversation between Socrates and his pupils is staged, and the successful philosophic initiation of a young man takes place behind closed doors.[56] Nevertheless, Aristophanes does suggest a solution to the problem he raises in *Clouds*. He appears himself as one of the Clouds for whom Socrates acts as a representative: philosophy, he indicates, can only endure in the city if it becomes subservient to poetry.

Aristophanes's challenge, Strauss suggests, was met by Xenophon and Plato. Their Socrates is versed in human affairs like no other: he is politically knowledgeable, a model of piety, an expert in the erotic things and a connoisseur of the arts. More importantly, he is a master of *eironeia* or dissimulation, and exceedingly cautious in communicating his views: his particular wisdom is always coupled with *sophrosunè*, self-knowledge and moderation. At the same time, through the irony and ambiguity of their own presentation, Xenophon and Plato acknowledge that Aristophanes's warning was not unjustified: philosophic questioning is indeed corrosive of the theological-political-legal order and may cause sons to revolt against their fathers.[57] By their own works, they show not only that they have heeded the warning, but also that philosophy is, in fact, able to outdo poetry on its own territory.[58]

Thus, Strauss points out, it is no accident that the introduction of communism in the *Republic* contains a host of allusions to Aristophanes's *Assembly of Women*, a comedy in which a similar political reform is staged.[59] Nor is it accidental that the blind spot of *Clouds*, Socrates's erotic attraction, is central in a dialogue where Aristophanes is twice prevented from speaking. In the *Symposium*, Plato subtly turns the tables on the poet, just as the Platonic "hologram" argues the superiority of philosophy over poetry.[60] When, in the *Republic*, Socrates alludes to "an old quarrel between philosophy and poetry," he concludes a long and well-known discussion in which poetry is criticized as an imitation of an imitation of reality and as a disturber of the soul's balance, and in which the poets are expelled from the best city, only to be readmitted when they submit to the authority of the philosopher-king.[61] This passage, which continues to be a stumbling block for those impervious to its subtle comedy, conveys what in fact happens in the Platonic dialogues: poetry is put in the service of philosophy. As Strauss's interpretation suggests, Aristophanes's friendly warning may also have played a role in Socrates's second sailing: his taking refuge in speeches as the sole access to the beings cannot be separated from his becoming aware of the importance of human affairs. Sharing this awareness, his two most famous pupils provided philosophy with the means to respond adequately to the challenge of politics and religion.

The intriguing wealth of their works notwithstanding, however, Strauss views his interpretations of Xenophon and Plato as merely "beginning to begin" to recover the Socratic question. This equally applies to all of the interpretations of other premodern writers he develops and publishes between 1940 and the year of his death, 1973: besides Xenophon, Plato, and Aristophanes, he also studies the art of writing of the Roman Epicurean poet Lucretius and the Greek historian Thucydides. Moreover, there is evidence that he traced the origins of the art of writing all the way back to the historian Herodotus, to the tragic poets Sophocles, Aeschylus, and Euripides, and even to the oldest epic poets, Homer and Hesiod.[62] In its way, each of these investigations is aimed at understanding the problem of Socrates in its complex relationship to pre- and post-Socratic thought.

## Machiavelli's Oblivion

If the discovery of the art of writing is of momentous importance for Strauss's approach to premodern thought, it is no less decisive for his approach of modern thought. In a series of interpretations of the founders of modern political thought, he argues that they were equally familiar with it. Like their predecessors, they faced political and religious persecution and were forced to adapt their writing to prevailing views. Unlike their predecessors, however, they used the art of writing to gradually overcome the distinction between philosophers and nonphilosophers and thus to eradicate the tension between philosophy and the city. From this perspective, Strauss rereads Spinoza and Hobbes, but also Locke and Rousseau.[63]

As a result of this reappraisal, he is compelled to revise his earlier view, according to which Spinoza and Hobbes are the founders of modern political thought. The break with the tradition of classical Greek philosophy and revealed religion in fact proves to have already been made in the sixteenth century. In the fifteenth chapter of The Prince (1513), Niccolò Machiavelli writes:

It seems to me better to follow the real truth of things (*la verità effet-uale della cosa*) than an imaginary view of them. For many Republics and Princedoms have been imagined that were never seen or known to exist in reality. And the manner in which we live, and that in which we ought to live, are things so wide asunder, that he who quits the one to betake himself to the other is more likely to destroy than to save himself; since any one who would act up to a perfect standard of good-ness in everything must be ruined among so many who are not good.[64]

This passage contains an unprecedented radical critique of classical political philosophy: instead of starting with the question of the good life, it insists, political thought worthy of the title should focus on the way human beings actually live. For Machiavelli, this is the point of departure for "new modes and orders" (*modi ed ordini nuovi*), the discovery of which, he says, is as dangerous as the exploration of "unknown waters and lands (*acque e terre incognite*)."[65] Because of these perils, the "greater Columbus" saw fit, when happening upon the truth, to "hide it between so many lies (*fra tante bugie*), that one is able to find it only with difficulty."[66]

Strauss makes this effort in a probing and complex study of Machi-avelli's two great political works, *The Prince* and the *Discourses on Livy*.[67] Starting once again from the surface, he shows that the Florentine, with a curious mixture of reticence and boldness, laid the philosophical founda-tions of modern politics as it was characterized in previous chapters: the re-volt against nature and religion in the name of culture and civilization based on a new morality rooted in the passions, the rise of practical reason to the detriment of theoretical reason, and the turn to history. In order to succeed, Machiavelli developed a literary and rhetorical strategy that would become a model for Hobbes, Spinoza, and other successors: he disguised his attack against tradition as an ostensible return to tradition, by means of an am-biguous appeal to the great Roman historian Livy.[68] With his strategy, Machiavelli intended to forge an alliance between philosophy and politics that would contribute to the improvement of the human condition. As the first Enlightenment thinker, however, he was responsible for casting the So-cratic question into oblivion. As Strauss notes, in his works the Florentine nowhere mentions the soul.[69] The principal reason, he asserts, is the fol-lowing: Machiavelli "is silent about the soul because he has forgotten the soul, just as he has forgotten tragedy and Socrates."[70] A little further, Strauss explains what this means: "wisdom is not a great theme for Machiavelli be-cause justice is not a great theme for him."[71] By the same token, the essen-tial Socratic combination of wisdom and moderation has vanished: with Machiavelli, practical reason begins its steep ascent in philosophy.

What is missing in the Florentine's field of vision is the connection between the problem of wisdom and the problem of justice, or between philosophy and politics, as Socrates discusses it in the *Republic*. Like Hobbes after him, Machiavelli dismisses classical, Socratic-Platonic political philosophy without having understood its core.[72] And like Hobbes, he lays claim to a deeper understanding of human nature, while in fact his new political philosophy rests on a major reduction of the political problem by the elimination of the question of the best regime. "The consequence is an enormous simplification and, above all, the appearance of the discovery of a hitherto wholly unsuspected whole continent. . . . [A] stupendous contraction of the horizon appears to Machiavelli and his successors as a wondrous enlargement of the horizon."[73] Strauss's choice of spatial metaphors is far from accidental. While it casts doubt on Machiavelli's claim to be a "greater Columbus," it also suggests that he has altogether given up the attempt to leave the Platonic cave, the realm of the city.

As Strauss also notes, however, "the narrowing of the horizon which Machiavelli was the first to effect, was caused, or at least facilitated, by anti-theological ire."[74] In order to succeed, the new philosophy is compelled to combat another tradition that claims there is something beyond the cave: revealed religion. According to Machiavelli, the success of Christianity in particular is, in fact, the success of the propaganda disseminated posthumously by an "unarmed prophet." Whoever wishes to install new modes and orders and is similarly unarmed is thus compelled to combat his opponent with the same means. In his political works, Machiavelli mounts a covert antireligious campaign with a view to posthumous victory: the conquest of the world by an alliance of philosophy and political power.[75] As in the case of Spinoza and Hobbes, however, the unparalleled success of this campaign obscured the fact that revealed religion survived the onslaught essentially intact. Thus, their "anti-theological ire" fueled the "Napoleonic strategy" of circumventing the "impregnable fortress of orthodoxy." As we saw in the previous chapter, this strategy eventually produced the second cave underneath the Platonic cave, where even the recollection of the Socratic question and Platonic politics has faded.

In fact, Platonic politics itself may be partly responsible for its decline, Strauss suggests. In an essay devoted to the art of writing, he observes about Alfarabi: "He substitutes politics for religion. He thus may be said to lay the foundation for the secular alliance between philosophers and princes friendly to philosophy, and so to initiate the tradition whose most famous representatives in the West are Marsilius of Padua and Machiavelli."[76] By underscoring the continuity between these thinkers, Strauss tacitly points to a fundamental discontinuity between East and West. Alfarabi's substitution of politics for religion influenced Western thought mainly through the reception of Averroës by so-called Latin Averroism.[77] In the course of this reception, however, the Platonic orientation of the *falasifa* was lost. Unlike Alfarabi, Marsilius and Machiavelli no longer viewed the substitution of politics for religion as an esoteric strategy for mediating the tension between philosophy and the city. Rather, they saw it as a first step on the way to eradicating this tension altogether. If they were unaware of the original design, Alfarabi may have concealed it too well for thinkers with a Christian background, Strauss suggests: "the political action of the philosophers on behalf of philosophy has achieved full success. One sometimes wonders whether it was not too successful."[78] If this is the case, Platonic politics may well have become a victim of its own success.

## Natural Right and the Socratic Question

Thus, taking our cue from Heidegger's notion of *Seinsvergessenheit* ("forget-fulness of Being"), we might encapsulate Strauss's diagnosis of modernity as *Sokratesvergessenheit* ("forgetfulness of Socrates"). That his thought remains focused on recovering the Socratic question, even if this is not always made explicit, is shown in *Natural Right and History* (1953), perhaps the best-known and most widely read of his works. All too often, this book is regarded as a neo-Aristotelian plea for the rehabilitation of the tradition of natural law, accompanied by a critique of modern positivism and historicism.[79] This interpretation is seriously misguided, however, if only because the title refers to "natural right" instead of "natural law." Strauss indeed launches an attack on positivism and historicism, but he does so from a position that is firmly rooted in his rediscovery of Socratic-Platonic philosophy of the 1930s. Regarding his understanding of natural right, he provides the following clarification: "The full understanding of the classic natural right doctrine would require a full understanding of the change in thought that was effected by Socrates. Such an understanding is not at our disposal."[80] Even if it is not at our disposal, it does not follow that it is completely beyond our reach. By studying the sources, we can try to understand the Socratic turn and its conditions:

> The classic natural right doctrine in its original form, if fully developed, is identical with the doctrine of the best regime. For the question as to what is by nature right or as to what is justice finds its complete answer only through the construction, in speech, of the best regime. The essentially political character of the classic natural right doctrine appears most clearly in Plato's *Republic*.[81]

In this way, it becomes apparent that for Strauss natural right is nothing other than the object of the Socratic question, as well as its paradoxical answer. The intention underlying *Natural Right and History* is to make the reader aware of natural right, not as a doctrine or an answer, but as a problem, a question, or, rather, "the primeval question."[82] Shortly after the publication of the book, Strauss writes to his colleague Eric Voegelin: "I do nothing more than present the *problem* of natural right as an unsolved problem."[83] This intention leads him to oppose positivism and historicism, on which point he continues the critique he had begun to elaborate at the beginning of the 1930s. The addressees of this critique have remained largely unchanged—Max Weber as the most important representative of positivism, and Nietzsche and Heidegger as the most thoughtful proponents of historicism—as have the main objections. Weberian positivism considers the Socratic question of the right life to be unanswerable, because the great value systems are locked in an irresolvable conflict that can only be settled by an individual, irrational decision. Nietzschean and Heideggerian historicism take one step further, by declaring the Socratic question to be altogether pointless. On the basis of modern historical consciousness, it stresses the relative character of all worldviews, values, and truths. Rejecting the notion of a natural horizon and an eternal order, it dismisses the beginning and end of philosophy in its original meaning.

In critical response, Strauss reiterates his foremost objection: both positivism and historicism unwarrantedly transform the historical fate of philosophy into its task. Instead, he argues, philosophy's fate should be taken as an inducement to renewed efforts.[84] As to what unites Nietzsche, Weber, and Heidegger in their rejection of classical political philosophy and the Socratic question, *Natural Right and History* provides no explicit answer. The few indications that can be found, however, suggest that here as well Strauss stands by his earlier analysis in *Philosophy and Law*: the atheism from probity, the rebellious heir to biblical faith and to the polemics against it.[85] If this is the case, we may surmise that he equally stands by the alternative to the atheism from probity that is adumbrated sotto voce in *Philosophy and Law*: "the old love of truth" or philosophic *eros*, the enigmatic desire for wisdom inseparably connected with the figure of Socrates. Recovering the Socratic question implies the rehabilitation of *eros*, which drove Socrates onto the streets of Athens and impelled Xenophon and Plato to write. Just as it is his "last word" against the antitheological ire of Machiavelli and his descendants, the unbelieving *eros* of Socrates is Strauss's last word, his response to the dogmatic, believing atheism of Nietzsche, Weber, and Heidegger.[86] Similarly, Strauss's emphasis on the

Socratic turn as philosophy's turn toward political self-awareness can be seen as a critical rejoinder to their "pre-Socratic" fascination with Being and the questionable political consequences of this fascination.[87]

## From Jerusalem to Athens (and Back)

For the same reasons, the Socratic life remains *the* alternative to a return to religious orthodoxy.[88] As we saw at the end of the second chapter, Strauss considered the way back to Jerusalem to be closed to him. From his critique of atheism from probity, we may infer that, as a result, the way to Athens was the only acceptable option. This option is by no means self-evident, however, not only because the Socratic philosopher requires permanent self-questioning, nor because the road to Athens is especially hard to travel, but also because it is not easy to turn one's back on Jerusalem. In *Natural Right and History*, Strauss offers a memorable formulation of the problem:

> Man cannot live without light, guidance, knowledge; only through knowledge of the good can he find the good that he needs. The fundamental question, therefore, is whether men can acquire that knowledge of the good without which they cannot guide their lives individually or collectively by the unaided efforts of their natural powers, or whether they are dependent for that knowledge on Divine Revelation. No alternative is more fundamental than this: human guidance of divine guidance. The first possibility is characteristic of philosophy or science in the original sense of the term, the second is presented in the Bible.[89]

The opposition between Jerusalem and Athens is essentially a theological-political conflict, according to Strauss. What is at stake is the relationship between man, society, and transcendence. Of the inscrutable God of Judaism, no more can be said than what he says of himself to Moses: *Ehyeh-Asher-Ehyeh*, or "I shall be what I shall be," establishing a covenant with man that requires his unconditional obedience.[90] The biblical God is a God who answers the question of the right life by revealing his divine guidance in the form of a divine law. As a political order, this law is the point of departure for philosophy, which thereby is essentially political philosophy. However, this does not do away with the fact that the philosophic question of the right life also has a theological dimension that is opposed to the Bible, Strauss holds. When he emphasizes that philosophy must begin with what is first "for us," he adds, "Only by beginning at this point will we be open to the full impact of the all-important question which is coeval with philosophy although the philosophers do not frequently pronounce it—the question *quid sit deus*."[91]

The question "What is God?" once more illustrates the paradoxical character of Socratic-Platonic political philosophy: while it calls into question the origin of the law and thus the highest authority of the city, it appears as the highest form of the concern for the divine that is presupposed in obedience to the law.[92] Like every other permutation of the Socratic question—What is virtue? What is courage? What is nobility?—it reflects the priorities of the city, and thus the intimate connection between theology and politics. By the same token, it is connected to the question of the right life: who or what is the God who rules the city, and who should be obeyed? And by the same token, it testifies to the Socratic question as an attempt to discover nature as that which is independent of both human artifice and divine power. As we saw, it is the fundamental claim of revealed religion to have definitely answered this question. With regard to the good life and "the one thing needful," therefore, philosophy and revelation are opposed as *the* question and *the* answer.

According to Strauss, Athens and Jerusalem represent two fundamentally irreconcilable and incompatible views of the right life. According to the first, only the philosophical, theoretical life leads to true human happiness. This view leads to an ambiguous relationship to the theological-political order of the city: philosophy as an activity is transmoral and transpolitical, but the philosopher is a political being subject to the authority of the city and its laws.[93] As a result, the philosopher's obedience to this authority can only be ambiguous. According to the second view, only the practical, moral life of pious obedience to the divine will leads to felicity.[94] This view cannot be dismissed forthwith, Strauss stresses. Revelation offers the most profound foundation and the most coherent defense of the superiority of the moral-practical life over the theoretical life as the way to happiness.[95] Because of this quality, it is the only worthy opponent of philosophy in its original meaning. The latter can call revelation into question, but it cannot refute it, for this would presuppose that it has found a definite answer to the question of the right life. Conversely, revelation cannot compel the philosopher's assent with the argument that such assent is of the greatest importance for his salvation: in the philosopher's view, this would only confirm the importance of raising the question of the right life, and thus demonstrate the necessity of philosophy.[96]

Despite their fundamental disagreement, both opponents share a common background that differs from the horizon erected by modern thought. To begin with, both Athens and Jerusalem acknowledge the importance of morality for human life, but they also point to its insufficiency. Their disagreement concerns precisely what is needed to supplement morality: free contemplation or pious obedience. In this respect, Strauss points to the importance of the *theioi nomoi* or divine laws, the theological-political order that is central to both classical political philosophy and revealed religion. A second common ground is the view that man remains incapable of creating the perfect society. From the perspective of classical political philosophy, such attempts are bound to come to grief on the unbridgeable rift between philosophers and nonphilosophers, and thus on the permanence of conflict among human beings regarding the good, the just, and the noble. For revealed religion, the creation of the perfect society is a divine privilege, and thus beyond the reach of man. Remarkably enough, as a result of this quasi agreement Strauss seems to come to an understanding of the Jewish question as a theological-political question on philosophical instead of theological grounds:

> Finite, relative problems can be solved; infinite, absolute problems cannot be solved. In other words, human beings will never create a society which is free of contradictions. From every point of view, it looks as if the Jewish people were the chosen people in the sense, at least, that the Jewish problem is the most manifest symbol of the human problem as a social or political problem.[97]

At the same time, this shows that Strauss did not acquiesce in a stalemate between Athens and Jerusalem. Near the middle of his life, he went as far as he could in trying to provide a genealogical–philosophical explanation of faith in revelation, guided by Socrates and Plato.[98] According to one observer, this means that ultimately he came to see that "the Athens side comprehends the Jerusalem side."[99] Whether this assessment is correct is hard to determine, even if it touches the core of Strauss's philosophic endeavor. What is clear, however, is that he remained determined to ascertain whether and how the philosopher would be able to face revelation while remaining a philosopher after the example of Socrates. This determination found a beautiful and noble expression in the following passage:

> Whether the Bible or philosophy is right is of course the only question which ultimately matters. But in order to understand that question one must first see philosophy as it is. One must not see it from the outset through Biblical glasses. Wherever each of us may stand, no respectable purpose is served by trying to prove that we eat the cake and have it. Socrates used all his powers to awaken those who can think out of the slumber of thoughtlessness. We ill follow his example if we use his authority for putting us to sleep."[100]

# Notes

## Introduction

1. Allan Bloom, "Leo Strauss, September 20, 1899–October 18, 1973," in *Giants and Dwarfs: Essays 1960–1990* (New York: Simon & Schuster, 1990), 235.

2. Robert Lacayo, "But Who Has the Power?" *Time*, June 1996, 41.

3. Cf. Myles Burnyeat, "Sphinx Without a Secret," *New York Review of Books* 32, no. 9 (1985): 30–36; Charles Larmore, "The Secrets of Philosophy," *New Republic* 3 (1989): 30–35; Shadia Drury, *The Political Ideas of Leo Strauss* (New York: St. Martin's Press, 1988; updated edition 2005) and *Leo Strauss and the American Right* (London: Palgrave Macmillan, 1999); Stephen Holmes, *The Anatomy of Antiliberalism* (Cambridge, MA: Harvard University Press, 1996); John G. Gunnell, "Political Theory and Politics: The Case of Leo Strauss," *Political Theory* 13, no. 3 (1985): 339–361. For opposite views, see Nathan Tarcov, "Philosophy and History: John Gunnell and Leo Strauss on Tradition and Interpretation," in *Tradition, Interpretation, and Science: Political Theory in the American Academy*, ed. John S. Nelson, 69–112 (Albany: State University of New York Press, 1986); Peter Berkowitz, "Liberal Zealotry," *Yale Law Journal* 103, no. 5 (1994): 1363–1382; Heinrich Meier, *Leo Strauss and the Theologico-Political Problem* (Cambridge: Cambridge University Press, 2006); Steven B. Smith, *Reading Leo Strauss: Politics, Philosophy, Judaism* (Chicago: University of Chicago Press, 2006).

4. Cf. Werner Dannhauser, "Leo Strauss: Becoming Naïve Again," *American Scholar* 44 (1975): 636–642; George Anastaplo, *The Artist as Thinker: From Shakespeare to Joyce* (Athens, OH: Swallow Press, 1983): 249–272; Kenneth L. Deutsch and John Murley, eds., *Leo Strauss, the Straussians, and the American Regime* (Lanham, MD: Rowman & Littlefield, 1999). For an impression of Strauss as a teacher, see the edited transcripts of his course on Plato's *Symposium*: Leo Strauss, *On Plato's Symposium*, ed. and with a foreword by Seth Benardete (Chicago: University of Chicago Press, 2001). Strauss even makes a brief appearance as the shadowy "Professor Davarr" in Saul Bellow's *Ravelstein* (Harmondsworth, UK: Penguin, 2000), a literary portrait of Allan Bloom.

5. See John A. Murley, ed., *Leo Strauss and His Legacy: A Bibliography* (Lanham, MD: Lexington Books, 2005).

6. See Steven Lenzner, "Leo Strauss and the Conservatives," *Policy Review*, April/May 2003.

7. Cf. Robert Devigne, *Recasting Conservatism: Oakeshott, Strauss and the Response to Postmodernism* (New Haven, CT: Yale University Press, 1994); David L. Schaefer, "Leo Strauss and American Democracy: A Response to Wood and Holmes," *Review of Politics* 53, no. 1 (1991): 187–199; Nasser Behnegar, "The Liberal Politics of Leo Strauss," in *Political Philosophy and the Human Soul: Essays in Memory of Allan Bloom*, ed. Michael Palmer and Thomas L. Pangle, 251–267 (Lanham, MD: Rowman & Littlefield, 1995).

8. Cf. Raymond Aron, Introduction to *Le savant et le politique*, by Max Weber, 31–52 (Paris: Plon, 1959); Claude Lefort, *Écrire: À l'épreuve du politique* (Paris: Calmann-Lévy, 1992), 261–301; Laurent Jaffro, Benoît Frydman, Emmanuel Cattin, and Alain Petit, eds., *Leo Strauss: art d'écrire, politique, philosophie* (Paris: Vrin, 2001); Daniel Tanguay, *Leo Strauss. An Intellectual Biography* (New Haven, CT: Yale University Press, 2007).

9. Leo Strauss, *Gesammelte Schriften*, Vols. 1–3 (Stuttgart/Weimar: Verlag J. B. Metzler, 1996—2001).

10. Quoted in Alan Udoff, "On Leo Strauss: An Introductory Account," in *Leo Strauss's Thought: Toward a Critical Engagement*, ed. Alan Udoff, 27 n. 63 (Boulder, CO: Lynne Rienner Publishers, 1991).

11. Rémi Brague, "Athènes, Jérusalem, La Mecque. L'interprétation 'musulmane' de la philosophie grecque chez Leo Strauss," *Revue de Métaphysique et de Morale* 94, no. 3 (1989): 311.

12. Bloom, "Leo Strauss," 239.

13. Udoff, "On Leo Strauss," 13.

14. V. Reinecke and J. Uhlaner, "The Problem of Leo Strauss: Religion, Philosophy, and Politics," *Graduate Philosophy Journal* 16, no. 1 (1992): 190.

15. Arnaldo Momigliano, "Hermeneutics and Classical Political Thought in Leo Strauss," in *Essays on Ancient and Modern Judaism* (Chicago: University of Chicago Press, 1994), 187 n. 22.

16. Meier, *Leo Strauss and the Theologico-Political Problem*, 64.

17. David Janssens, *Tussen Athene en Jeruzalem: filosofie, profetie en politiek in het werk van Leo Strauss* (Amsterdam: Boom, 2001). I owe many thanks to Theo Dunkelgrün, who gave an early impulse to the present volume by preparing a draft translation of the introduction.

## Chapter 1. "In the Grip of the Theological-Political Predicament"

1. Strauss, *Spinoza's Critique of Religion*, trans. Elsa M. Sinclair (New York: Schocken Books, 1965). This volume will henceforth be referred to as "SCR." Original edition: *Die Religionskritik Spinozas als Grundlage seiner Bibelwissenschaft: Unter-*

*suchungen zu Spinozas Theologisch-politischem Traktat* (Berlin: Akademie-Verlag, 1930); reprinted in Leo Strauss, *Gesammelte Schriften, Bd. 1: Die Religionskritik Spinozas und zugehörige Schriften*, ed. Heinrich Meier (Stuttgart/Weimar: Verlag J. B. Metzler, 1996), henceforth referred to as "GS 1."

2. Strauss, *The Political Philosophy of Hobbes: Its Basis and Its Genesis*, trans. Elsa M. Sinclair (Oxford: Clarendon Press, 1936), henceforth "PPH." See Strauss's correspondence with Karl Löwith, in Leo Strauss, *Gesammelte Schriften Bd 3: Hobbes' politische Wissenschaft und zugehörige Schriften*, ed. Heinrich Meier, 641, 655–656 (Stuttgart/Weimar: Verlag J. B. Metzler, 2001), henceforth referred to as "GS 3." Cf. Strauss, *On Tyranny: Revised and Expanded Edition—Including the Strauss-Kojève Correspondence*, ed. Victor Gourevitch and Michael S. Roth (New York: Free Press, 1991), 230, henceforth "OT." Cf. Heinrich Meier's preface in Strauss, *Gesammelte Schriften Bd. 2: Philosophie und Gesetz—Frühe Schriften*, ed. Heinrich Meier, x n. 3 (Stuttgart/Weimar: Verlag J. B. Metzler, 1997), henceforth "GS 2." Although all available English translations of Strauss's early German writings were used, at times I have made slight alterations in order to bring the text closer to the German original.

3. Strauss, SCR, 1.

4. Strauss, "Preface to *Hobbes' politische Wissenschaft*," in *Jewish Philosophy and the Crisis of Modernity: Essays and Lectures in Modern Jewish Thought*, ed. and intro. by Kenneth Hart Green (Albany: State University of New York Press, 1997), 453; henceforth "JPCM."

5. Strauss, "Why We Remain Jews: Can Jewish Faith and History Still Speak to Us?" in JPCM, 312.

6. Quoted in ibid., 313. See also 286, 322–323.

7. Cf. Strauss, "Freud on Moses and Monotheism," in JPCM, 286, and "Why We Remain Jews," in JPCM, 322–323.

8. Strauss himself relates how a childhood encounter with Russian-Jewish refugees made a profound impression. See Strauss, "Why We Remain Jews," in JPCM, 312–313.

9. Cf. Michael Morgan, *Dilemmas in Modern Jewish Thought: The Dialectics of Revelation and History* (Bloomington: Indiana University Press, 1992), 42.

10. Cf. Shlomo Avineri, *The Making of Modern Zionism: The Intellectual Origins of the Jewish State* (London: Weidenfeld and Nicolson, 1981), 88–100. Herzl's political and voluntaristic approach appears very clearly in the motto to his other major work, the utopian novel *Old New Land* (*Altneuland*): "If you want, it is no fairy tale" (*Wenn Ihr wollt, ist es kein Märchen*). See Theodor Herzl, *Old New Land* (Princeton, NJ: Markus Wiener Publishers, 1997).

11. Jehudah Reinharz, "Ideology and Structure in German Zionism, 1882–1933," in *Essential Papers on Zionism*, ed. J. Reinharz and A. Shapira, 279–284 (New York: New York University Press, 1996).

12. Strauss, "A Giving of Accounts" (with Jacob Klein), in JPCM, 460. Strauss's conversion to political Zionism probably antedates his military service,

which he performed between July 1917 and December 1918 as a translator in the German army stationed in Belgium. See Edward C. Banfield, "Leo Strauss: 1899–1973," in *Remembering the University of Chicago: Teachers, Scientists, and Scholars*, ed. Edward Shils, 493 (Chicago: University of Chicago Press, 1991).

13. For a thorough and well-documented treatment of Strauss's involvement in political Zionism, see the editor's introduction in Strauss, *The Early Writings (1921–1932)*, trans. and ed. Michael Zank (Albany: State University of New York Press, 2002), 3–36; henceforth "EW".

14. Strauss, "The Zionism of Max Nordau," in EW, 83.

15. Strauss, "Sigmund Freud, *The Future of an Illusion*," in EW, 202.

16. Strauss, "On the Argument with European Science," in EW, 108.

17. Strauss, "Sigmund Freud, *The Future of an Illusion*," in EW, 204.

18. Strauss, "Zur Ideologie des politischen Zionismus" ("On the Ideology of Political Zionism"), in GS 2, 445.

19. Cf. Strauss, "Response to Frankfurt's 'Word of Principle'" and "The Zionism of Nordau," in EW, 68 and 86.

20. Strauss, "The Zionism of Nordau," in EW, 85.

21. Cf. Strauss, "Response to Frankfurt's 'Word of Principle'" and "Paul de Lagarde," in EW, 67 and 93–94. Cf. Emil Fackenheim, *The Jewish Return into History: Reflections in the Age of Auschwitz and a New Jerusalem* (New York: Schocken Books, 1978).

22. Cf. Strauss, "Response to Frankfurt's 'Word of Principle,'" in EW, 68. With regard to the historicization of Judaism and the influence of Hegelianism in particular, see Avineri, *The Making of Modern Zionism: The Intellectual Origins of the Jewish State* (London: Weidenfeld and Nicolson, 1981).

23. Cf. Strauss, "Response to Frankfurt's 'Word of Principle'" and "The Zionism of Nordau," in EW, 67 and 87. Vladimir (Ze'ev) Jabotinsky, the founder of the radical Revisionist movement, similarly regarded Zionism as an exponent of European culture and therefore rejected every form of "orientalism." See Avineri, *The Making of Modern Zionism*, 179–180.

24. Strauss, "Response to Frankfurt's 'Word of Principle,'" in EW, 69.

25. Strauss, "Response to Frankfurt's 'Word of Principle," in EW, 70.

26. Strauss, "Why We Remain Jews," in JPCM, 319–320.

27. Strauss, SCR, 6.

28. Cf. Strauss, "Ecclesia Militans," in EW, 127.

29. Cf. Strauss, "Ecclesia Militans" and "Biblical History and Science," in EW, 125–126 and 132–133.

30. Ibid., 133 (translation slightly altered). Strauss sums up his critique in the words of the eighteenth-century playwright, poet, philosopher, and theologian

Gotthold Ephraim Lessing: "Thus, what is so nauseating is not orthodoxy itself, but a certain squinting, limping orthodoxy which is unequal to itself!" (Gotthold Ephraim Lessing, "Gegensätze des Herausgebers," in *Werke in drei Bänden* (München: Carl Hanser Verlag, 1982), 3:342. Quoted in Strauss, "Biblical History and Science," in EW, 133. Lessing conducted a polemic with the Christian orthodoxy of his time in which he reproached his opponent for defending faith by one-sidedly and dishonestly stressing its salutary effects. As we shall see, Lessing's influence on Strauss's thought is considerable.

31. Strauss, "Ecclesia Militans," in EW, 126.

32. Ibid., 128.

33. Strauss, "Comment on Weinberg's Critique," in EW, 118.

34. Strauss, SCR, 6.

35. Ibid.

36. Strauss, "The Zionism of Nordau," in EW, 85.

37. Cf. Strauss, "The Zionism of Nordau," in EW, 86–87; SCR, 5; and "Why We Remain Jews," in JPCM, 318.

38. Cf. Strauss, SCR, 4: "Zionism was almost never wholly divorced from the traditional Jewish hopes."

39. Strauss, "Response to Frankfurt's 'Word of Principle,'" in EW, 68.

40. Strauss, "Ecclesia Militans," in EW, 128.

41. Cf. Joseph Cropsey, "Leo Strauss," in *Biographical Supplement to the International Encyclopaedia of the Social Sciences* (London: Free Press, 1979), 18:746–750.

42. Strauss, "A Giving of Accounts," in JPCM, 458. Cf. Ernest L. Fortin, "Gadamer on Strauss: An Interview," *Interpretation* 12, no. 1 (1984): 1–13.

43. Simon M. Dubnow, *Die Weltgeschichte des jüdischen Volkes*, 10 vols. (Berlin: Jüdischer Verlag, 1925–1930).

44. Strauss, "Biblical History and Science," in EW, 135.

45. Cf. Strauss, "Sociological Historiography?" and "Biblical History and Science," in EW, 104 and 134.

46. Strauss, "On the Argument with European Science," in EW, 109.

47. Ibid.

48. Ibid.

49. See Hermann Cohen, *Die Religion der Vernunft aus den Quellen des Judentums* (Leipzich: Fock, 1919). The English translation (*Religion of Reason Out of the Sources of Judaism* [New York: Frederick Ungar Publishing, 1972]) contains an introductory essay by Strauss, reprinted in JPCM, 267–282.

50. Strauss, "On the Argument with European Science," in EW, 111.

51. Franz Rosenzweig, *Hegel und der Staat* (München: R. Oldenbourg, 1920).

52. Strauss, "On the Argument with European Science," in EW, 110. In the same vein, Strauss wonders in his first publication "whether 'science' and 'state' . . . are perhaps more closely related to the innermost Jewish tendency . . . a 'perhaps' at which one may very well arrive if one thinks of the biblical origins of modern science, of the equally *uncanny* character of the biblical world" (Strauss, "Response to Frankfurt's 'Word of Principle,'" in EW, 65).

53. Rudolf Otto, *Das Heilige: Über das Irrationale in der Idee des Göttlichen und sein Verhältnis zum Rationalen* (Breslau: Trewendt & Granier, 1917). English translation by J. W. Harvey, *The Idea of the Holy: An Inquiry into the Non-Rational Factor in the Idea of the Divine and Its Relation to the Rational* (New York: Galaxy Books, 1958).

54. Cf. Strauss, "On the Argument with European Science," in EW, 111: "Theology is needed as an autonomous science, insofar as it makes sense to speak of God's being-in-Himself, and insofar as there is knowledge of this being-in-Himself."

55. Strauss, "On the Argument with European Science," in EW, 111.

56. Strauss, "The Holy," in EW, 76.

57. Ibid., 77.

58. Martin Buber, *Eclipse of God: Studies in the Relation between Religion and Philosophy* (New York: Harper, 1952), quoted in Strauss, SCR, 10–11.

59. Strauss, SCR, 13.

60. Ibid., 14.

61. Strauss, "On the Argument with European Science," in EW, 108 (translation slightly altered).

62. Strauss, "The Holy," in EW, 75.

63. Strauss, "On the Argument with European Science," in EW, 109.

64. Strauss, SCR, 15.

65. Strauss, "Die geistige Lage der Gegenwart" ("The Spiritual Situation of the Present"), in GS 2, 444.

66. Strauss, "Response to Frankfurt's 'Word of Principle,'" in EW, 65 (emphasis added).

67. Strauss, "On the Argument with European Science," in EW, 109.

68. Cf. Strauss, *What Is Political Philosophy? And Other Studies* (Glencoe, IL: Free Press, 1959), 225 (henceforth "WPP").

69. Cf. Strauss, WPP, 171; Strauss, *Thoughts on Machiavelli* (Glencoe, IL: Free Press, 1958), 294 (henceforth "TM"); Strauss, *Persecution and the Art of Writing* (Glencoe, IL: Free Press, 1952), 35 n. 17 (henceforth "PAW").

70. Cf. Strauss, *The Rebirth of Classical Political Rationalism* (Chicago: University of Chicago Press, 1989), 23 (henceforth "RCPR").

71. Strauss, "The Testament of Spinoza," in EW, 217–218.

72. Baruch Spinoza, *Tractatus Theologico-Politicus*, Ed. Pr. (in Spinoza, *Opera/Werke* (Darmstadt: Wissenschaftliche Buchgesellschaft, 1979), 43. References in this and the following chapter are to this edition, henceforth "TTP."

73. Cf. Strauss, "The Testament of Spinoza," in EW, 219–220; RCPR, 231; SCR, 5.

74. Cf. Strauss, WPP, 13; "Why We Remain Jews," in JPCM, 318–319.

75. Strauss, SCR, 15.

76. Strauss, *Philosophy and Law: Contributions to the Understanding of Maimonides and his Predecessors*, trans. Eve Adler (Albany: State University of New York Press, 1995), 27–28 (henceforth "PL").

77. Strauss, "On the Argument with European Science," in EW, 109.

78. Strauss, "A Giving of Accounts," in JPCM, 460.

## Chapter 2.  The Shadow of Spinoza

1. Strauss, "The Testament of Spinoza," in EW, 216; SCR, 15–17.

2. See Hermann Cohen, "Spinoza über Staat und Religion Judentum und Christentum," in *Gesammelte Schriften*, vol. 3 (Berlin: C. A. Schwetschke, 1924), 290–372.

3. Cf. Strauss, "Cohen's Analysis of Spinoza's Bible Science," in EW, 161; "On the Bible Science of Spinoza and His Precursors," in EW, 173; SCR, 15, 208; "The Testament of Spinoza," in EW, 216.

4. Strauss, "Cohen's Analysis," in EW, 141.

5. Spinoza, TTP, in pr.

6. Strauss, "Cohen's Analysis," in EW, 142. Cf. Thomas L. Pangle's introduction to *Studies in Platonic Political Philosophy*, by Leo Strauss (Chicago: University of Chicago Press, 1983), 18–20 (henceforth "SPPP").

7. Cf. Strauss, "Cohen's Analysis," in EW, 158–159.

8. Ibid., 146.

9. Cf. ibid., 144–145, 151–152, 156–157; WPP, 225–226.

10. Cf. Strauss, "Cohen's Analysis," in EW, 148; Spinoza, TTP, v.

11. Strauss, "Cohen's Analysis," in EW, 146.

12. Spinoza, TTP, v.

13. Ibid., 153.

14. Cf. Strauss, SCR, 119–123.

15. Strauss, "Cohen's Analysis," in EW, 156.

16. This does not prevent Strauss from agreeing with Cohen that the *herem* was fully justified from the orthodox point of view. See Strauss, "Cohen's Analysis," in EW, 160.

17. Strauss, "Cohen's Analysis," in EW, 160 (translation slightly altered).

18. Rosenzweig had laid the foundations of the academy in "It is Time" (*Zeit ists*), an essay addressed to Cohen. See Strauss's tribute to Rosenzweig, "Franz Rosenzweig and the Academy for the Science of Judaism," in EW, 212. Cf. Nahum Glatzer, *Franz Rosenzweig: His Life and Thought* (New York: Schocken Books, 1976), 49.

19. Cf. Strauss, "On the Bible Science of Spinoza and His Precursors," in EW, 173; "Vorwort," GS 1, 55.

20. Apparently, this change was not well received by Strauss's supervisor at the academy, Julius Guttmann. In a letter of October 3, 1931, Strauss tells his colleague Gerhard Krüger about certain "deficiencies" (*Fehler*) in the book that are due to "the censorship I was under" (GS 3, 393). According to Heinrich Meier, Strauss was forced to alter or omit certain passages Guttmann objected to (Meier, "Vorwort des Herausgebers," in Strauss, GS 2, n. 10). This probably explains the exceptionally complex and oblique structure of the book.

21. Spinoza, TTP, 84–85. Cf. Strauss, "On Spinoza's Bible Science," in EW, 174; SCR, 259; PAW, 144.

22. Strauss, SCR, 114, 143, 173, 263; PAW, 149, 193–194.

23. Strauss, SCR, 115, 259; PAW, 147.

24. Cf. Strauss, "On Spinoza's Bible Science," in EW, 174

25. Strauss, SCR, 263.

26. Spinoza, TTP, 48: "God's will and God's intellect are in truth one and the same; and they can only be distinguished with respect to our thoughts, which we form of God's intellect."

27. Spinoza, TTP, 51. Cf. Strauss, SCR, 151–154.

28. On the same grounds, Spinoza rejects the idea of God as a lawgiver and of the revealed law as a set of moral or legal norms. The fact that he nevertheless continues to use the term "law" while fundamentally changing its content and meaning testifies to the consistency with which he practices his motto (*caute*). Cf. David Lachterman, "Laying Down the Law: The Theological-Political Matrix of Spinoza's Physics," in *Leo Strauss's Thought: Toward a Critical Engagement*, ed. Alan Udoff, 123–153 (Boulder, CO: Lynne Rienner Publishers, 1991).

29. Cf. Strauss, SCR, 206, 153–155, 201; "On the Bible Science of Spinoza," in EW, 176–177; PL, 135 n. 2.

30. Cf. Spinoza, TTP, ii.

31. Cf. Strauss, SCR, 217: "Radically understood striving after self-preservation evolves into interest in theory."

32. Spinoza, TTP, i.

33. Cf. Strauss, SCR, 28, 111–112, 129–130; PAW, 162–163.

34. Cf. Strauss, SCR, 258–259.

35. Ibid., 259 (translation slightly altered; emphasis added). This crucial sentence occurs near the end of the book, possibly as a consequence of the censorship Strauss was under (see note 20). Cf. Strauss, SCR, 114 n. 141.

36. Cf. ibid., 37 n. 2.

37. Strauss, "On Spinoza's Bible Science," in EW, 174.

38. Strauss, SCR, 108.

39. Spinoza, TTP, iv.

40. Ibid., v.

41. Ibid., 166, 168.

42. Cf. SCR, 75, 92–93, 94, 196–97. Strauss later upholds this analysis, as becomes apparent from PAW, 193–194:

> The return to the literal sense of the Bible fulfils an entirely different function within the context of the criticism, based on the Bible, of traditional theology on the one hand and within the context of the attack on the authority of the Bible on the other. . . . [V]iewed as the standard and corrective for all later religion and theology, the Bible is the document of "the ancient religion"; viewed as the object of philosophic criticism, the Bible is a document transmitting "the prejudices of an ancient nation."

As we shall see in the section "Fighting the Kingdom of Darkness" in Chapter 5, Thomas Hobbes, like Spinoza a critic of religion and founder of modern liberalism, deploys a similar double strategy. Cf. Pierre Manent, *Naissances de la politique moderne: Machiavel, Hobbes, Rousseau* (Paris: Payot, 1977), 106.

43. According to Strauss, there is no contradiction between the two strategies "since both of these occur in Scripture, 'pure doctrine,' and 'prejudices,' quite apart from the fact that in each of the two cases his argument proceeds on a different plane" (Strauss, SCR, 138).

44. Cf. Strauss, PAW, 193.

45. Cf. Spinoza, TTP, 84–92, especially 88: "from the investigation of Scripture this must first be sought that is the most universal and the basis and the foundation of the whole of Scripture."

46. Strauss, SCR, 117. Cf. Strauss, RCPR, 230.

47. Cf. Strauss, SCR, 141.

48. Ibid., 144. Cf. ibid., 123.

49. Ibid., 121.

50. 1 Kings 18. Cf. Strauss, SCR, 213–214; RCPR, 265.

51. As Strauss points out, tradition views physical tangibleness as the most important characteristic of a miracle. As a consequence of the critique of religion as well as of later attempts to rehabilitate miracles, "the fact has been glossed over or suppressed that the genuine significance of miracles is direct action by God on corporeal things" (Strauss, SCR, 291 n. 166). This remark echoes Strauss's interest in the factual and material aspect of revelation, which also animates his critique of the religious a priori's of idealist theology (see the section "Biblical Politics, Biblical Science, and the New Theology" in chapter 1). Cf. Strauss, SCR, 212: "miracles as works of God occurring within the corporeal world, and affecting the corporeal world."

52. In his review of *Spinoza's Critique of Religion*, Gerhard Krüger defines the demonstrative power of miracles as "the direct, univocal manifestation of a divine creative power to the 'simple experience' (*bloße Erfahrung*) of all." See his "Besprechung von L. Strauss, *Die Religionskritik Spinozas als Grundlage seiner Bibelwissenschaft*," *Deutsche Literaturzeitung* 51 (1931): 2409.

53. Cf. Strauss, PAW, 167.

54. Strauss, SCR, 126. Cf. Walter Soffer, "Modern Rationalism, Miracles, and Revelation: Strauss's Critique of Spinoza," in *Leo Strauss: Political Philosopher and Jewish Thinker*, ed. Kenneth L. Deutsch and Walter Nicgorski, 146 (Lanham, MD: Rowman & Littlefield Publishers, 1994).

55. Strauss, SCR, 131.

56. Cf. Strauss, "On the Bible Science of Spinoza," in EW, 178.

57. Cf. Strauss, SCR, 187; RCPR, 263; *Natural Right and History* (Chicago: University of Chicago Press, 1953), 210 (henceforth "NRH").

58. Spinoza, Letter 75.

59. Cf. Strauss, SCR, 215–223.

60. Cf. Ibid., 140–144.

61. Cf. Strauss, SPPP, 150.

62. Strauss, SCR, 136.

63. Cf. ibid., 177; Soffer, "Modern Rationalism," 151–152.

64. Strauss, SCR, 136; PL, 32–33; RCPR, 265; Soffer, "Modern Rationalism," 153

65. Cf. Strauss, SCR, 132.

66. Cf. ibid., 213.

67. Ibid., 135.

68. Cf. ibid., 263.

69. Cf. ibid., 181: "'Prejudice' is an historical category."

70. Ibid., 136.

71. Cf. ibid., 263.

72. Ibid., 178.

73. Cf. Strauss, *The City and Man* (Chicago: Rand McNally, 1964), 45 (henceforth "CM"):

> The rights of man are the moral equivalent of the *Ego cogitans*. The *Ego cogitans* has emancipated itself entirely from the "tutelage of nature" and eventually refuses to obey any law which it has not originated in its entirety or to dedicate itself to any "value" of which it does not know that it is its own creation.

Cf. Strauss, "The Crisis of Our Times," in *The Predicament of Modern Politics*, ed. Harold J. Spaeth, 97 (Detroit, MI: University of Detroit Press, 1964).

74. Cf. Strauss, SCR, 181–182. See also Strauss's letter of July 17, 1935, to Karl Löwith in GS 3, 656.

75. Strauss, SCR, 179.

76. Cf. Exodus 20:18–19, quoted in Strauss, SCR, 179.

77. Cf. Strauss, SPPP, 163.

78. Strauss, SCR, 179 (see also n. 229). See also Strauss, "The Holy," in EW, 76–77. Cf. Susan Shell, "Taking Evil Seriously: Schmitt's 'Concept of the Political' and Strauss's 'True Politics,'" in *Leo Strauss: Political Philosopher and Jewish Thinker*, ed. Kenneth L. Deutsch and Walter Nicgorski, 179 (Lanham, MD: Rowman & Littlefield Publishers, 1994).

79. Cf. Strauss, RCPR, 264: "No miracle was performed in the presence of first-rate physicists."

80. Cf. ibid., 265; SPPP, 151; PAW, 105.

81. Strauss, SCR, 214. Cf. Strauss, "On the Interpretation of *Genesis*," in JPCM, 360; Strauss, *Liberalism Ancient and Modern* (New York: Basic Books, 1968), 166 (henceforth "LAM").

82. Spinoza, TTP, 166

83. Ibid., 167.

84. Strauss, SCR, 173.

85. Cf. ibid., 148–149; "On the Bible Science of Spinoza," in EW, 177.

86. Spinoza, TTP, 100.

87. Strauss, SCR, 174–176.

88. The English translation alternately uses "theory of prophecy" and "doctrine of prophecy" where the German original systematically has "Prophetologie." Cf. Strauss, SCR, 155, 172, 183.

89. Cf. Strauss, "On the Bible Science of Spinoza," in EW, 180; SCR, 175.

90. Cf. Strauss, "On the Bible Science of Spinoza," in EW, 180; SCR, 171–172.

91. Cf. Strauss, SCR, 185–191.

92. Strauss, "On the Bible Science of Spinoza," in EW, 179. Cf. Strauss, SCR, 229.

93. Cf. Strauss, "On the Bible Science of Spinoza," in EW, 177–178.

94. Cf. Strauss, SCR, 1–19; CM, 15.

95. Compare the title of the first part of the *Ethics* with that of the first part of Hobbes's *Leviathan*: "De Deo" (*Of God*) and "Of Man," respectively.

96. Cf. Strauss, SCR, 239: "Spinoza's doctrine of natural right is free from any consideration of the specifically human; it is conceived in terms of the cosmos alone." Hobbes's concern for a human concept of justice, on the other hand, impels him to seek a meaningful distinction between right and might. See chapter 5.

97. In Letter 50, Spinoza writes to Jarig Jelles that his difference with Hobbes consists therein "that I always preserve natural right intact, and only allot to the chief magistrates in every state a right over their subjects commensurate with the excess of their power over the power of the subjects. This is what always takes place in the state of nature."

98. Cf. Strauss, SCR, 228–229. A striking example can be found in the introduction to third chapter of the *Ethics*:

> Nothing comes to pass in nature, which can be set down to a flaw therein; for nature is always the same, and everywhere one and the same in her efficacy and power of action; that is, nature's laws and ordinances, whereby all things come to pass and change from one form to another, are everywhere and always the same. . . . Thus the passions of hatred, anger, envy, and so on, considered in themselves, follow from this same necessity and efficacy of nature; they answer to certain definite causes, through which they are understood, and possess certain properties as worthy of being known as the properties of anything else, whereof the contemplation in itself affords us delight.

99. Cf. Strauss, SPPP, 212–213.

100. Cf. Strauss, LAM, 201.

101. Cf. Strauss, "On Spinoza's Bible Science," in EW, 177; SCR, 165–166, 171.

102. Cf. Strauss, SCR, 188–189.

103. Cf. ibid., 168–169.

104. Ibid., SCR, 164. Cf. Strauss, RCPR, 234.

105. Cf. Strauss, SCR, 164, 169, 171. As in his critical review of Cohen's

analysis, Strauss rejects a psychological explanation of Spinoza's attitude: whoever invokes rancor and vengefulness on Spinoza's part to explain the *herem* inverts cause and consequence. Cf. Strauss, "Cohen's Analysis," in EW, 160, where Strauss already mentions Spinoza's "alienation from Judaism."

106. Cf. Strauss, "On Spinoza's Bible Science," in EW, 182; SCR, 156–160.

107. Spinoza, TTP, i.

108. Strauss, SCR, 164.

109. Ibid., 194 (translation slightly altered).

110. Strauss, "On Spinoza's Bible Science," in EW, 184; SCR, 195. Strauss quotes from Letter 21, where Spinoza writes to Willem van Blijenbergh: "I feel that when I have obtained a firm proof, I cannot fall into a state of doubt concerning it, I acquiesce entirely in what is commended to me by my understanding, without any suspicion that I am being deceived in the matter." Cf. Strauss, RCPR, 258.

111. Strauss, SCR, 195–196.

112. Remarkably enough, Spinoza also reduces his opponent's position to one of subservience to carnal desires. Cf. Shell, "Taking Evil Seriously," 182.

113. Strauss, SCR, 208. In this respect, Spinoza's appeal to Paul's critique of Jewish Law is entirely unjustified, Strauss judges: "In Paul, the deepest awareness of sin rebels against legalism, while Spinoza's rejection of the Law rests on the rejection of obedience as such, and rests ultimately on the absence of any awareness of sin" (Strauss, "On Spinoza's Bible Science," in EW, 185). Cf. Spinoza, TTP, 40–41. In this context, we may again refer to Rudolf Otto's views on the numinous character of divine transcendence, which made a profound impression on the young Strauss (see the section "Biblical Politics, Biblical Science, and the New Theology" in chapter 1).

114. Jeremiah 18:6, quoted by Spinoza in Letter 75. Although Strauss does not mention it, Maimonides quotes the same verse in his *Letter on Astrology* to the Jewish community of Marseille. Spinoza, who refers to Maimonides's correspondence in the *Theological-Political Treatise*, may also have seen this epistle. See Moses Maimonides, "Letter on Astrology," in *Medieval Political Philosophy: A Sourcebook*, ed. Ralph Lerner and Muhsin Mahdi, 188–229 (Ithaca, NY: Cornell University Press, 1963); Spinoza, TTP, 167.

115. As Soffer rightly remarks, Calvin's view is the exact opposite of Spinoza's. For both, the difference between the ordinary and the extraordinary is merely statistical, not ontological: all phenomena are attributed to a single power, either God or nature. See Soffer, "Modern Rationalism," 156 n. 20. Cf. Shell, "Taking Evil Seriously," 181.

116. Cf. Strauss, SCR, 197: "God in His limitless power and freedom can use the things created by Him as tools, as His will; He was able to make the plants grow before the creation of the sun, thus without the apparently necessary sunshine; he could stay the sun in its course at the prayer of Joshua." Cf. Strauss, "On the Interpretation of *Genesis*," in JPCM, 363–364; SPPP, 151–163.

117. Strauss, SCR, 213.

118. Ibid., 204.

119. Cf. ibid., 28–29; Soffer, "Modern Rationalism," 143.

120. Cf. Strauss, SCR, 205–206; PL, 31–32; "On the Interpretation of *Genesis*," in JPCM, 360; NRH, 59–62, 60 n. 20.

121. Strauss, SCR, 206.

122. Cf. Yirmiyahu Yovel, *Spinoza and Other Heretics* (Princeton. NJ: Princeton University Press 1989), vol. 2, ix.

123. Cf. Strauss, "On the Bible Science of Spinoza," in EW, 186; SCR, 29; NRH, 30; "The Mutual Influence of Theology and Philosophy," *Independent Journal of Philosophy* 3 (1979): 117. In the wake of Strauss's analysis, Michael Morgan (*Dilemmas in Modern Thought*, 48) makes the interesting suggestion that Spinoza is an "as if" thinker, in the sense of Hans Vaihinger's "philosophy of the As If." Cf. Hans Vaihinger, *The Philosophy of "As If": A System of the Theoretical, Practical and Religious Fictions of Mankind* (London: Kegan Paul, 1945).

124. Strauss, SCR, 196 (punctuation slightly altered).

125. Cf. Strauss, SCR, 29; Kenneth Hart Green, *Jew and Philosopher: The Return to Maimonides in the Jewish Thought of Leo Strauss* (Albany: State University of New York Press, 1993), 11.

126. Cf. Strauss "On the Bible Science of Spinoza," in EW, 184–185. See also Krüger, "Besprechung von Leo Strauss," 2407: "Thus *one* unjustifiable (*unbegründbare*) tendency of the experience of the world is opposed to the other: to this extent, the opponents talk at cross-purposes."

127. Cf. Strauss, "On the Bible Science of Spinoza," in EW, 186; SCR, 208–211.

128. Strauss, SCR, 29, 37–46. In Letter 56, Spinoza writes to Hugo Boxel: "The authority of Plato, Aristotle, and Socrates, does not carry much weight with me. I should have been astonished, if you had brought forward Epicurus, Democritus, Lucretius, or any of the atomists, or upholders of the atomic theory." Cf. Strauss, PAW, 152; PL, 35.

129. Strauss, SCR, 209. As the most important representatives of this tradition, Strauss names Da Costa, La Peyrère, Hobbes, Hume, Holbach, Feuerbach, Bauer, and Marx (Strauss, SCR, 45).

130. Strauss, SCR, 46.

131. Ibid., 299–300 n. 276.

132. Ibid., 71.

133. Cf. Strauss, NRH, 169. Cf. ibid., 279–280.

134. Cf. Strauss, SCR, 37–38, 59, 70, 88; LAM, x.

135. Strauss, SCR, 146. In the same context, Strauss acknowledges his debt for this insight: "The Enlightenment, as Lessing put it, had to laugh orthodoxy out of a position from which it could not be driven by any other means" (Strauss, SCR, 143).

136. Strauss, "On the Argument with European Science," in EW, 108.

137. Strauss, "The Testament of Spinoza," in EW, 216–223.

138. Ibid., 221.

139. Cf. Strauss, SCR, 21.

140. Cf. ibid., 4; "Why We Remain Jews," in JPCM, 317–318; RCPR, 233; "On Husik's Work in Medieval Jewish Philosophy," in JPCM, 254.

141. Strauss, SCR, 5. Cf Strauss, WPP, 13; "Why We Remain Jews," in JPCM, 318–319. Cf. Ralph Lerner, "Leo Strauss (1899–1973)," *American Jewish Year Book* 76, no. 91–97 (1976): 95–96.

142. Strauss, SCR, 5. See also Strauss's letter on the State of Israel to the editor of *National Review* in JPCM, 413–414.

143. Strauss, SCR, 15.

144. Strauss, letter of January 7, 1930, in GS 3, 380–381.

145. Strauss, SCR, 31.

## Chapter 3.  The Second Cave

1. Strauss, SCR, 204.

2. Ibid.

3. Strauss, "Das Erkenntnisproblem in der philosophischen Lehre Fr. H. Jacobis" ("The Problem of Knowledge in the Philosophical Doctrine of Friedrich Heinrich Jacobi"), reprinted in GS 2, 237–292. Strauss wrote his dissertation under the supervision of Ernst Cassirer (a student of Hermann Cohen), and defended it in Hamburg on September 17, 1921. Strauss's research was part of Cassirer's large-scale project on the problem of knowledge in modern philosophy. Cf. Ernst. Cassirer, *Das Erkenntnisproblem in der Philosophie und Wissenschaft der neueren Zeit* (Berlin: Cassirer, 1920). Cf. Strauss, "Das Erkenntnisproblem," in GS 2, 291.

4. Strauss's introductions were published in volumes 2, 3.1, and 3.2 of the *Jubiläumsausgabe* (Stuttgart: Friedrich Fromman Verlag [Günther Holzboog], 1974). The edition, begun in 1929, was interrupted in 1936 as a result of the political situation, so that only volumes 1 to 3.1 were published. Only when the edition was resumed in 1974, did volume 3.2—which contains all of Strauss's writings on the Pantheism Controversy—become available. In 1946, Strauss wrote the plan of a book to be entitled *Philosophy and the Law: Historical Essays*, which was never published. The tenth chapter of this book was to be devoted to the Pantheism Controversy. See Strauss, JPCM, 470.

5. Strauss, "Das Erkenntnisproblem," in GS 2, 249. Cf. Strauss, NRH, 173–174, 201; RCPR, 243–244; LAM, 212.

6. Cf. Strauss, "Das Erkenntnisproblem," in GS 2, 249.

7. Cf. ibid., 285. Cf. Frederick C. Beiser, *The Fate of Reason: German Philosophy from Kant to Fichte* (London: Cambridge University Press, 1987), 81, 89–91.

8. Strauss, "Das Erkenntnisproblem," in GS 2, 252.

9. Strauss, "Das Erkenntnisproblem," in GS 2, 281.

10. Strauss, "Einleitung zu *Morgenstunden* und *An die Freunde Lessings*," in GS 2, 537–538. Cf. Strauss, "Das Erkenntnisproblem," in GS 2, 278.

11. Strauss, "Einleitung zu *Morgenstunden*," in GS 2, 549.

12. Ibid., 533–535. See Frederick C. Beiser, *Enlightenment, Revolution, and Romanticism: The Genesis of Modern Political Thought, 1790–1800* (Cambridge, MA: Harvard University Press, 1992).

13. Cf. Beiser, *The Fate of Reason*, 89.

14. Strauss, "Das Erkenntnisproblem," in GS 2, 242–243, 270, 274–275, 277, 279–280, 282.

15. Ibid., 245–247, 252.

16. Strauss, SCR, 183–186.

17. Strauss, "Progress or Return? The Contemporary Crisis of Western Civilization," in JPCM, 117. Cf. Strauss, SCR, 28–29: "The *Ethics* thus begs the decisive question, the question as to whether the clear and distinct account is as such true and not merely a plausible hypothesis. . . . Spinoza's *Ethics* attempts to be the system but does not succeed; the clear and distinct account of everything that it presents remains fundamentally hypothetical."

18. Strauss, NRH, 30.

19. Strauss "Das Erkenntnisproblem," in GS 2, 251–252.

20. See chapter 1.

21. Strauss, "On the Bible Science of Spinoza," in EW, 186.

22. Strauss, SCR, 209.

23. Strauss, "Das Erkenntnisproblem," in GS 2, 247.

24. Ibid., 247–248.

25. Strauss, SCR, 178–182.

26. Strauss, "Das Erkenntnisproblem," in GS 2, 282 n. 135.

27. Ibid., 282.

28. See chapters 2, 3, and 4 of Beiser, *The Fate of Reason*. In his account, Beiser names Strauss's introductions among the "best treatments" of the controversy. Cf. Beiser, *The Fate of Reason*, 335 n. 12. See also Alexander Altmann, *Moses Mendelssohn: A Biographical Study* (London: Routledge & Kegan Paul, 1973) and Hermann Timm, *Gott und die Freiheit: Studien zur Religionsphilosophie der Goethezeit* (Frankfurt: Klostermann, 1974). The main documents of the Controversy were edited and published in H. Scholz, ed., *Die Hauptschriften zum Pantheismusstreit zwischen Jacobi und Mendelssohn* (Berlin: Reuther and Reichard, 1916). A concise discussion of Mendelssohn's position in the controversy, critical of Strauss's account, can be found in Allan Arkush, *Moses Mendelssohn and the Enlightenment* (Albany: State University of New York Press, 1994).

29. Strauss, "Einleitung zu *Morgenstunden*," in GS 2, 531. Cf. Beiser, *The Fate of Reason*, 61.

30. Strauss, "Einleitung zu *Morgenstunden*," in GS 2, 572.

31. Ibid., 587.

32. Cf. Moses Mendelssohn, *Jerusalem, or On Religious Power and Judaism*, trans. Allan Arkush, with a commentary by Alexander Altmann (Hanover, NH: University Press of New England, 1984).

33. Leo Strauss, "Einleitung zu *Phädon*," in GS 2, 491. Cf. Strauss, PL, 44.

34. Strauss, "Einleitung zu *Morgenstunden*," in GS 2, 583–586.

35. Ibid., 585.

36. In PL, 78 n. 28, Strauss renders this criticism more explicit by pointing out the Hobbesian pedigree of Mendelssohn's "surrender of the ancient natural right of duty in favor of the modern natural right of claim."

37. Strauss, "Einleitung zu *Morgenstunden*," in GS 2, 573–574.

38. Leo Strauss, "Einleitung zu *Sache Gottes, oder die gerettete Vorsehung*," in GS 2, 527.

39. Strauss, "Einleitung zu *Morgenstunden*," GS 2, 578. Challenging Strauss's thesis, Arkush argues that Mendelssohn "could have defended Judaism without downplaying the importance or denying the possibility of philosophical knowledge of religious truths," because he never did "place such an absolute value on philosophical knowledge" in the first place. Rather, Mendelssohn regarded the balance between reason and common sense he tried to strike as a temporary settlement, in anticipation of an ultimate demonstrative proof of God's existence. Arkush, *Moses Mendelssohn and the Enlightenment*, 88–93.

40. Strauss, "Einleitung zu *Morgenstunden*," in GS 2, 581.

41. Ibid., 587.

42. Ibid., 575–576.

43. Ibid., 573. On 577, Strauss comments on Mendelssohn's "pride in this progress [of metaphysics] and, at the same time, the concomitant inability to understand the character of Aristotelian ethics, which had been adopted by Maimonides."

44. Ibid., 588. With slight alterations, I reproduce Beiser's translation of both quotations in *The Fate of Reason*, 88–89. On 88, Beiser aptly dubs Jacobi's doctrine an "epistemology of action."

45. Strauss, "Einleitung zu *Morgenstunden*," in GS 2, 588.

46. See Strauss's letter of May 12, 1935, to Gerhard Krüger and Hans-Georg Gadamer, where he writes that in the introduction to *Philosophy and Law* he had tried to repair the "formal shortcomings" of the Spinoza book (GS 3, 446–447).

47. Strauss, PL, 32. Cf. Green, *Jew and Philosopher*, 17.

48. Krüger, "Besprechung von Leo Strauss," 2410.

49. Strauss, PL, 33–34.

50. Ibid., 37.

51. Perhaps Sigmund Freud may be added to this list. Although the young Strauss initially appreciates the frank unreligious outlook of Freud's *The Future of an Illusion*, he later becomes more critical of his Spinozist, Machiavellian, and Nietzschean antecedents, as becomes apparent from a lecture he gave in 1958 on Freud's *Moses and Monotheism* (probably in 1958). Compare Strauss, "Sigmund Freud, *The Future of an Illusion*," in EW, 202–208 and Strauss, "Freud on Moses and Monotheism," in JPCM, 285–309).

52. Strauss, PL, 37–38.

53. Strauss, SCR, 30.

54. See also Strauss, "Introductory Essay to Hermann Cohen, *Religion of Reason*," in JPCM, 281; Strauss's letter of December 12, 1932, to Gerhard Krüger, in GS 3, 414.

55. See Strauss's letter of December 12, 1932, in GS 3, 414–415.

56. Strauss, SCR, 12–13.

57. Strauss's critique of intellectual probity and its roots in biblical morality is a recurring topic in his correspondence with Gerhard Krüger and Karl Löwith. See GS 3, 380, 414, 620, 632, 636, 662, 676, 686, 696. See also Strauss, "The Living Issues of German Postwar Philosophy," in Heinrich Meier, *Leo Strauss and the Theologico-Political Problem* (Cambridge: Cambridge University Press, 2006), 130.

58. Strauss, SCR, 30.

59. Strauss, PL, 38. In 1934, shortly before the publication of *Philosophy and Law*, Strauss still defends political Zionism as "the most *decent* Jewish movement" and the only acceptable alternative to orthodoxy in a letter to his friend Jacob Klein (letter of June 23, 1934, in GS 3, 516).

60. Strauss, letter of December 27, 1932, in GS 3, 420. In a lecture delivered in 1932, we find the rhetorical question, "How shall he pray who does not believe in God?" (Strauss, "Die geistige Lage der Gegenwart," in GS 2, 444)

61. Strauss, PL, 38.

62. Ibid., 137 n. 13.

63. Strauss, SCR, 181.

64. Strauss, "Religiöse Lage der Gegenwart," in GS 2, 377–391; "Die geistige Lage der Gegenwart," in GS 2, 441–464.

65. Strauss, "Religiöse Lage der Gegenwart," in GS 2, 389. Cf. Strauss, "Die geistige Lage der Gegenwart," in GS 2, 446; PL, 135 n. 2.

66. That Strauss regards Nietzsche as part of the Enlightenment is further borne out in his correspondence with Karl Löwith, where he interprets the Will to Power and the Eternal Return as attempts to liberate man from the deeply rooted "pampering" (Verwöhnung) by faith in creation and providence. In the same context, Strauss connects Nietzsche's rejection of "it was" (es war) to Descartes's critique of the Aristotelian analysis of the manifest order of the world, in the name of a philosophy that focuses on what is immediately given. Cf. Strauss's letters to Löwith of June 23 and July 17, 1935, in GS 3, 649 and 656. See the section "Spinoza's Twofold Strategy" in chapter 2.

67. Strauss, "Religiöse Lage der Gegenwart," in GS 2, 387.

68. Cf. Strauss, "Die geistige Lage der Gegenwart," in GS 2, 450–451; LAM, 23; SPPP, 147–149; RCPR, 34.

69. Strauss refers to the "polytheism of values" that Max Weber views as the central characteristic of modernity. Strauss reiterates this critique of Weber twenty years later in Natural Right and History (cf. NRH, 36–80). See also Strauss, "Review of Julius Ebbinghaus, On the Progress of Metaphysics," in EW, 214–215; "Der Konspektivismus," in GS 2, 374; "Die geistige Lage der Gegenwart," in GS 2, 447–448.

70. In particular, Strauss has in mind the so-called Conspectivism developed by the sociologist Karl Mannheim. Cf. Strauss, "Der Konspektivismus," in GS 2, 365–375; "Die geistige Lage der Gegenwart," in GS 2, 449; RCPR, 34–35.

71. In particular, Strauss envisages the philosophy of history developed by Oswald Spengler in Decline of the West. Cf. Strauss, "Review of Ebbinghaus," in EW, 214; "Die geistige Lage der Gegenwart," in GS 2, 452; "The Crisis of Our Time," 43, 48; RCPR, 41, 241; "The Three Waves of Modernity," in Hilail Gildin, ed., An Introduction to Political Philosophy: Ten Essays by Leo Strauss (Detroit, MI: Wayne State University Press, 1975), 81, 94; "On Collingwood's Philosophy of History," Review of Metaphysics 5, no. 4 (1952), 563; CM, 2–3; SPPP, 32.

72. Strauss, "Der Konspektivismus," in GS 2, 372.

73. Strauss, "Religiöse Lage der Gegenwart," in GS 2, 284. Cf. Strauss, "Der Konspektivismus," in GS 2, 373; NRH, 20; "Vorwort zu einem geplanten Buch über Hobbes," in GS 3, 213–214; letter to Karl Löwith of July 11, 1964, in GS 3, 693.

74. Strauss, "Die geistige Lage der Gegenwart," in GS 2, 452.

75. Ibid., 452. Cf. Strauss, RCPR, 32.

76. Eighteen years later, Strauss repeats this diagnosis in similar terms: "If the 'anarchy of systems' exhibited by the history of philosophy proves anything, it proves our ignorance concerning the most important subjects . . . , and therewith it proves the necessity of philosophy. It may be added that the 'anarchy' . . . of our time, or of present-day interpretations of the past, is not conspicuously smaller than that of . . . the past" (Strauss, WPP, 62).

77. Strauss, "Die geistige Lage der Gegenwart," in GS 2, 447.

78. Plato, *Gorgias*, 500c (all references to Platonic dialogues are based on the Stephanus edition). Cf. Strauss, "Religiöse Lage der Gegenwart," in GS 2, 379–385, 389–390; "Die geistige Lage der Gegenwart," in GS 2, 445–446. Cf. Peter Emberley and Barry Cooper, eds. and trans., *Faith and Political Philosophy: The Correspondence between Leo Strauss and Eric Voegelin, 1934–1964* (University Park: Pennsylvania State University Press, 1993), 90 (henceforth "FPP").

79. Plato, *Apology*, 38a.

80. The only one to perceive the importance of this distinction at the time of the publication of *Philosophy and Law* is Strauss's friend Jacob Klein. See Klein's letter of May 6, 1935, to Strauss in GS 3, 539.

81. Plato, *Republic*, 514a–519d.

82. Cf. Strauss, WPP, 70.

83. Strauss, "Religiöse Lage der Gegenwart," in GS 2, 386.

84. Cf. Strauss, "Die geistige Lage der Gegenwart," in GS 2, 445; NRH, 83–84.

85. Strauss, "Die geistige Lage der Gegenwart," in GS 2, 446.

86. Cf. Strauss, "The Crisis of Our Time," 37.

87. Strauss, "Die geistige Lage der Gegenwart," in GS 2, 448–452. Cf. Strauss, "On Collingwood's Philosophy of History," 575–576.

88. Cf. Strauss, "Die geistige Lage der Gegenwart," in GS 2, 446, 452, 455; NRH, 25, 28; WPP, 72–73, 255; RCPR, 327; "On Collingwood's Philosophy of History," 585; "The Crisis of Our Time," 42.

89. Maimonides, *The Guide of the Perplexed*, vol. 1, 31, quoted in Strauss, "Die geistige Lage der Gegenwart," in GS 2, 455–456 and PL, 57.

90. Strauss, "Die geistige Lage der Gegenwart," in GS 2, 456.

91. Cf. Strauss, "Die geistige Lage der Gegenwart," in GS 2, 456; "Religiöse Lage der Gegenwart," in GS 2, 387. Already in 1929, Strauss sees it as his primary task to discover "what the world, in which science originated, looked like before the irruption (*Einbruch*) of biblical consciousness[.] Only by turning to this world can

the horizon be gained in which alone radical questioning and answering are now possible" (Strauss, "Der Konspektivismus," in GS 2, 375).

92. Strauss, "Religiöse Lage der Gegenwart," in GS 2, 387.

93. See Strauss's letters to Karl Löwith of August 20, 1946, of March 15, 1962, and of March 12, 1970, in GS 3, 666, 686, 696.

94. Cf. Strauss, "Die geistige Lage der Gegenwart," in GS 2, 456; PL, 46 n. 2; TM, 231; LAM, 201; PAW, 33; WPP, 44.

95. Cf. Strauss's letter to Karl Löwith of August 15, 1946, in GS 3, 660–663; Strauss, "Existentialism," *Interpretation* 22, no. 3 (1995): 301–320.

96. Strauss, "Religiöse Lage der Gegenwart," in GS 2, 390. Cf. Strauss, "On Collingwood's Philosophy of History," 578; CM, 1, 9; "The Crisis of Our Time," 53.

97. Cf. Strauss, "Die geistige Lage der Gegenwart," in GS 2, 461; CM, 55; RCPR, 152, 150–156, 187; "On Collingwood's Philosophy of History," 582–586; "On a New Interpretation of Plato's Political Philosophy," *Social Research* 13, no. 3 (1946): 347–352; SPPP, 38, 67; PAW, 16; LAM, 45–46, 54, 58, 61, 65; *The Argument and the Action of Plato's Laws* (Chicago: University of Chicago Press, 1975), 1–2 (henceforth AAPL); FPP, 78–79.

98. Cf. Strauss, "A Giving of Accounts," in JPCM, 462: "[Heidegger] intended to uproot Greek philosophy, especially Aristotle, but this presupposed the laying bare of its roots, the laying bare of it as it was and not just as it had come to appear in the light of the tradition and of modern philosophy"; SCR, 10: "with the questioning of traditional philosophy the traditional understanding of the tradition becomes questionable."

99. Strauss, "An Unspoken Prologue to a Public Lecture at St. John's College in Honor of Jacob Klein," in JPCM, 450.

100. Cf. Strauss, "On Collingwood's Philosophy of History," 585; FPP, 58.

101. Strauss, "Review of Julius Ebbinghaus," in EW, 214. Cf. Strauss, "On a New Interpretation of Plato's Political Philosophy," 330 n. 3; "On Collingwood's Philosophy of History," 577, 584–585; WPP, 68. This "prejudice against prejudices" is the basis of the modern concept of progress. Cf. Frederick Lawrence, "Leo Strauss and the Fourth Wave of Modernity," in *Leo Strauss and Judaism: Athens and Jerusalem Critically Revisited*, ed. David Novak, 141(Lanham, MD: Rowman & Littlefield, 1996).

102. Strauss is thinking of nineteenth-century German philology as developed by Friedrich Schleiermacher and Ulrich von Wilamowitz-Moellendorf. This approach, he judges, has destroyed every motivation to read texts seriously and in a nonhistoricist manner. Cf. FPP, 79, 90; CM, 10. For a critique of modern philology's reading of classical philosophy in Strauss's spirit, see Thomas L. Pangle, ed., *The Roots of Political Philosophy: Ten Forgotten Socratic Dialogues* (Ithaca, NY: Cornell University Press, 1987), 1–20.

103. Cf. Strauss, RCPR, 34. This readiness underlies the "ministerial" manner of interpreting Strauss defends in his brief but captivating correspondence with

Hans-Georg Gadamer. Cf. Strauss, "Correspondence with Hans-Georg Gadamer concerning *Wahrheit und Methode*," *Independent Journal of Philosophy* 2 (1978): 6–7, 9, 11. Cf. Hans-Georg Gadamer, *Wahrheit und Methode: Grundzüge einer philosophischen Hermeneutik* (Tübingen: J. C. B. Mohr, 1972), 20 n. 4, 255 n. 1, 278 n. 2, 302 n. 1, and *Gesammelte Werke* (Tübingen: J. C. B. Mohr, 1986), 299–300, 401, 414–424, 501. See also Fortin, "Gadamer on Strauss: An Interview"; Catherine H. Zuckert, *Postmodern Platos: Nietzsche, Heidegger, Gadamer, Strauss, Derrida* (Chicago: University of Chicago Press, 1996).

104. Strauss, "Review of Julius Ebbinghaus," in EW, 215. Heinrich Meier fittingly speaks of "a retrial of philosophy that advances in a direction contrary to that of 'historical progress'" (Meier, *Leo Strauss and the Theologico-Political Problem*, 62). In a letter of August 15, 1946, Strauss writes to Karl Löwith, "We agree that today we need historical reflection—only I assert that it is neither a progress nor a fate to submit to with resignation, but an unavoidable means for the overcoming of modernity. . . . [W]e attempt to *learn* from the ancients" (GS 3, 662). Cf. Thomas L. Pangle and Nathan Tarcov, "Epilogue: Leo Strauss and the History of Political Philosophy," in *History of Political Philosophy*, ed. Leo Strauss and Joseph Cropsey, 911 (Chicago: University of Chicago Press, 1987).

105. Cf. Strauss, "Die geistige Lage der Gegenwart," in GS 2, 451; LAM, 75; FPP, 88.

106. Fifteen years later, Strauss repeats this view in a telling passage:

> People may become so frightened of the ascent to the light of the sun, and so desirous of making that ascent utterly impossible to any of their descendants, that they dig a deep pit beneath the cave in which they were born, and withdraw into that pit. If one of the descendants desired to ascend to the light of the sun, he would first have to try to reach the level of the natural cave, and he would have to invent new and most artificial tools unknown and unnecessary to those who dwelt in the natural cave. He would be a fool, he would never see the light of the sun, he would lose the last vestige of memory of the sun, if he perversely thought that by inventing his new tools he had progressed beyond the ancestral cave-dwellers." (PAW, 155–156)

Notice the suggestion that man has become frightened of the philosophic ascent from the first cave due to the additional, historical obstacle. Cf. Strauss, "The Crisis of Our Time," 54.

107. Compare the lapidary formulation in *Philosophy and Law*: "To that end and only to that end is the 'historicizing' of philosophy justified and necessary: only the history of philosophy makes possible the ascent from the second, 'unnatural' cave" (Strauss, PL, 136 n. 2). Cf. Strauss, "Religiöse Lage der Gegenwart," in GS 2, 390, 462; "On a New Interpretation of Plato's Political Philosophy," 328; FPP, 12.

108. Strauss, "Die geistige Lage der Gegenwart," in GS 2, 461. Strauss immediately adds that Nietzsche only laid bare the Socratic question, but failed to raise it again with the necessary seriousness. Cf. Strauss, NRH, 26; letter to Karl Löwith of June 23, 1935, in GS 3, 648–650.

109. Strauss developed the idea of reopening the quarrel right after *Spinoza's Critique of Religion*. See Strauss, "The Testament of Spinoza," in EW, 217, where he speaks of "the moment when the 'querelle des anciens et des modernes' within philosophy had been decided on the main point in favor of the moderns." Cf. Strauss, RCPR, 243; "On a New Interpretation of Plato's Political Philosophy," 326; TM, 112.

# Chapter 4. The Order of Human Things

1. Hermann Cohen, "Charakteristik der Ethik Maimunis," in *Mose ben Maimon: Sein Leben, seine Werke und sein Einfluß*, vol. 1, ed. W. Bacher, M. Brann, and D. Simonsen, 63–134, 105 (Leipzig: Gustav Fock, 1908). See A. S. Bruckstein, trans., *Ethics of Maimonides* (Madison: University of Wisconsin Press, 2003).

2. Strauss, "Cohen und Maimuni," in GS 2, 393–436. The lecture was given on May 4, 1931, at the Hochschule für die Wissenschaft des Judentums in Berlin (see the editor's notice in GS 2, 619–620).

3. Cf. Strauss, "Cohen und Maimuni," in GS 2, 395–397, 403–405.

4. Cohen, "Charakteristik der Ethik Maimunis," 81, quoted in Strauss, "Cohen und Maimuni," in GS 2, 416. Cf. ibid., 421.

5. Cf. Strauss, "Cohen und Maimuni," in GS 2, 416, 421.

6. Cf. ibid., 394, 402, 417; RCPR, 28; SPPP, 172, 236–239.

7. Ibid., 396.

8. See Strauss's letter of May 7, 1931, to Gerhard Krüger, in GS 3, 385.

9. Cf. Strauss, "Cohen und Maimuni," in GS 2, 420; PL, 130–131.

10. Plato, *Republic*, 519d–520a.

11. Cf. Rémi Brague, "Leo Strauss et Maïmonide," in *Maimonides and Philosophy: Papers Presented at the Sixth Jerusalem Philosophic Encounter, May 1985*, ed. Shlomo Pines and Yirmiyahu Yovel, 246–268 (Dordrecht: Martinus Nijhoff, 1986).

12. See the section "Maimonides: The Limits of Reason and the Interest in Revelation" in chapter 2.

13. Cf. Strauss, PL, 103–104; "Quelques remarques sur la science politique de Maïmonide et de Fârâbî," in, GS 2, 140–141; PAW, 10.

14. Cf. Strauss, PL, 109–110, 65. One may also think of Strauss's remarks in *Spinoza's Critique of Religion* on the "will to mediacy" characteristic of the reception of prophecy. See the section "Spinoza's Twofold Strategy" in chapter 2.

15. Strauss, "Cohen und Maimuni," in GS 2, 422. Cf. Strauss, PL, 106–120; "Quelques remarques," in GS 2, 140–142; "Eine vermißte Schrift Farâbîs," in GS 2, 168–169 n. 1a.

16. Strauss, "Cohen und Maimuni," in GS 2, 423.

17. Strauss, "Cohen und Maimuni," in GS 2, 424. Cf. Strauss, PL, in GS 2, 73–74, 118–122; "Quelques remarques," in GS 2, 145–147. See also the section "Maimonides" in chapter 2.

18. *Falasifa* is the Arabic transliteration of the Greek *philosophoi*, "philosophers."

19. Avicenna adopts the Aristotelian division of philosophy or science: (1) the theoretical sciences: logic, physics, and metaphysics; (2) the practical sciences: economics, ethics and politics.

20. Avicenna, "On the Parts of the Sciences," in *Tis' Rasâ'il* (Constantinople, 1298), quoted in Strauss, PL, 122 (in the English translation, the date of publication has erroneously been changed to 1928).

21. Strauss, "Cohen und Maimuni," in GS 2, 425; PL, in GS 2, 122; "Quelques remarques," in GS 2, 140; "Eine vermißte Schrift Farâbîs," in GS 2, 92, 97 n. 1, 98; "Der Ort der Vorsehungslehre nach der Ansicht Maimunis," in GS 2, 184; "On Abravanel's Philosophical Tendency and Political Teaching," in GS 2, 195, 198; PAW, 10–11; WPP, 161; RCPR, 218, 223–224. In 1933, Strauss writes about his research: "The research . . . led me from Maimonides to Islamic philosophers, of whom I studied several in Arabic manuscripts—and made me realize that the connection between medieval Jewish and Islamic teaching on prophecy and Plato's *Statesman* and *Laws* has not yet been thoroughly evaluated" (letter of November 30, 1933, to Cyrus Adler, quoted in Hildegard Korth, *Guide to the Leo Strauss Papers* [Chicago: University of Chicago Library, Department of Special Collections, 1978], 5).

22. Cf. FPP, 17: "the basis of their political doctrine is expressly Plato's own thoughts."

23. Strauss, "Cohen und Maimuni," in GS 2, 425: "Avicenna understands the action of the prophets in accordance with the instructions given by Plato's State." Cf. Strauss, PL, 124–125: "*The prophet is the founder of the ideal state*. The classic model of the ideal state is the *Platonic* state. . . . The prophet is the founder of the Platonic state; the prophet carries out what Plato called for. . . . Here politics are to be understood in the Platonic sense: for Alfarabi it is not a matter of a state in general, but of the state directed to the specific excellence of man, the 'excellent state', the ideal state"; "Quelques remarques," in GS 2, 125–126.

24. Plato, *Republic*, 519d.

25. Ibid., 520c.

26. Strauss, "Cohen und Maimuni," in GS 2, 426; PL, 81–82.

27. Plato, *Laws*, 631c. Cf. Strauss, "Quelques remarques," in GS 2, 146–148; "On Abravanel's Philosophical Tendency and Political Teaching," in GS 2, 198.

28. Cf. Strauss, PL, 131–132.

29. See the section "Maimonides" in chapter 2.

30. Strauss, PL, 132; "Cohen und Maimuni," in GS 2, 427.

31. Strauss even wonders whether the *falasifa* may have refrained deliberately from translating or commenting on the *Politics*. Cf. Strauss, "Cohen und Maimuni," in GS 2, 426–427; PL, 129; "Quelques remarques," in GS 2, 127–128; "On Abravanel's Philosophical Tendency and Political Teaching," in GS 2, 197.

32. Cf. Strauss, RCPR, 213–216.

33. Strauss, "Cohen und Maimuni," in GS 2, 428. Besides Jews and Greeks, the ancient concept of law also includes the Muslims: the Arabic *namús*, which signifies "custom," "usage," or "norm," is related to the Greek *nomos*.

34. Cf. Romans 7; Galatians 3–4.

35. Strauss already offers this view in his research on the Pantheism Controversy. In its struggle against Calvinism in particular, the Enlightenment gave precedence to divine goodness over divine justice. According to Strauss, Leibniz's "restoration" of the orthodox identification of justice and goodness "by the dissolution of the classic concept of justice, in which the original sense of justice as obedience to the law had been preserved, considerably furthered the process that aimed at pushing back the law as duty in favor of right as claim" (Strauss, GS 2, 527). Cf. Strauss, "Quelques remarques," in GS 2, 126: "it is not the Bible and the Koran, it is perhaps the New Testament, it is certainly the Reformation and modern philosophy that have brought about the break with ancient thought." See the section "The Crisis of Enlightment: Jacobi, Mendelssohn, and the Pantheism Controversy" in chapter 3.

36. Cf. Strauss, SPPP, 168.

37. Three years before his death, Strauss said of his discovery of the passage in Avicenna: "Then I began to begin [*sic*] to understand Maimonides's prophetology and eventually, as I believe, the whole *Guide of the Perplexed*" ("A Giving of Accounts," in JPCM, 463). Cf. Heinrich Meier, "Vorwort des Herausgebers," in GS 2, xviii.

38. Strauss, PL, 73. Cf. Strauss, PAW, 8: "If Islamic and Jewish medieval philosophy must be understood properly, they must be of philosophic and not merely of antiquarian interest, and this in turn requires that one ceases to regard them as counterparts of Christian scholasticism." See Strauss's letter of October 2, 1935 to Gerschom Scholem, in GS 3, 715–716. Cf. Strauss, RCPR, 221–223; Brague, "Athènes, Jérusalem, La Mecque," 327–333; Green, *Jew and Philosopher*, 104; Clark A. Merrill, "Christianity and Politics: Leo Strauss's Indictment of Christian Philosophy," *Review of Politics* 62, no. 1 (2000): 77–106.

39. Cf. Strauss, PL, 55–56; Richard Kennington, "Strauss's *Natural Right and History*," *Review of Metaphysics* 35 (1981): 57–86, 60; Victor Gourevitch, "The Problem of Natural Right and the Fundamental Alternatives in *Natural Right and History*," in *The Crisis of Liberal Democracy: A Straussian Perspective*, ed. Kenneth L. Deutsch and Walter Soffer, 30 (Albany: State University of New York Press, 1987).

40. Strauss, "Cohen und Maimuni," in GS 2, 429.

41. Cf. Strauss, PL, 78: "the necessary connection between politics and theology (metaphysics), on which we have stumbled as if by accident."

42. Strauss, FPP, 78. Cf. Strauss, RCPR, 248.

43. Strauss, PL, 82. Cf. ibid., 57; PAW, 20.

44. Strauss, PL, 76. Cf. Strauss, "Quelques remarques," in GS 2, 156.

45. Strauss, PL, 128.

46. Ibid., 75.

47. Ibid.

48. Ibid., 78–79. Cf. Strauss, "On Abravanel's Philosophical Tendency and Political Teaching," in GS 2, 189.

49. Strauss, "Maimunis Lehre von der Prophetie und ihre Quellen," *Le Monde Oriental: Revue des Études Orientales* 28 (1934): 99–139.

50. See the editor's notes, in GS 2, 610.

51. Quoted in Strauss, "Cohen und Maimuni," in GS 2, 414.

52. Ibid.

53. Ibid., 410.

54. Ibid., 412.

55. Plato, *Apology*, 21a–22a.

56. Strauss, "Cohen und Maimuni," in GS 2, 412.

57. Cf. Strauss, LAM, 214–215.

58. Strauss, "Cohen und Maimuni," in GS 2, 413. Cf. Plato, *Apology*, 31c, 33a; *Gorgias*, 490e. Cf. Strauss, *On Plato's Symposium* (Chicago: University of Chicago Press, 2001), 246–247.

59. Cf. Strauss, CM, 69, 109, 112, 115, 128. Cf. David Janssens, "Questions and Caves: Philosophy, Politics, and History in Leo Strauss's Early Work," *Journal of Jewish Thought and Philosophy* 10 (2000): 111–144.

60. Quoted in Stendhal, *The Red and the Black*, (Harmondsworth, UK: Penguin 2002), ch. 22, beginning.

61. For an English translation, see Lerner and Mahdi, eds., *Medieval Political Philosophy*, 163–186.

62. As we saw, this view was a principal target in Spinoza's critique of Maimonides. See the section "Maimonides" in chapter 2.

63. Cf. Strauss, PL, 118–119.

64. For this reason, Strauss rejects the popular view that the *falasifa* developed a doctrine of a "twofold truth" (i.e., a philosophic and a religious truth). Instead of a double truth, he argues, the *falasifa* acknowledge only one truth, albeit with an outer (exoteric) and an inner (esoteric) dimension. Cf. Strauss, PL, 65–66; RCPR, 224–225.

65. Cf. Strauss, PL, 84–85, 102–103; "Eine vermißte Schrift Farâbîs," in GS 2, 99 nn. 2 and 3; Lerner and Mahdi, *Medieval Political Philosophy*, 172.

66. Maimonides, *The Guide of the Perplexed*, prefatory remarks. Cf. Strauss, PL, 95–96.

67. Quoted in Strauss, PL, 153, n. 65.

68. Maimonides, *The Guide of the Perplexed*, vol. 1, 17. Cf. Strauss, PAW, 47.

69. Gotthold Ephraim Lessing, "Leibniz von den ewigen Strafen," in *Werke in acht Bänden*, vol. 7 (München: Carl Hanser Verlag, 1979), 180. Strauss quotes this passage in RCPR, 65, but omits the final sentence. Cf. Strauss, "Einleitung zu *Sache Gottes oder die gerettete Vorsehung*," in GS 2, 522: "with the ideal of contemplation, the division (*Aufspaltung*) of humanity in 'the wise' and 'the many' is given, and therewith the recognition of a twofold way of communicating truths, an esoteric and an exoteric."

70. Lessing, "Leibniz von den ewigen Strafen," 196. Cf. Strauss, PAW, 182.

71. Strauss, "Einleitung zu *Morgenstunden*," in GS 2, 543.

72. Strauss, RCPR, 64. Cf. Strauss, "Einleitung zu *Morgenstunden*," in GS 2, 541–542:

> If one pays attention to the How rather than to the What—and for Jacobi and Lessing alike, the great manner of thinking held more weight than the recognition of this or that opinion—one will be inclined to reckon with the possibility that Jacobi was the most intelligent follower Lessing found among his contemporaries. . . . Jacobi felt himself to be, not entirely without justification, the legitimate heir of Lessing and the latter's radical, i.e., undogmatic way of thinking.

Furthermore, Strauss suggests that even Jacobi did not fully fathom the extent of Lessing's irony, and may have become its dupe. As Strauss observes, before admitting to Jacobi that "there is no other philosophy than that of Spinoza," Lessing had already qualified his commitment: "*If* I were to name myself after anyone, then I know no one better." Similarly, to Jacobi's avowal that "my creed is not in Spinoza," Lessing rejoined ironically: "I hope it is in no book," that is, not even in Spinoza. See Strauss, "Einleitung zu *Morgenstunden*," in GS 2, 546. Referring to Jacobi's conversation with Lessing, Strauss praises the latter as "the author of the only improvised live dialogue on a philosophic subject known to me." In the same context, looking back on *Spinoza's Critique of Religion*, he states, "In this study, I was greatly assisted by Lessing," that is, not Jacobi. See Strauss, "A Giving of Accounts," in JPCM, 462. Cf. Strauss, "Eine Erinnerung an Lessing" (A Recollection/Reminder of Lessing), in GS 2, 607; PAW, 28, 76, 182; RCPR, 63–71; the letters to Karl Löwith of July 17 and August 15, 1935, in GS 3, 657 and 661, respectively. Cf. Green, *Jew and Philosopher*, 23 n. 105, 14 n. 49, 19 n. 78, 57–58, 165 n. 105; Clemens Kauffmann, *Strauss und Rawls: Das philosophische Dilemma der Politik* (Berlin: Duncker & Humblot, 2000), 129–141; Heinrich Meier, "Vorwort," in GS 2, xxxiii.

73. In 1747, Lessing completed a comedy entitled *Der junge Gelehrte*. At the beginning of the play, the protagonist, a young scholar, is reading Maimonides's

*Mishneh Torah* (cf. Lessing, *Werke*, vol. 1, 282). At the end of the "Notes on Philosophy and Revelation" that accompany his lecture on "Reason and Revelation," Strauss refers to "the man to whom I owe, so to say, everything I have been able to discern in the labyrinth of that grave question: Lessing. I do not mean the Lessing of a certain tradition, the Lessing celebrated by a type of oratory, but the true and unknown Lessing" (Strauss, "Notes on Philosophy and Revelation," in Meier, *Leo Strauss and the Theologico-Political Problem*, 178).

74. Strauss, "Plan of a Book Tentatively Titled *Philosophy and the Law*," in JPCM, 470. In the same context, Strauss announces, "While preparing the edition of Mendelssohn's metaphysical writings for the *Jubilee-Edition* of Mendelssohn's works, I discovered some unknown material which throws new light on that controversy." However, it is not clear from the text, nor does it become clear in the introductions what this material consists of. Although the book was never published, there is fragmentary evidence in Strauss's *Nachlaß* in the University of Chicago Library that he worked on an interpretation of *Nathan the Wise*. Cf. *Leo Strauss Papers*, Box 11, Folder 7.

75. Strauss, "Einleitung zu *Morgenstunden*," GS 2, 535. Consider also Strauss's comment on Mendelssohn's art of writing in casting *Morgenstunden* as a dialogue: "A dialogue is a kind of drama; a drama, being a product of poetry, is an ideal presentation of nature, in specific cases an ideal presentation of real occurrences; and art is playful, whereas life is serious" (590).

76. Plato, *Apology*, 23a.

77. Cf. Strauss, WPP, 93: "From this point of view the adjective 'political' designates not so much a subject matter as a manner of treatment; from this point of view, I say, 'political philosophy' means primarily not the philosophic treatment of politics, but the political, or popular, treatment of philosophy, or the political introduction to philosophy." Cf. Strauss, "Farabi's Plato," in *Louis Ginzberg Jubilee Volume* (New York: American Academy for Jewish Research, 1945), 362.

78. Strauss, PL, 116.

79. Cf. Strauss, "Quelques remarques," in GS 2, 133–134; PAW, 99; "Farabi's Plato," 378.

80. Plato, *Laws*, 899d–910d. Compare Plato, *Laws* 905a–b and Amos 9:1–3.

81. Plato, *Laws*, 663d–e.

82. Ibid., 663e–664a.

83. Strauss, "Quelques remarques," in GS 2, 152; PAW, 182; WPP, 144, 299.

84. Strauss, "Quelques remarques," in GS 2, 129. It is perhaps no accident that Strauss uses Nietzschean terms to define an opposition that is transcended and surpassed by Alfarabi's "right mean." See Strauss's letter of December 7, 1933, to Gerschom Scholem, in GS 3, 706–707.

85. Strauss, "Quelques remarques," in GS 2, 129.

86. Strauss, PL, 76. Strauss's "Farabian turn" is carefully analyzed in Daniel Tanguay's excellent study *Leo Strauss: An Intellectual Biography*.

87. Alfarabi, *The Philosophy of Plato and Aristotle*, quoted in Strauss, PAW, 12. Cf. Strauss, WPP, 144: "Fârâbî may have rewritten the *Laws*, as it were, with a view to the situation that was created by the rise of Islam or of revealed religion generally. He may have tried to preserve Plato's purpose by adapting the expression of that purpose to the new medium."

88. Cf. Strauss, "Quelques remarques," in GS2, 148–149; "Eine vermißte Schrift Farâbîs," in GS 2, 101, 105; PAW, 12.

89. Cf. Strauss, "Quelques remarques," in GS 2, 150–151; RCPR, 214.

90. Yeshayahu Leibovitz also observes that Maimonides tries to mitigate Jewish messianism, while pointing out that what remains unsaid in Maimonides's writings is as important as what is said. Cf. Yeshayahu Leibovitz, *La foi de Maïmonide* (Paris: Cerf, 1992), 72.

91. Cf. Strauss, "On Abravanel's Philosophical Tendency and Political Teaching," in GS 2, 199:

> Now this property of law had to be imitated by Maimonides in his philosophic interpretation of the law. For if he had distinguished explicitly between true and necessary beliefs, he would have endangered the acceptance of the necessary beliefs on which the authority of the law with the vulgar, i.e., with the great majority, rests. Consequently, he could make this essential distinction only in a disguised way, partly by allusions, partly by the composition of his whole work, but mainly by the rhetorical character, recognizable only to philosophers, of the arguments by which he defends the necessary beliefs.

92. Strauss, "On Abravanel's Philosophical Tendency and Political Teaching," in GS 2, 199.

93. See Strauss's remarkable letters to Jacob Klein of January 20, February 16, and July 23, 1938, in GS 3, 544–546, 548–550, and 553–554, respectively. These letters show that Strauss was keenly aware of the implications of his view that Maimonides "was *absolutely* not a Jew in his belief," and that *The Guide of the Perplexed* in fact reveals the "incompatibility in principle of philosophy and Judaism" (GS 3, 549–550). See also Meier, *Leo Strauss and the Theologico-Political Problem*, 23–24.

94. Strauss, PL, 103. Cf. Daniel Tanguay, "La querelle des Anciens et des Modernes et le statut de la raison pratique chez Leo Strauss," in *Carrefour* 21, no. 2 (1999): 21–35.

95. Denis Diderot, *Pensées sur l'interpretation de la nature*, xl, in *Œuvres complètes*, vol. 9 (Paris: Hermann, 1981), 69; quoted in Meier, *Leo Strauss and the Theologico-Political Problem*, 58.

96. See Strauss's letter of February 7, 1933, to Gerhard Krüger, where he defends himself against Krüger's objection that he takes his unbelief for granted: "I know nothing, but I am merely of the opinion (*ich meine nur*); in the first place, I want to figure out for myself what my opinion is (and my *doxa* [opinion] is atheism), what it is about, what its problems are, in order to find, by raising these questions, the road that will perhaps lead me to knowledge" (GS 3, 425).

97. Strauss, SCR, 31. As becomes apparent from a letter to Klein written on June 23, 1934 (GS 3, 516), Strauss was prepared to accept the consequences of his rediscovery:

> And even if we were to be huddled into the ghetto once again and thus be compelled to go to the synagogue and to observe the law in its entirety, then this too we would have to do as philosophers, i.e., with a reserve (*Vorbehalt*) that, if ever so tacit, must for that very reason be all the more determined. . . . That revelation and philosophy are at one in their opposition to sophistry, i.e., the whole of modern philosophy, I deny as little as you do. However, this doesn't change anything regarding the fundamental difference between philosophy and revelation: philosophy, while it may perhaps be brought under one roof with faith, prayer and preaching, can never be brought into agreement with them.

98. Strauss, letter of October 2, 1935, to Gerschom Scholem, in GS 3, 716.

99. Strauss's review was reprinted in an English translation in *Spinoza's Critique of Religion*. All references are to this edition.

100. The importance of Strauss's review for the understanding of Schmitt's thought has been widely recognized. The most detailed study is Heinrich Meier's *Carl Schmitt and Leo Strauss: The Hidden Dialogue* (Chicago: University of Chicago Press, 1995). Subsequently Meier elaborated his insight in a comprehensive interpretation of Schmitt's entire work: *The Lesson of Carl Schmitt: Four Chapters on the Distinction between Political Theology and Political Philosophy* (Chicago: University of Chicago Press, 1998).

101. Strauss, SCR, 351.

102. Ibid. 335.

103. See Meier, *Carl Schmitt and Leo Strauss*, and *Leo Strauss and the Theologico-Political Problem*, 16.

104. Cf. Strauss, CM, 33.

105. Cf. Strauss, SCR, 71, 335.

106. Ibid., 335. Cf. Strauss, CM, 2.

107. Strauss, SCR, 335–336. Cf. Strauss, "On a New Interpretation of Plato's Political Philosophy," 355.

108. Ibid., 336.

109. Cf. Ibid., 339 n. 2.

110. Cf. Strauss, RCPR, 326.

111. Cf. Strauss, SCR, 342.

112. Ibid., 338.

113. Ibid., 339. Cf. Strauss, LAM, 220.

114. Thomas Hobbes, *De Cive*, "Epistle Dedicatory." Later on, Strauss will define this view as the core of Hobbes's anthropology: "the traditional definition implies that man is by nature a social animal, and Hobbes must reject this implication" (Strauss, WPP, 176 n. 2). Cf. Strauss, "Preface to *Hobbes' politische Wissenschaft*," in JPCM, 453–454; SPPP, 144.

115. Aristotle, *Politics*, 1253a8.

116. Cf. Strauss, NRH, 184 n. 23: "According to the classics, the state of nature would be the life in a healthy society and not the life antedating civil society."

117. Cicero, *Tusculan Disputations*, II.v.13.

118. Strauss, SCR, 342.

119. To support this point, Strauss quotes another classical source: Plutarch's *Life of Pyrrhus*, where the Roman commander Caius Fabricius, hearing an exposition of the teaching that pleasure is the highest human good, is reported to have said, "'O Hercules, may Pyrrhus and the Samnites cherish these doctrines as long as they are at war with us'" (*Life of Pyrrhus*, 20.4, quoted in Strauss, SCR, 342). In other words, viewed from what according to Schmitt is the political perspective par excellence, human dangerousness is seen to point *beyond* itself. Simply affirming it thus proves to be insufficient to explain the political. In fact, Plutarch not only explicitly identifies the philosophic teaching as Epicurean, but he also spells out both its political and its theological implications. As he explains in the same passage, and as Strauss doubtless knew, the Epicureans "would have nothing to do with civil government on the ground that it was injurious and the ruin of felicity, and . . . they removed the divine as far as possible from feelings of kindness or anger or concern for us, into a life that knew no care and was filled with ease and comfort" (*Life of Pyrrhus*, 20.3). In the context of Strauss's debate with Schmitt, this remark is not without significance. The Epicurean position, as described by Plutarch, is squarely at odds with the political theology that Strauss discreetly brings to light underneath Schmitt's position. It denies both the importance of politics and of special divine providence for human life, two crucial tenets of the Schmittian teaching (see Meier, *Leo Straus and the Theologico-Political Problem*, 77–78). Moreover, a reader of *Spinoza's Critique of Religion* like Schmitt is likely to have been aware of the influence of Epicureanism's apolitical hedonism and antitheism on early modern political thinkers such as Spinoza and Hobbes, which Strauss traces with great care (see the section "Happiness and Ridicule: The Epicurean Connection" in chapter 2). Needless to say, this connection deals an additional blow to Schmitt's putative alliance with Hobbes.

120. Another point on which Schmitt deviates from his predecessors is his sympathy, even his admiration for the amoral evil of man in the state of nature. In a review of *The Concept of the Political*, Helmut Kuhn calls Schmitt "an inverted Rousseau," since he offers a "predator idyll" instead of a "pastoral idyll." See Helmut Kuhn, "Besprechung von Carl Schmitt, *Der Begriff des Politischen*," *Kant-Studien* 38 (1933): 190–196.

121. Strauss, SCR, 346.

122. Ibid., 347.

123. Ibid.

124. Plato, *Euthyphro*, 7d.

125. Plato, *Phaedrus*, 263a.

126. Cf. Strauss, SPPP, 171.

127. Strauss, SCR, 349.

128. Cf. Strauss, LAM, 207: "the political is *sui generis* and cannot be understood as derivative of the subpolitical"; LAM, 215: "the political proper, the essentially controversial"; RCPR, 143: "By recognizing that the political is irreducible to the nonpolitical, that the political is *sui generis*, Socrates does justice to the claim raised on behalf of the political, or even by the political itself, namely by the political community, by the *polis*." See also Strauss, *Xenophon's Socrates* (Ithaca, NY: Cornell University Press, 1972), 69; "Why We Remain Jews," in JPCM, 331.

129. See Meier, *Carl Schmitt and Leo Strauss*. Because of this "affinity," some critics have charged Strauss with harboring authoritarian, even totalitarian sympathies, and of being Schmitt's ally in a kind of neo-Hobbesian conspiracy against the Weimar Republic. Cf. Drury, *The Political Ideas of Leo Strauss* and *Leo Strauss and the American Right*; Holmes, *The Anatomy of Antiliberalism*. None of these critics, however, correctly perceive the Socratic-Platonic orientation that distinguishes Strauss from Schmitt (and Hobbes). As a result, their arguments mostly amount to imputing guilt by association and using the fallacious reasoning Strauss himself has disparaged as *reductio ad Hitlerum* (cf. Strauss, NRH, 42). Precisely because of his classical inspiration, Strauss was deeply critical of the authoritarian decisionism of "revolutionary conservatives" like Schmitt and Ernst Jünger. See Strauss, "German Nihilism," *Interpretation*, 26, no. 3 (1999): 353–378; "The Living Issues of German Postwar Philosophy," in Meier, *Leo Strauss and the Theologico-Political Problem*, 127–130.

130. Cf. Strauss, RCPR, 102: "The orientation by civilizations thus appears to be based on a remarkable estrangement from those life-and-death issues which animate societies and keep them in motion."

131. Strauss, SCR, 352.

132. Ibid., 348, 351.

133. Ibid., 351.

134. Ibid., 339 (emphasis in the original).

135. See Strauss's letter of August 19, 1932, to Gerhard Krüger, in GS 3, 399, and his letter of August 15, 1946, to Karl Löwith, in GS 3, 662–663.

136. Strauss, SCR, 351.

137. Ibid., 348 (emphasis added).

138. Ibid., 332.

139. Ibid., 351.

140. Strauss, PL, 138 n. 2.

141. Ibid.

142. Consider the opening paragraph of *Philosophy and Law*: "Maimonides' rationalism is the true natural model, the standard to be carefully protected from any distortion, and thus the stumbling block on which modern rationalism fails. To awaken a prejudice in favor of this view of Maimonides and, even more, to arouse suspicion against the powerful opposing prejudice, is the aim of the present work" (Strauss, PL, 21).

143. Strauss, SCR, 31.

144. Strauss, "Cohen und Maimuni," in GS 2, 412. Cf. Strauss, "Reason and Revelation," in Meier, *Leo Strauss and the Theologico-Political Problem*, 146–148.

145. Cf. Meier, *Leo Strauss and the Theologico-Political Problem*, 6–11.

## Chapter 5.  Socrates and the Leviathan

1. Strauss, "Einige Anmerkungen über die politische Wissenschaft des Hobbes," in GS 3, 243–261.The work under review is Zbigniew Lubienski, *Die Grundlagen des ethisch-politischen Systems von Hobbes* (Munich: Reinhardt, 1932). The review was originally written in German, and subsequently translated into French by Strauss's friend Alexandre Kojève. See the editor's note in GS 3, 779.

2. Cf. Strauss, "Einige Anmerkungen," in GS 3, 245. Cf. Strauss, WPP, 172.

3. Strauss acknowledges his debt for this insight to the sociologist Ferdinand Tönnies, who devoted several influential studies to Hobbes. See Strauss, "Einige Anmerkungen," in GS 3, 249–250; PAW, 28 n. 10.

4. Strauss, "Einige Anmerkungen," in GS 3, 250.

5. Hobbes, *Leviathan*, ch. 14.

6. Strauss, "Einige Anmerkungen," in GS 3, 259.

7. Ibid.

8. Ibid., 260.

9. Strauss, SCR, 108.

10. The original German titles are *Die Religionskritik des Hobbes: Ein Beitrag zum Verständnis der Aufklärung* and *Hobbes' politische Wissenschaft in ihrer Genesis*. The first manuscript remained unfinished and was never published during Strauss's lifetime. The second was published in an English translation in 1936 (see chapter 1). A meticulous edition of both original manuscripts by Heinrich and Wiebke Meier is now available in the third volume of Strauss's *Gesammelte Schriften*.

11. Strauss, "Die Religionskritik des Hobbes," in GS 3, 270.

12. Cf. Strauss, SPPP 231. Cf. Aristotle, *Nicomachean Ethics*, 1095b.

13. Strauss, *The Political Philosophy of Hobbes*, 1. Where the English edition reads "the ideal of life," the German original reads "die Frage nach dem richtigen

Leben" (the question of the right life) (see GS 3, 13). In 1952, the University of Chicago Press issued an American edition (references are to this edition, henceforth "PPH"). In the preface, Strauss repeats his thesis: "the real basis of his political philosophy is not modern science" (ix).

14. Strauss, PPH, 5.

15. Ibid.

16. As Strauss points out, Hobbes calls the Leviathan, the contractual state, "King of the Proud." Cf. Strauss, PPH, 13; Hobbes, *Leviathan*, ch. 28, *in fine*.

17. Strauss, PPH, 15.

18. Cf. ibid., 16. This interpretation is already adumbrated in *Spinoza's Critique of Religion*. Compare ibid., 16–17 and Strauss, SCR, 284 n. 95. In the same context, Strauss already points to the discrepancy between the anthropological basis of Hobbes's politics and his natural science. Cf. Strauss, SCR, 284 n. 96. In Strauss's later studies of Hobbes, the fear of violent death remains central; cf. Strauss, NRH, 186; WPP, 192.

19. Strauss, PPH, 27.

20. Ibid., 29. Cf. Strauss, ibid., 168–170. As an example of an entirely naturalistic political theory, Strauss points to Spinoza, while referring the reader to his comparative analysis in *Spinoza's Critique of Religion*. Cf. Strauss, WPP, 192; NRH, 192 n. 33.

21. Cf. Strauss, NRH, 187. In this respect, Strauss views Hobbes as a precursor of Kant; cf. Strauss, PPH, 23, 54; CM, 88–89.

22. Strauss, PPH, 55.

23. Strauss draws an interesting parallel between Hobbesian fear and Cartesian doubt, pointing out that in fact Hobbes's ethics are in better accord with Descartes's basic intention than Cartesian ethics itself, with its emphasis on *générosité*:

> Radical doubt, whose moral correlate is distrust and fear, comes earlier than the self-confidence of the ego grown conscious of its independence and freedom, whose moral correlate is *générosité*. Descartes begins the groundwork of philosophy with distrust of his own prejudices, with distrust above all of the potential *deus deceptor*, just as Hobbes begins interpreting the State and therewith all morality by starting from men's natural distrust. It is, however, not Descartes's morals, but Hobbes's, which explains the concrete meaning and the concrete implications of fundamental distrust. For Hobbes . . . sees the origin of virtue not in magnanimity, but in fear, in fear of violent death. He considers not magnanimity but fear of violent death as the only adequate self-consciousness. (Strauss, PPH, 56)

It is tempting to see the influence of Jacobi on this issue (see the section "The Crisis of the Enlightenment" in chapter 3). Cf. Strauss, NRH, 17; Manent, *Naissances de la politique moderne*, 86.

24. Hobbes, *Leviathan*, ch. 21.

25. Cf. Strauss, PPH, 118, 121; NRH, 187. On this point, Strauss refers the reader to his review of Schmitt: "Hobbes 'prefers' these terrors of the state of nature because only on awareness of these terrors can a true and permanent society rest. The bourgeois existence which no longer experiences these terrors will endure only as long as it remembers them. By this finding Hobbes differs from those of his opponents who in principle share his bourgeois ideal, but reject his conception of the state of nature" (Strauss, PPH, 122).

26. Strauss, PPH, 27. Cf. ibid., 125.

27. Cf. ibid., 119.

28. Ibid., 34. To some extent, this instrumental approach also characterizes the other founder of the modern liberal horizon. For Spinoza as well, philosophy is a means to achieving the supreme happiness, rather than an end in itself. See the section "Maimonides" in chapter 2.

29. Strauss, PPH, 35.

30. Cf. ibid., 84; OT, 228.

31. In this context, Strauss makes a statement that will prove to be far-sighted: "The reference to Machiavelli's programme (15th chapter of *Il Principe*) shows the direction and the lines which further investigation of the origins of the modern interest in history should take" (Strauss, PPH, 88 n. 5). See the epilogue to this book.

32. Cf. Strauss, PPH, 104: "Hobbes considered the philosophic grounding of the principles of all judgement on political subjects more fundamental, incomparably more important than the most thoroughly founded historical knowledge. . . . The state of nature is thus for Hobbes not an historical fact, but a necessary construction."

33. Cf. ibid., 101; NRH, 180; SPPP, 212.

34. Cf. Strauss, PPH, 123.

35. Cf. ibid., 107, 168.

36. Cf. ibid., 81, 92–93.

37. Cf. ibid., 110; NRH, 180.

38. Ibid., 128.

39. Ibid., 81. Cf. ibid., 130.

40. Cf. Strauss, "Die Religionskritik des Hobbes," in GS 3, 273. Cf. Meier, *Leo Strauss and the Theologico-Political Question*, 91–111.

41. Strauss, PPH, 152. Cf. ibid., 136. In an unpublished manuscript written in 1931 and 1932, Strauss encapsulates his fundamental objection in an exemplary manner: "Hobbes *omits* (*versäumt*) the question without the answering of which political science cannot be science. He does not begin with the question: what is the

right order of human living together?—or with the equivalent question: *ti estin aretè* [what is virtue?]" (quoted in GS 3, xviii). For the use of the expression "omits," Strauss acknowledges his debt to Heidegger's *Destruktion* of tradition (ibid., xix). In the same manuscript, Strauss observes that Hobbes's "being caught up in the tradition already determines his outset in this way, that he is unable to repeat the Socratic question" (Cf. Strauss, PPH, 163). When Strauss argues in *Natural Right and History* that Socrates "was as much concerned with understanding what justice is . . . as with preaching justice," he adds the following caveat: "For if one is concerned with understanding the problem of justice, one must go through the stage in which justice presents itself as identical with citizen-morality, and one must not merely rush through that stage" (Strauss, NRH, 150). Could this be an implicit censure of modern thinkers like Hobbes and Heidegger, who rashly disparaged citizen morality and its accompanying understanding of justice, and who thereby "rushed" through the crucial stage?

42. On this point, Strauss is exceptionally critical: "[Hobbes's] judgment appears at first sight to be a caricature of the actual position, a caricature which was almost inevitable, for Hobbes, as a result of his disdain for classical philosophy, did not consider an unbiased study of the sources necessary" (Strauss, PPH, 141).

43. Strauss, PPH, 142. Cf. Strauss, letter of August 20, 1946, to Karl Löwith, in GS 3, 668; OT, 278; NRH, 124.

44. Strauss, PPH, 143–144. In a footnote to this passage, Strauss refers to Plato, *Euthyphro* 7b–d and *Phaedrus* 263a (Strauss, PPH, 143 n. 5; see also 141 n. 3).

45. A similar observation applies to Mendelssohn: in his commentary on the Pantheism Controversy, Strauss relates Mendelssohn's rejection of a paradoxical truth to his Cartesian distrust of ordinary language (see the section "The Crisis of the Enlightenment" in chapter 3).

46. One is entitled to wonder whether "ontology" includes "fundamental ontology." See also Strauss's letter of December 7, 1934, to Jacob Klein, in GS 3, 534.

47. "The virtue which is not found in the works of men is found in speech alone, in the divinatory, 'supposing' and 'founding' knowledge incorporated in speech. Speech alone, and not the always equivocal deeds, originally reveals to man the standard by which he can order his actions and test himself, take his bearings in life and nature, in a way completely undistorted, and, in principle, independent of the possibility of realization. This is the reason for Plato's 'escape' into speech, and for the theory thereby given of the transcendence of ideas; only by means of speech does man know of the transcendence of virtue'" (Strauss, PPH, 144). Cf. Strauss, NRH, 146.

48. Plato, *Republic*, 549d–550a; *Gorgias*, 495c. Cf. Strauss, PPH, 147; CM, 88–89.

49. Strauss, PPH, 147. Plato, *Laws*, 631c–d. In the German manuscript, the final sentence reads: "In itself wisdom (*die Einsicht*) stands supreme, for man (*für den Menschen*), however, justice" (GS 3, 168). As Strauss explains in his letter of December 12, 1932, to Gerhard Krüger, Nietzsche opposed the depreciation of courage by religion and modern philosophy by violently reaffirming the ancient ideal of courage. His intellectual probity, however, prevented him from progress-

ing "to the *unbelieving* critique of this ideal," the covert critique developed by Plato (GS 3, 414–415).

50. Cf. Plato, *Apology*, 23a. Cf. Seth Benardete, *Socrates' Second Sailing* (Chicago: University of Chicago Press, 1989), 179: "Wisdom is an idol of the cave."

51. Strauss, PPH, 149.

52. Ibid., 151.

53. Ibid., 153.

54. Ibid.

55. Cf. ibid., 154.

56. By the same token, Hobbes excludes the possibility of philosophical agreement regarding the fundamental problems. Cf. Strauss, CM, 115.

57. As Strauss will later observe, the problem of sovereignty is coeval with the problem of representation: because an irrevocable discrepancy remains between the will of the sovereign and the wills of the individual citizens, the former has to be regarded *as if* it were the will of all and each. Cf. Strauss, NRH, 190 n. 30.

58. Strauss, PPH, 159–160.

59. Cf. Strauss, SPPP, 166.

60. Strauss, PPH, 163.

61. Cf. Strauss, NRH, 167: "Hobbes was indebted to tradition for a single, but momentous, idea: he accepted on trust the view that political philosophy or political science is necessary."

62. In 1935, having completed the manuscript of *The Political Philosophy of Hobbes*, Strauss writes to Alexandre Kojève that "it is the first attempt at a radical liberation from the modern prejudice" (Strauss, OT, 230).

63. Strauss, "Die Religionskritik des Hobbes," in GS 3, 272. Cf. ibid., 267, 275.

64. Ibid., 344.

65. Cf. Strauss, PPH, 75: "The fact that Hobbes accommodated not his unbelief but his utterances of that unbelief to what was permissible in a good, and, in addition, prudent subject justifies the assumption that in the decades before the Civil War, and particularly in his humanist period, Hobbes hid his true opinions and was mindful of the maintenance of theological conventions."

66. Cf. Strauss, "Die Religionskritik des Hobbes," in GS 3, 276–278, 286, 339. Cf. Strauss, PPH, 71: "Hobbes's three presentations of political philosophy may with scarcely less justice than Spinoza's expressly so entitled work be called theological-political treatises. Exactly as Spinoza did later, Hobbes with double intention becomes an interpreter of the Bible, in the first place in order to make use of the authority of the Scriptures for his own theory, and next and particularly in order to shake the authority of the Scriptures." See the section "Spinoza's Twofold Strategy" in chapter 2.

67. Hobbes, *Leviathan*, pt. IV.

68. Cf. Strauss, WPP, 194.

69. Strauss, "Die Religionskritik des Hobbes," in GS 3, 313.

70. Ibid., 323.

71. Ibid., 327.

72. Cf. ibid., 343.

73. Ibid., 348.

74. Ibid., 358. Cf. ibid., 362. See also Strauss's letter of April 9, 1934, to Jacob Klein, in GS 3, 496.

75. Cf. Strauss, NRH, 174–177.

76. Strauss, "Die Religionskritik des Hobbes," in GS 3, 366.

77. Ibid.

78. Ibid., 270.

79. See Strauss's letters of October 15, 1931, and November 17, 1932, to Gerhard Krüger, in GS 3, 394, 404–409.

80. Strauss, "Einige Anmerkungen," in GS 3, 260.

81. Strauss, letter to Gerhard Krüger of December 27, 1932, in GS 3, 416.

82. Cf. Merrill, "Christianity and Politics."

83. The only occurrence is in a quote. Cf. Strauss, PPH, 155.

84. Ibid., 153.

85. Cf. Strauss, "Preface to *Hobbes' politische Wissenschaft*," in JPCM, 454.

86. Gerhard Krüger, *Philosophie und Moral in der kantischen Kritik* (Tübingen: J. C. B. Mohr, 1931), 236.

87. Strauss, PL, 136 n. 2.

# Chapter 6. Epilogue

1. When the Academy for the Science of Judaism encounters financial difficulties in 1931, Strauss obtains a stipend of the Rockefeller Foundation, endorsed by Ernst Cassirer and Carl Schmitt. In 1932, he moves to Paris, where he conducts the research on medieval Jewish and Islamic philosophy that will culminate in *Philosophy and Law*. One year later, he relocates to England, in order to continue his research on Hobbes.

2. In 1937, Strauss briefly worked as a researcher in the Department of History at Columbia University, New York City. From 1938–1948, he joined the faculty of political science at the New School for Social Research, also in New York

City, obtaining American citizenship in 1944. In 1949, he was appointed as a professor in the Department of Political Science at the University of Chicago, where he stayed until his retirement in 1968. Subsequently, Strauss went to Claremont Men's College in California, where he taught for a year and a half, from January 1968 through June 1969, after which he moved to St. John's College in Annapolis, Maryland, until his death in 1973.

3. On this point, Strauss's letters to Jacob Klein of the period between 1937 and 1939 are fascinating and compelling reading. Cf. GS 3, 542–587.

4. Cf. Meier, *Leo Strauss and the Theologico-Political Problem*, 53–73.

5. Cf. Strauss, WPP, 126–127, 222.

6. Cf. Strauss, "Farabi's Plato," 375; PAW, 182, 111 n. 45.

7. Strauss, TM, 13. Cf. Strauss, NRH, 123–124; WPP, 251. Cf. Bloom, "Leo Strauss, September 20, 1899, October 18, 1973," in *Giants and Dwarfs*, 253: "the surface is the core."

8. In his correspondence to Hans-Georg Gadamer, Strauss writes that he has no theory of hermeneutic experience, while emphasizing the "ministerial" and "irretrievably 'occasional' character of every worthwhile interpretation" (Strauss, "Correspondence concerning *Wahrheit und Methode*," 5–6, 11). Cf. Gadamer, *Wahrheit und Methode*, 20 n. 4, 255 n. 1, 278 n. 2, 302 n. 1; Gadamer, *Gesammelte Werke*, 299–300, 401, 414–424, 501. See also Fortin, "Gadamer on Strauss: An Interview."

9. Lessing, "Leibniz von den ewigen Strafen," quoted in Strauss, "Farabi's Plato," 357. Cf. Strauss, PAW, 65.

10. Cf. Xenophon, *On Hunting*, 13.6.

11. Strauss, PAW, 60–78.

12. Strauss, WPP, 136: "the public will interpret the absolutely unexpected speech in terms of the customary and expected meaning of the surroundings rather than it will interpret the surroundings in terms of the dangerous character of the speech."

13. Cf. Strauss, "Farabi's Plato," 386–387.

14. Discussing the requirements for an adequate interpretation of Maimonides's *The Guide of the Perplexed*, Strauss characterizes his own approach as follows: "Since the *Guide* contains an esoteric interpretation of an esoteric teaching, an adequate interpretation of the *Guide* would thus have to take the form of an esoteric interpretation of an esoteric interpretation of an esoteric teaching" (Strauss, PAW, 56). Cf. Bloom, "Leo Strauss," 247–248.

15. Strauss, PAW, 14. Cf. Strauss, "Farabi's Plato," 375.

16. For some interpretations of Strauss's works that take account of his art of writing, see Laurence Lampert, "The Argument of Leo Strauss in *What Is Political Philosophy?*" *Modern Age*, 22, no. 1 (1978): 38–46, *Leo Strauss and Nietzsche* (Chicago:

University of Chicago Press, 1996); Seth Benardete, "Leo Strauss' *The City and Man*," *Political Science Reviewer* 8 (1978): 1–20; Susan Orr, *Jerusalem and Athens: Reason and Revelation in the Work of Leo Strauss* (Lanham, MD: Rowman & Littlefield, 1995); Nathan Tarcov, "On a Certain Critique of 'Straussianism,'" *Review of Politics* 53, no. 1 (1991): 3–18; Smith, *Reading Leo Strauss*.

17. Strauss met Kojève during his sojourn in Paris. A plan to collaborate on a book on the connection between Hobbes and Hegel never materialized (see Strauss, PPH, 58 n. 1). The debate between Strauss and Kojève on tyranny, the end of history, and the relationship between philosophy and politics constitutes the backdrop to Francis Fukuyama's *The End of History and the Last Man* (Harmondsworth, UK: Penguin, 1992). Although the title captures the disagreement between Kojève and Strauss, the latter is never mentioned explicitly in the text, but only in the footnotes and the bibliography. Cf. Alexandre Kojève, *Introduction to the Reading of Hegel* (Ithaca, NY: Cornell University Press, 1980); George Grant, "Tyranny and Wisdom: A Comment on the Controversy between Leo Strauss and Alexandre Kojève," *Social Research* 31 (1964): 45–72; Victor Gourevitch, "Philosophy and Politics" I and II, *Review of Metaphysics* 22, no. 1 (1968): 58–84 and 281–328; Dominique Auffret, *Alexandre Kojève: La philosophie, L'État, la fin de l'Histoire* (Paris: Grasset, 1990); Robert Pippin, "Being, Time, and Politics: The Strauss-Kojève Debate," in *Idealism as Modernism: Hegelian Variations* (Cambridge: Cambridge University Press, 1997), 233–261.

18. A "classic" reading of Plato along these lines is Karl Popper, *The Open Society and Its Enemies I: The Spell of Plato* (London: Routledge & Kegan Paul, 1993).

19. Cf. Strauss, "On a New Interpretation of Plato's Political Philosophy"; Stanley Rosen, *The Quarrel between Philosophy and Poetry* (New York: Routledge, 1988), 187–188; John Ferrari, "Strauss's Plato," *Arion* 5, no. 2 (1997): 61–62.

20. Cf. Strauss, CM, 61–62. Cf. Jacob Klein, *A Commentary on Plato's Meno* (Chapel Hill: University of North Carolina Press, 1965), 3–31. Klein stresses the importance of the dramatic context in interpreting Platonic dialogues, as well as the necessity for the reader to participate in the reconstruction of this context.

21. Strauss, CM, 60. Cf. Strauss, "On the Interpretation of *Genesis*," in JPCM, 374.

22. Cf. *Matthew* 10:29.

23. James Joyce, *Ulysses*, ch. 9.

24. Cf. Strauss, *On Plato's Symposium*, 11–12.

25. Cf. Strauss, CM, 50–59; *On Plato's Symposium*, 5.

26. Strauss, CM, 51.

27. Cf. Seth Benardete, *The Argument of the Action: Essays on Greek Poetry and Philosophy* (Chicago: University of Chicago Press, 2000).

28. Strauss, CM, 62.

29. Plato, *Republic*, 368e.

30. Ibid., 369a.

31. Ibid., 331c–d.

32. Cf. Strauss, CM, 69.

33. Cf. Plato, *Republic*, 452a–456b. Cf. Strauss, CM, 79.

34. Cf. Plato, *Republic*, 238a, 354a–b. Cf. Strauss, CM, 83, 91, 109.

35. Cf. Plato, *Republic*, 573b–d.

36. Cf. Strauss, CM, 105, 117, 127, 133. Cf. Allan Bloom, *Love and Friendship* (New York: Simon & Schuster 1993), 440–443.

37. Plato, *Republic*, 414b–415c; Strauss, CM, 102.

38. Plato, *Republic*, 440e. Cf. Strauss, CM, 110–111; Benardete, *Socrates' Second Sailing*, 93.

39. Cf. Rosen, *The Quarrel between Philosophy and Poetry*, 109.

40. Plato, *Republic*, 473c–e.

41. Cf. Strauss, CM, 125.

42. Plato, *Republic*, 515c–516a. Cf. Strauss, CM, 128.

43. Plato, *Republic*, 327c. Cf. Rosen, *The Quarrel between Philosophy and Poetry*, 106–107.

44. Strauss, CM, 127. Cf. Strauss, CM, 65; Benardete, *Socrates' Second Sailing*, 149.

45. Plato, *Republic*, 611b–c.

46. Cf. Strauss, WPP, 39: "Socrates, then, viewed man in the light of the mysterious character of the whole. He held therefore that we are more familiar with the situation of man as man than with the ultimate causes of that situation. We may also say he viewed man in the light of the unchangeable ideas, i.e., of the fundamental and permanent problems." NRH, 150 n. 24: "Socrates was . . . concerned with understanding what justice *is*, i.e., with understanding the whole complexity of the problem of justice."

47. Cf. Seth Benardete, *The Tragedy and Comedy of Life: Plato's Philebus* (Chicago: University of Chicago Press, 1993), x; Ferrari, "Strauss's Plato," 52, 56–60; Stanley Rosen, *Plato's Statesman: The Web of Politics* (New Haven, CT: Yale University Press, 1995), 190.

48. Cicero, *On the Republic*, II, 52. Cf. Strauss, SPPP, 128; CM, 138.

49. Plato, *Republic*, 498c–d.

50. Ibid. Cf. Strauss, "Farabi's Plato," 382; WPP, 153–154; NRH, 6. Cf. Alfarabi, *Philosophy of Plato and Aristotle* (Ithaca, NY: Cornell University Press, 2001), 66–67.

51. Plato, *Phaedo*, 99d–e. Cf. Ronna Burger, *The Phaedo: A Platonic Labyrinth* (New Haven, CT: Yale University Press, 1984), 144–147, 254, n. 26. Cf. Strauss, PPH, 141–149.

52. Cf. Strauss, TM, 19: "we have learned from Socrates that the political things, or the human things, are the key to the understanding of all things."

53. Cf. Strauss, WPP, 10: "All political action has then in itself a directedness towards knowledge of the good, or of the good society. For the good society is the complete political good. If this directedness becomes explicit, if men make it their explicit goal to acquire knowledge of the good life and of the good society, political philosophy emerges."

54. Meier, *Leo Strauss and the Theologico-Political Problem*, 103.

55. Cf. Strauss, *Socrates and Aristophanes* (New York: Basic Books, 1966), henceforth "SA."

56. Strauss, SA, 5, 34, 50–52; RCPR, 105. Aristophanes shares the incapacity to penetrate Socrates's enigmatic core with Alcibiades: as Strauss suggests, this may be related to the fact that, unlike Socrates, both the poet and the politician are essentially dependent on the acclaim of their audience. Cf. Plato, *Symposium*, 221a–b and *Philebus*, 48a–50a. Cf. Strauss, *On Plato's Symposium*, 137, 140, 149, 265–269. See also Strauss's letter of December 12, 1938, to Jacob Klein, in GS 3, 561.

57. In the *Apology*, Socrates tells his audience that "many accusers have risen up against me before you," who claimed that "there is a certain Socrates, a wise man, a ponderer over the things in the air and one who has investigated the things beneath the earth and who makes the weaker argument the stronger." As Socrates goes on to say, "it is not even possible to know and speak their names, except when one of them happens to be a writer of comedies" (Plato, *Apology*, 18b–d). Cf. Strauss, NRH, 93; *On Plato's Symposium*, 267; Harry Neumann, "Civic Piety and Socratic Atheism: An Interpretation of Strauss' *Socrates and Aristophanes*," *Independent Journal of Philosophy* 2 (1978): 33–37.

58. Cf. Bloom, *Love and Friendship*, 477; Benardete, *The Tragedy and Comedy of Life*, 224.

59. Cf. Strauss, SA, 282; RCPR, 104. Cf. Aristophanes, *Lysistrata*, 565–586. See also George Steiner, *No Passion Spent: Essays 1978–1996* (London: Faber and Faber 1997), 406.

60. Cf. Strauss, *On Plato's Symposium*, 6–7, 40–41.

61. Plato, *Republic*, 607b.

62. See especially Strauss's letters to Jacob Klein from October 15, 1938, to November 28, 1939, GS 3, 556–587. Cf. Strauss, LAM, 34–37, 41–43; Benardete, *The Argument of the Action*, 415–416.

63. Cf. Strauss, "On the Intention of Rousseau," *Social Research* 14, no. 4 (1947): 455–87; PAW, 142–201; "The Three Waves of Modernity," in *An Introduction to Political Philosophy: Ten Essays by Leo Strauss*, ed. Hilail Gildin, 81–98 (Detroit, MI: Wayne State University Press, 1975).

64. Niccolò Machiavelli, *The Prince*, ch. 15. Cf. Strauss, SCR, 321–323.

65. Niccolò Machiavelli, *Discourses on Livy*, preface.

66. Machiavelli, letter to Francesco Guicciardini of May 17, 1521, quoted in Kauffmann, *Strauss und Rawls*, 127. Introducing the first book of the *Discourses*, Machiavelli tells his addressee: "And even if this enterprise may be difficult, nonetheless, aided by those who have advised me to begin carrying this load, I believe I can carry it *so that there will remain for others a short way to bring it to its destined place*" (emphasis added).

67. Strauss, TM. Cf. Claude Lefort, *Le travail de l'œuvre Machiavel* (Paris: Gallimard, 1972); Kim A. Sorensen, *Discourses on Strauss: Revelation and Reason in Leo Strauss and His Critical Study of Machiavelli* (Notre Dame, IN: University of Notre Dame Press, 2006).

68. Cf. Strauss, "Machiavelli and Classical Literature," *Review of National Literatures* 1, no. 1 (1970): 7–25. See also Strauss's letter to Karl Löwith of August 15, 1946, in GS 3, 661. See the section "Spinoza's Twofold Strategy" in chapter 2 and the section "Fighting the Kingdom of Darkness" in chapter 5.

69. Cf. Strauss, TM, 31.

70. Ibid., 294.

71. Ibid., 295.

72. Cf. Strauss, *On Plato's Symposium*, 230. In the fourteenth chapter of *The Prince*, Machiavelli advises his addressee to imitate the models of antiquity, in particular the Persian ruler Cyrus and "those things which have been written of Cyrus by Xenophon." However, Machiavelli fails to see the profound critical irony in Xenophon's depiction of Cyrus, as well as the fact that Cyrus is only one of the two *foci* of Xenophon's field of vision, the other of which is Socrates. Cf. Strauss, TM, 290–291. Cf. Christopher C. Nadon, *Xenophon's Prince: Republic and Empire in the Cyropaedeia* (Berkeley: University of California Press, 2001).

73. Strauss, TM, 295.

74. Strauss, WPP, 44. Cf. Daniel Tanguay, "'Colère anti-théologique' et sécularisation: quelques remarques sur l'interprétation straussienne de la rupture moderne," *Science et Esprit* 52, no. 2 (1999): 185–197.

75. Cf. Strauss, TM, 297; WPP, 44–46.

76. Strauss, PAW, 15.

77. Cf. Strauss, TM, 202–203.

78. Strauss, WPP, 127.

79. Cf. Aron, introduction to *Le savant et le politique*, 31–52; Helmut Kuhn, "Naturrecht und Historismus," *Independent Journal of Philosophy* 2 (1978): 13–21; Luc Ferry, *Philosophie Politique 1 Le Droit: La nouvelle querelle des anciens et des modernes* (Paris: Presses Universitaires de France, 1984). But see Kennington, "Strauss's *Natural Right and History*," 57–86, and Terence Marshall, "Leo Strauss, la philosophie et

la science politique" (1) and (2), *Revue française de science politique* 35, no. 4 (1985): 605–638 and 35, no. 5 (1985): 801–838.

80. Strauss, NRH, 120.

81. Ibid., 144. In the same context, Strauss once again points to the ambiguity of the Platonic dialogues: "Many interpreters of Plato do not sufficiently consider the possibility that his Socrates was as much concerned with understanding what justice is, i.e., with understanding the whole complexity of the problem of justice, as with preaching justice" (ibid., 150 n. 24).

82. Strauss, "Religiöse Lage der Gegenwart," in GS 2, 380.

83. Strauss, FPP, 74.

84. Interestingly enough, on this point Strauss quotes Lessing, who warns against identifying "the goal of our thinking with the point at which we have become tired of thinking" (Lessing, letter to Mendelssohn of January 9, 1771, quoted in Strauss, NRH, 22). During his early investigations on Hobbes, Strauss wrote a "preface to a projected book on Hobbes," in which he took to task two prominent legal theorists and critics of natural right: Hans Kelsen and Carl Bergbohm. Both of these authors, he argued, commit the historicist fallacy of concluding the impossibility of natural right from the historical failure of the quest for natural right, out of intellectual probity. See Strauss, "Vorwort zu einem geplanten Buch über Hobbes," in GS 3, 201–215. Cf. Strauss, NRH, 4, 10.

85. Cf. Strauss, NRH, 13, 18, 26–28, 64–66

86. Cf. Strauss, SPPP, 176–181, 188.

87. Cf. Strauss, "Restatement on Xenophon's *Hiero*," in JPCM, 472: "those who lacked the courage to face the issue of Tyranny, who therefore *et humiliter serviebant et superbe dominabantur* [themselves obsequiously subservient while arrogantly lording it over others], were forced to evade the issue of Being as well, precisely because they did nothing but talk of Being." See also Meier, *Leo Strauss and the Theologico-Political Problem*, 45–51, 105–106.

88. See Strauss's letters of August 11, 1960, November 22, 1960, and November 17, 1972, to Gerschom Scholem, in GS 3, 740, 742, 765.

89. Strauss, NRH, 74. Strauss offers a lengthy and profound meditation on this alternative in a lecture on "Reason and Revelation" he gave in 1948 at the Hartford Theological Seminary. In the lecture, he makes extensive use of his findings in *Spinoza's Critique of Religion*. The lecture is published in Meier, *Leo Strauss and the Theologico-Political Problem*, 141–180, esp. 150–155.

90. The Christian point of view is fittingly encapsulated by Eric Voegelin: "The *qui est* [he who is] is the name most appropriate for God, because it does not refer to specific forms of immanent being" (Eric Voegelin, *Anamnesis* [München: Piper Verlag, 1966], 338; cf. Thomas Aquinas, *Summa Theologiae* I, XIII, 11). Cf. Strauss, SPPP, 122, 162–163, 166, 170; RCPR, 256–257; "On the Interpretation of *Genesis*," 6, 16–20.

91. Strauss, CM, 241. See also ibid., 98, where Strauss refers to "the gravity of the failure to raise and answer the question 'what is a God?' or 'who are the gods?'" See also Strauss, OT, 109; *Xenophon's Socrates*, 118; SA, 53. See also Meier, *Leo Strauss and the Theologico-Political Problem*, 25–27 n. 42. Cf. Benardete, "Leo Strauss' *The City and Man*," 1.

92. Strauss, CM, 240.

93. Cf. Strauss, RCPR, 246–252.

94. Strauss, PAW, 114.

95. Cf. Strauss, SPPP, 232. In "On the Interpretation of *Genesis*," Strauss shows that Genesis begins with the disparagement of the two themes that are characteristic of philosophy: the investigation of the heavens and the knowledge of good and evil. Cf. Strauss, "Reason and Revelation," in Meier, *Leo Strauss and the Theologico-Political Problem*, 147, 162. See also Thomas L. Pangle, *Political Philosophy and the God of Abraham* (Baltimore, MD: Johns Hopkins University Press, 2003).

96. Cf. Strauss, RCPR, 258–260; "Reason and Revelation," 178.

97. Strauss, SCR, 6.

98. Strauss, "Reason and Revelation," 141–180.

99. Seth Benardete, *Encounters and Reflections: Conversations with Seth Benardete*, ed. Ronna Burger, 176–178 (Chicago: University of Chicago Press, 2002).

100. Strauss, RCPR, 206. This passage concludes Strauss's interpretation of Plato's *Euthyphro*, in which the problem of piety is central.

# Bibliography

## Works by Leo Strauss

*The Argument and the Action of Plato's Laws.* Chicago: University of Chicago Press, 1975.

*The City and Man.* Chicago: Rand McNally, 1964.

"Correspondence with Hans-Georg Gadamer concerning *Wahrheit und Methode.*" *Independent Journal of Philosophy* 2 (1978): 5–12.

"The Crisis of Our Time." In *The Predicament of Modern Politics,* ed. Harold J. Spaeth, 41–54. Detroit: University of Detroit Press, 1964.

*The Early Writings (1921–1932).* Translated and edited by Michael Zank. Albany: State University of New York Press, 2002.

"Existentialism." *Interpretation,* 22, no. 3 (1995): 301–320.

*Faith and Political Philosophy: The Correspondence between Leo Strauss and Eric Voegelin, 1934–1964.* Edited and translated by Peter Emberley and Barry Cooper. University Park: Pennsylvania State University Press, 1993.

"Farabi's Plato." In *Louis Ginzberg Jubilee Volume.* New York: American Academy for Jewish Research, 1945, 357–393.

"German Nihilism." *Interpretation,* 26, no. 3 (1999): 353–378.

*Gesammelte Schriften Bd. 1: Die Religionskritik Spinozas und zugehörige Schriften.* Edited by Heinrich Meier. Stuttgart/Weimar: Verlag J. B. Metzler, 1996.

*Gesammelte Schriften Bd. 2: Philosophie und Gesetz—Frühe Schriften.* Edited by Heinrich Meier. Stuttgart/Weimar: Verlag J. B. Metzler, 1997.

*Gesammelte Schriften Bd 3: Hobbes' politische Wissenschaft und zugehörige Schriften.* Edited by Heinrich Meier. Stuttgart/Weimar: Verlag J. B. Metzler, 2001.

*History of Political Philosophy,* with Joseph Cropsey, eds. Chicago: University of Chicago Press, 1987.

*Jewish Philosophy and the Crisis of Modernity: Essays and Lectures in Modern Jewish Thought.* Edited with an introduction by Kenneth Hart Green. Albany: State University of New York Press, 1997.

*Liberalism Ancient and Modern.* New York: Basic Books, 1968.

"The Living Issues of German Postwar Philosophy." In *Leo Strauss and the Theologico-Political Problem* by Heinrich Meier, 115–139. Cambridge: Cambridge University Press, 2006.

"Machiavelli and Classical Literature." *Review of National Literatures*, 1, 1 (1970): 7–25.

*Natural Right and History.* Chicago: University of Chicago Press, 1953.

"On Collingwood's Philosophy of History." *Review of Metaphysics* 5, no. 4 (1952): 559–586.

"On the Intention of Rousseau." *Social Research* 14, no. 4 (1947): 455–487.

"On a New Interpretation of Plato's Political Philosophy." *Social Research* 13, no. 3 (1946): 326–367.

*On Plato's Symposium.* Edited and with a foreword by Seth Benardete. Chicago: University of Chicago Press, 2001.

*On Tyranny: Revised and Expanded Edition—Including the Strauss-Kojève Correspondence.* Edited by Victor Gourevitch and Michael S. Roth. New York: Free Press, 1991.

*Persecution and the Art of Writing.* Glencoe, IL: Free Press, 1952.

*Philosophy and Law: Contributions to the Understanding of Maimonides and his Predecessors.* Translated and with an introduction by Eve Adler. Albany: State University of New York Press, 1995.

*The Political Philosophy of Hobbes: Its Basis and Its Genesis.* Translated by Elsa M. Sinclair. Oxford, UK: Clarendon Press, 1936; reprint, Chicago: University of Chicago Press, 1952.

"Reason and Revelation." In *Leo Strauss and the Theologico-Political Problem* by Heinrich Meier, 141–180. Cambridge: Cambridge University Press, 2006.

*The Rebirth of Classical Political Rationalism: Essays and Lectures by Leo Strauss.* Selected and introduced by Thomas L. Pangle. Chicago: University of Chicago Press, 1989.

*Socrates and Aristophanes.* New York: Basic Books, 1966.

*Spinoza's Critique of Religion.* Translated by Elsa M. Sinclair. New York: Schocken Books, 1965.

*Studies in Platonic Political Philosophy.* With an introduction by Thomas L. Pangle. Chicago: University of Chicago Press, 1983.

*Thoughts on Machiavelli.* Glencoe, IL: Free Press, 1958.

"The Three Waves of Modernity." In *An Introduction to Political Philosophy: Ten Essays by Leo Strauss*, ed. Hilail Gildin, 81–98. Detroit.MI: Wayne State University Press, 1975.

*What Is Political Philosophy? And Other Studies*. Glencoe, IL: Free Press, 1959.

*Xenophon's Socrates*. Ithaca, NY: Cornell University Press, 1972.

*Xenophon's Socratic Discourse: An Interpretation of the Oeconomicus*. Ithaca, NY: Cornell University Press, 1970.

For a complete bibliography, see John A. Murley, ed., *Leo Strauss and His Legacy: A Bibliography*. Lanham, MD: Lexington Books, 2005.

## Secondary Sources

Altmann, Alexander. *Moses Mendelssohn: A Biographical Study*. London: Routledge & Kegan Paul, 1973.

———. "Necrology: Leo Strauss (1899–1973)." *Proceedings of the American Academy for Jewish Research* 41–42 (1973): xxxiii–xxxvi.

Anastaplo, George. *The Artist as Thinker: From Shakespeare to Joyce*. Athens, OH: Swallow Press, 1983.

Aron, Raymond. Introduction. In *Le savant et le politique* by Max Weber, 31–52, Paris: Plon, 1959.

Auffret, Dominique. *Alexandre Kojève La philosophie, L'État, la fin de l'Histoire*. Paris: Grasset, 1990.

Avineri, Shlomo. *The Making of Modern Zionism: The Intellectual Origins of the Jewish State*. London: Weidenfeld and Nicolson, 1981.

Banfield, Edward. C. "Leo Strauss: 1899–1973." In *Remembering the University of Chicago: Teachers, Scientists, and Scholars*, ed. Edward Shils, 490–501. Chicago: University of Chicago Press, 1991.

Behnegar, Nasser. "The Liberal Politics of Leo Strauss." In *Political Philosophy and the Human Soul: Essays in Memory of Allan Bloom*, ed. Michael Palmer and Thomas L. Pangle, 251–267. Lanham, MD: Rowman & Littlefield, 1995.

Beiser, Frederick C. *Enlightenment, Revolution, and Romanticism: The Genesis of Modern Political Thought, 1790–1800*. Cambridge, MA: Harvard University Press, 1992.

———. *The Fate of Reason: German Philosophy from Kant to Fichte*. London: Cambridge University Press, 1987.

Benardete, Seth. *The Argument of the Action: Essays on Greek Poetry and Philosophy*. Chicago: University of Chicago Press, 2002.

————. *Encounters and Reflections: Conversations with Seth Benardete*. Chicago: University of Chicago Press, 2002.

————. "Leo Strauss' *The City and Man*." *Political Science Reviewer* 8 (1978): 1–20.

————. *Socrates' Second Sailing*. Chicago: University of Chicago Press, 1989.

————. *The Tragedy and Comedy of Life: Plato's Philebus*. Chicago: University of Chicago Press, 1993.

Berkowitz, Peter. "Liberal Zealotry." *Yale Law Journal* 103, no. 5 (1994): 1363–1382.

Bloom, Allan. *The Closing of the American Mind*. New York: Simon & Schuster, 1988.

————. *Giants and Dwarfs: Essays 1960–1990*. New York: Simon & Schuster, 1990.

————. *Love and Friendship*. New York: Simon & Schuster, 1993.

Bolotin, David. "Leo Strauss and Classical Political Philosophy." *Interpretation* 22, no. 1 (1994): 129–142.

Brague, Rémi. "Athènes, Jérusalem, La Mecque: L'interprétation 'musulmane' de la philosophie grecque chez Leo Strauss." *Revue de Métaphysique et de Morale* 94, no. 3 (1989): 309–336.

————. "Leo Strauss et Maïmonide." In *Maimonides and Philosophy: Papers Presented at the Sixth Jerusalem Philosophic Encounter, May 1985*, ed. Shlomo Pines and Yirmiyahu Yovel, 246–268. Dordrecht: Martinus Nijhoff, 1986.

Burger, Ronna. *The Phaedo: A Platonic Labyrinth*. New Haven, CT: Yale University Press, 1984.

Burnyeat, Myles. "Sphinx Without a Secret." *New York Review of Books* 32, no. 9 (1985): 30–36.

Cropsey, Joseph. "Leo Strauss." In *Biographical Supplement to the International Encyclopaedia of the Social Sciences*, 18:746–750. London: Free Press, 1979.

Dannhauser, Werner. "Leo Strauss: Becoming Naïve Again." *American Scholar* 44 (1975): 636–642.

Deutsch, Kenneth L., and John Murley, eds. *Leo Strauss, the Straussians, and the American Regime*. Lanham: Rowman & Littlefield, 1999.

Deutsch, Kenneth L., and Walter Nicgorski, eds. *Leo Strauss: Political Philosopher and Jewish Thinker*. Lanham, MD: Rowman & Littlefield, 1994.

Deutsch, Kenneth L., and Walter Soffer, eds. *The Crisis of Liberal Democracy: A Straussian Perspective*. Albany: State University of New York Press, 1987.

Devigne, Robert. *Recasting Conservatism: Oakeshott, Strauss and the Response to Postmodernism*. New Haven, CT: Yale University Press, 1994.

Drury, Shadia B. *Leo Strauss and the American Right*. London: Palgrave Macmillan, 1979.

————. *The Political Ideas of Leo Strauss*. New York: St. Martin's Press, 1988; updated edition 2005.

Fackenheim, Emil. *Jewish Philosophers and Jewish Philosophy*. Bloomington: Indiana University Press, 1996.

Ferrari, John. "Strauss's Plato." *Arion* 5, no. 2 (1997): 36–65.

Ferry, Luc. *Philosophie Politique 1 Le Droit: La nouvelle querelle des anciens et des modernes*. Paris: Presses Universitaires de France, 1984.

Fortin, Ernest L. "Gadamer on Strauss: An Interview." *Interpretation* 12, no. 1 (1984): 1–13.

Fradkin, Hillel. "Leo Strauss." In *Interpreters of Judaism in the Late Twentieth Century*, ed. Steven T. Katz, 344–365. Washington, DC: B'nai B'rith Books, 1993.

Fukuyama, Francis. *The End of History and the Last Man*. Harmondsworth, UK: Penguin, 1992.

Gadamer, Hans-Georg. *Gesammelte Werke*. Tübingen: J. C. B. Mohr, 1986.

————. *Wahrheit und Methode: Grundzüge einer philosophischen Hermeneutik*. Tübingen: J. C. B. Mohr, 1972.

Gildin, Hilail. "Leo Strauss and the Crisis of Liberal Democracy." In *The Crisis of Liberal Democracy: A Straussian Perspective*, ed. Kenneth L. Deutsch and Walter Soffer, 91–103. Albany: State University of New York Press, 1987.

Glatzer, Nahum. *Franz Rosenzweig: His Life and Thought*. New York: Schocken Books, 1976.

Gourevitch, Victor. "Philosophy and Politics I." *Review of Metaphysics* 22, no. 1 (1968): 58–84.

————. "Philosophy and Politics II." *Review of Metaphysics* 22, no. 2 (1968): 281–328.

————. "The Problem of Natural Right and the Fundamental Alternatives in *Natural Right and History*." In *The Crisis of Liberal Democracy: A Straussian Perspective*, ed. Kenneth L. Deutsch and Walter Soffer, 30–47. Albany: State University of New York Press, 1987.

Grant, George. "Tyranny and Wisdom: A Comment on the Controversy between Leo Strauss and Alexandre Kojève." *Social Research* 31 (1964): 45–72.

Green, Kenneth Hart. "'In the Grip of the Theological-Political Predicament': The Turn to Maimonides in the Jewish Thought of Leo Strauss." In *Leo Strauss's Thought: Toward a Critical Engagement*, ed. Alan Udoff, 41–74. Boulder, CO: Lynne Rienner Publishers, 1991.

————. *Jew and Philosopher: The Return to Maimonides in the Jewish Thought of Leo Strauss*. Albany: State University of New York Press, 1993.

Gunnell, John G. "Political Theory and Politics: The Case of Leo Strauss." *Political Theory* 13, no. 3 (1985): 339–361.

———. "Strauss before Straussianism: Reason, Revelation and Nature." *Review of Politics* 53, no. 1 (1991): 53–74.

Holmes, Stephen. *The Anatomy of Antiliberalism*. Cambridge, MA: Harvard University Press, 1996.

Jaffro, Laurent, Benoît Frydman, Emmanuel Cattin, and Alain Petit, eds. *Leo Strauss: art d'écrire, politique, philosophie*. Paris: Vrin, 2001.

Janssens, David. "A Change of Orientation: Leo Strauss's 'Comments' on Carl Schmitt Revisited." *Interpretation* 33, no. 1 (2006): 93–104.

———. "The Problem of the Enlightenment: Strauss, Jacobi, and the Pantheism Controversy." *Review of Metaphysics* 56 (2003): 605–632.

———. "Questions and Caves: Philosophy, Politics, and History in Leo Strauss's Early Work." *Journal of Jewish Thought and Philosophy* 10 (2000): 111–144.

Kauffmann, Clemens. *Leo Strauss zur Einführung*. Hamburg: Junius, 1997.

——— *Strauss und Rawls: Das philosophische Dilemma der Politik*. Berlin: Duncker & Humblot, 2000.

Kennington, Richard. "Strauss's *Natural Right and History*." *Review of Metaphysics* 35 (1981): 57–86.

Kielmansegg, Peter Graf, Horst Mewes, and Elisabeth Glaser-Schmidt, eds. *Hannah Arendt and Leo Strauss: German Emigrés and American Political Thought after World War II*. Cambridge: Cambridge University Press, 1995.

Klein, Jacob. *A Commentary on Plato's* Meno. Chapel Hill: University of North Carolina Press, 1965.

Kojève, Alexandre. *Introduction to the Reading of Hegel*. Ithaca, NY: Cornell University Press, 1980.

Korth, Hildegard. *Guide to the Leo Strauss Papers*. Chicago: University of Chicago Library, Department of Special Collections, 1978.

Krüger, Gerhard. "Besprechung von L. Strauss, *Die Religionskritik Spinozas als Grundlage seiner Bibelwissenschaft*." *Deutsche Literaturzeitung* 51 (1931): 2407–2412.

———. *Philosophie und Moral in der kantischen Kritik*. Tübingen: J. C. B. Mohr, 1931.

Kuhn, Helmut. "Naturrecht und Historismus." *Independent Journal of Philosophy* 2 (1978): 13–21.

Lachterman, David. "Laying Down the Law: The Theological-Political Matrix of Spinoza's Physics." In *Leo Strauss's Thought: Toward a Critical Engagement*, ed. Alan Udoff, 123–153. Boulder, CO: Lynne Rienner Publishers, 1991.

Lampert, Laurence. "The Argument of Leo Strauss in *What Is Political Philosophy?*" *Modern Age* 22, no. 1 (1978): 38–46.

———. *Leo Strauss and Nietzsche*. Chicago: University of Chicago Press, 1996.

Larmore, Charles. "The Secrets of Philosophy." *New Republic* 3 (1989): 30–35.

Lefort, Claude. *Écrire: À l'épreuve du politique*. Paris: Calmann-Lévy, 1992.

———. *Le travail de l'œuvre Machiavel*. Paris: Gallimard, 1972.

Leibovitz, Yeshayahu. *La foi de Maïmonide*. Paris: Cerf, 1992.

Lerner, Ralph. "Leo Strauss (1899–1973)." *American Jewish Year Book* 76 (1976): 91–97.

Lerner, Ralph, and Muhsin Mahdi, eds. *Medieval Political Philosophy: A Sourcebook*. Ithaca, NY: Cornell University Press, 1963.

Lessing, Gotthold Ephraim. *Werke in acht Bänden*. München: Carl Hanser Verlag, 1979.

———. *Werke in drei Bänden*. München: Carl Hanser Verlag, 1982.

Levine, David. "Without Malice But with Forethought: A Response to Burnyeat." *Review of Politics* 53, no. 1 (1991): 200–218.

Manent, Pierre. *Naissances de la politique moderne: Machiavel, Hobbes, Rousseau*. Paris: Payot, 1977.

Marshall, Terence. "Leo Strauss, la philosophie et la science politique (1)." *Revue française de science politique* 35, no. 4 (1985): 605–638.

———. "Leo Strauss, la philosophie et la science politique (2)." *Revue française de science politique* 35, no. 5 (1985): 801–838.

McAllister, Ted V. *Revolt Against Modernity: Leo Strauss, Eric Voegelin, and the Search for a Postliberal Order*. Lawrence: University Press of Kansas, 1996.

Meier, Heinrich. *Carl Schmitt and Leo Strauss: The Hidden Dialogue*. Chicago: University of Chicago Press, 1995.

———. *Leo Strauss and the Theologico-Political Problem*. Cambridge: Cambridge University Press, 2006.

———. *The Lesson of Carl Schmitt: Four Chapters on the Distinction between Political Theology and Political Philosophy*. Chicago: University of Chicago Press, 1998.

Mendelssohn, Moses. *Gesammelte Schriften Jubiläumsausgabe*. Stuttgart: Friedrich Fromman Verlag (Günther Holzboog), 1974.

Merrill, Clark A. "Christianity and Politics: Leo Strauss's Indictment of Christian Philosophy." *Review of Politics* 62, no. 1 (2000): 77–106.

———. "Spelunking in the Unnatural Cave: Leo Strauss's Ambiguous Tribute to Max Weber." *Interpretation* 27, no. 1 (1999): 3–26.

Momigliano, Arnaldo. *Essays on Ancient and Modern Judaism*. Chicago: University of Chicago Press, 1994.

———. "Review of Leo Strauss, *Socrates and Aristophanes*." *Commentary* (October 1967): 102–104.

Morgan, Michael. *Dilemmas in Modern Jewish Thought: The Dialectics of Revelation and History*. Bloomington: Indiana University Press, 1992

Murley, John A., ed. *Leo Strauss and His Legacy: A Bibliography*. Lanham, MD: Lexington Books, 2005.

Nadon, Christopher C. *Xenophon's Prince: Republic and Empire in the Cyropaedeia*. Berkeley: University of California Press, 2001.

Neumann, Harry. "Civic Piety and Socratic Atheism: An Interpretation of Strauss' *Socrates and Aristophanes*." *Independent Journal of Philosophy* 2 (1978): 33–37.

Novak, David, ed. *Leo Strauss and Judaism: Athens and Jerusalem Critically Revisited*. Lanham, MD: Rowman & Littlefield, 1996.

Orr, Susan. *Jerusalem and Athens: Reason and Revelation in the Works of Leo Strauss*. Lanham, MD: Rowman & Littlefield, 1995.

Pangle, Thomas L. *Political Philosophy and the God of Abraham*. Baltimore: Johns Hopkins University Press, 2003.

———, ed. *The Roots of Political Philosophy: Ten Forgotten Socratic Dialogues*. Ithaca, NY: Cornell University Press, 1987.

Paraboschi, Germana. *Leo Strauss e la destra americana*. Rome: Editori Reuniti, 1988.

Pines, Shlomo. "On Leo Strauss." *Independent Journal of Philosophy* 5/6 (1988): 169–171.

Pippin, Robert B. *Idealism as Modernism: Hegelian Variations*. Cambridge: Cambridge University Press, 1997.

Reinecke, Volker, and Jonathan Uhlaner. "The Problem of Leo Strauss: Religion, Philosophy, and Politics." *Graduate Philosophy Journal* 16, no. 1 (1992): 189–208.

Reinharz, Jehuda. "Ideology and Structure in German Zionism, 1882–1933." In *Essential Papers on Zionism*, ed. Jehuda Reinharz and Anita Shapira, 279–284. New York: New York University Press, 1996.

Rosen, Stanley. *Hermeneutics as Politics*. Oxford: Oxford University Press, 1987.

———. *Plato's Statesman: The Web of Politics*. New Haven, CT: Yale University Press, 1995.

———. *The Quarrel between Philosophy and Poetry*. New York: Routledge, 1988.

Rosenzweig, Franz. *Der Mensch und sein Werk: Gesammelte Schriften*, 4 vols. The Hague: Martinus Nijhoff, 1979.

Schaefer, David L. "Leo Strauss and American Democracy: A Response to Wood and Holmes." *Review of Politics* 53, no. 1 (1991): 187–199.

Shell, Susan M. "Meier on Strauss and Schmitt." *Review of Politics* 53, no. 1 (1991): 219–223.

Smith, Steven B. *Reading Leo Strauss: Politics, Philosophy, Judaism*. Chicago: University of Chicago Press, 2006.

Sorensen, Kim A. *Discourses on Strauss: Revelation and Reason in Leo Strauss and His Critical Study of Machiavelli*. Notre Dame, IN: University of Notre Dame Press, 2006.

Tanguay, Daniel. "'Colère anti-théologique' et sécularisation: quelques remarques sur l'interprétation straussienne de la rupture moderne." *Science et Esprit* 52, no. 2 (1999): 185–197.

———. *Leo Strauss: An Intellectual Biography*. New Haven, CT: Yale University Press, 2007.

———. "La querelle des Anciens et des Modernes et le statut de la raison pratique chez Leo Strauss." *Carrefour* 21, no. 2 (1999): 21–35.

———. "Strauss, disciple de Nietzsche? À propos d'une hypothèse récente sur le sens 'caché' de l'œuvre de Leo Strauss. " *Les études philosophiques* 1 (2000): 105–132.

Tarcov, Nathan. "On a Certain Critique of 'Straussianism.'" *The Review of Politics* 53, no. 1 (1991): 3–18.

———. "Philosophy and History: John Gunnell and Leo Strauss on Tradition and Interpretation." In *Tradition, Interpretation, and Science: Political Theory in the American Academy*, ed. John S. Nelson, 69–112, Albany: State University of New York Press, 1986.

Udoff, Alan, ed. *Leo Strauss's Thought: Toward a Critical Engagement*. Boulder, CO: Lynne Rienner Publishers, 1991.

Voegelin, Eric. *Anamnesis*. Munich: Piper Verlag, 1966.

Yovel, Yirmiyahu. *Spinoza and Other Heretics*. Princeton, NJ: Princeton University Press, 1989.

Zuckert, Catherine H. *Postmodern Platos: Nietzsche, Heidegger, Gadamer, Strauss, Derrida*. Chicago: University of Chicago Press, 1966.

# Index